Western Financial Assistance to the Developing World

Chuku-Dinka R. Spencer

Western Financial Assistance to the Developing World

Perceptions of the Power Imbalance and its Impact on Fiscal Terms

palgrave
macmillan

Chuku-Dinka R. Spencer

ISBN 978-1-137-58398-7 ISBN 978-1-137-58399-4 (eBook)
DOI 10.1057/978-1-137-58399-4

Library of Congress Control Number: 2016949422

Printed on acid-free paper

This Palgrave Macmillan imprint is published by Springer Nature
The registered company is Nature America Inc. New York

This book is dedicated to the memory of all my departed relatives and in-laws and especially to the memory of my late sister, Lemuella. It is also dedicated to Dr. H.L. van der Laan, former professor of economics at Fourah Bay College, then part of the University of Durham.

Foreword

The perception or the actual forces of influence in the world of development finance leads the different participants to think about the institutions or the countries that provide financial assistance as having different declared or concealed objectives. In Africa, criticisms have been dynamic and have evolved in the course of the recent history of development. From bitter criticism of so-called "odious" aid, through "tied aid," to structural adjustment programs, the world of development finance has been the object of differentiated perceptions of the participants in development.

The author excellently captures the state of affairs through a well-researched and expert analysis, drawing factual data from his experience in development finance. Chuku-Dinka is an accomplished development practitioner with more than three decades of experience in development finance. He is accustomed to conducting in-depth analyses on contemporary subjects relating to development finance as evidenced by his prior works on the subject. He has no hesitation to use arguments which are both empirical and theoretical, to lead the reader into a world of development inquiry, which by nature is a world of divergent and at times contradictory interests. It is a world where donors, beneficiaries, the media, and so-called external and internal forces can, because of one reason or another, wish to enlarge one characteristic or another, thus creating a clear difference between perception and reality.

I have been involved on both sides of the development finance divide, having been for over 30 years an active player in the world of development finance. I now find myself among the decision-makers at the national public/political scene. Readers interested in the world of development finance can relate to the book. The author brings out the roles played by the various actors in the development process, roles which are buttressed by the specific case of Africa. In these different roles, it is important not to lose sight of the critical questions: what is, in fact, in the end, the crucial expectation of the recipients of development finance and from there what is important to those who provide financial solutions? What lessons can African countries draw from the awareness of the forces in play in order to better structure their discussions and their search for the optimum financial solutions for their development programs? Using his pen with the skill of an authoritative writer, Chuku-Dinka endeavors to provide answers to these and other pertinent questions.

Welcome to an incisive reading about the contemporary world of development finance, in which the traditional as well as the new players are analyzed with a fine-tooth comb, whether they are countries, international non-governmental organizations, or multilateral or bilateral institutions.

Chuku-Dinka adroitly takes the reader into an analysis where theoretical references are reinforced by decades of experience in the world of development finance, specifically in Africa. I invite readers to read the book and draw their own conclusions, about the book which is addressed to the informed general observers, participants in the world of development, the political decision-makers, academics, university teaching staff, and development practitioners.

Bedoumra Kordjé
Former Vice President African Development Bank,
Tunis-Belvedere, Tunisia
Former Minister of Economy, Development Planning, and
International Cooperation, N'Djamena, Republic of Chad
Former Minister of Finance and Budget, N'Djamena, Republic of Chad

Preface

In the preface of my previous book (*Politics, Agricultural Development, and Conflict Resolution*) which dealt with a specific program in Mali, I had asked the question "how did the government and the population of the developing countries view the interventions of the donors (especially international non-governmental organizations—INGOs)?" In answering this question, it became obvious that while INGOs intervene in the development efforts of developing countries, many other players are also involved in these development efforts. These include bilateral and multilateral financiers.

In researching for the present book, and from my experience of over three decades in agricultural economics research and the operational side of development finance, I realized that there was and still is a great imbalance of power among the players in the development finance arena. I wanted to look at the power imbalance from the point of view of the recipients of external financial assistance. In order to examine development finance from this point of view, it became apparent and important to examine in detail the perceptions and emotions of the population in developing countries, recipient of financial development assistance. What factors influence their perceptions of this power imbalance? In the interest of rigor and thoroughness and in order to be able to capture the whole spectrum of development finance, it was critical to examine both the traditional and non-traditional financial assistance. The traditional is defined as the North-South, financial assistance from developed countries (i.e. in Western and Northern Europe, North America, and the Far East) to developing countries, and the non-traditional, South-South financial assistance, as such assistance that includes emerging economic/financial powers as China, Brazil, India, South Africa, and even less-endowed countries that provide development finance or other technical assistance, as Cuba and Egypt.

The book explores in great depth such conceptual and key issues as power, perception, accountability, legitimacy, and globalization. As part of the conceptual and key issues, development finance is discussed in all its guises. The extensive and in-depth discussion of these conceptual and key issues prepares the reader for the ensuing analysis. Models, examples, and scenarios help the reader to ascertain the emotions and perceptions of the various segments of the populations in developing countries. Another question I asked in the preface of my previous book related to the effect that the interventions in development finance of the external donors, both traditional and non-traditional, have on the expected and actual outcomes.

Many of the reports of the bilateral and multilateral donors and agencies show adequately the expected and actual outcomes in terms of socioeconomic outputs and financial returns. I therefore felt that these aspects receive satisfactory attention. Rather than deal with purely socioeconomic data to show outcomes, I preferred to look at power from a different perspective. I analyze such factors that affect perception as media, source of information, current situation, and what the Gibsons. Husband & wife call "affordances." Finally, I studied the manifestations of power that are the conditions which accompany development finance packages. How does the power imbalance (i.e. the power play) affect the developing countries as viewed from the perspectives of the population in the developing countries? How do they view conditions that accompany the financial assistance packages? Did such manifestations of power as embodied in the conditions have positive or negative effects on the socioeconomic well-being of the population? How did they affect the economy and the finances of the countries concerned? These and other questions are answered as the perceptions of the population are rigorously and thoroughly explored and analyzed.

Acknowledgments

My first gratitude goes to the ALMIGHTY for making everything possible. My thanks go to my spouse Waltina, sons, Chuku-Dinka, W., Dr. Chuku-Dima, R., and Dr. Cheka, R. Spencer for their constant support, encouragement, valuable comments and suggestions, and for willingly accepting to be my sounding boards for some of the positions espoused in the book. Thanks also go to my sister Mrs. Ethel Greene, nee Spencer, and my nephews Drs. Harold and Raymond Greene, for constantly spurring me on to finish what I started. I also thank the anonymous reviewers. I also appreciate the assistance of my former colleagues in the African Development Bank, especially Mamadou Abdoul Kane and Foday Turay, for their invaluable assistance.

The views expressed are not necessarily those of any institution or organization, past or present, with which the author may be or may have been associated. Any errors and omissions are the sole responsibility of the author.

Contents

Abbreviations and Acronyms

ADDAX	Addax Bioenergy company
AfDB	African Development Bank
AfDF	African Development Fund
ALLAT	Action for Large Scale Land Acquisition Transparency
AsDB	Asian Development Bank
ASEAN	Association of Southeast Asian Nations
BADEA	Arab Bank for Economic Development in Africa
BBC	British Broadcasting Corporation
BRICS	Brazil, Russia, India, China, and South Africa
CGIAR	Consultative Group for International Agricultural Research
CII	Confederation of Indian Industry
COMESA	Common Market for Eastern and Southern Africa
DAC	Development Assistance Committee
DFI	Development Finance Institution
DRC	Democratic Republic of Congo
ECOWAS	Economic Community of West African States
EEZ	Exclusive Economic Zone
Ex Ante	Expected or intended outcome before the event
Ex Post	Actual outcome after the event
FAO	Food and Agriculture Organization
GDP	Gross Domestic Product
GNI	Gross National Income
GNP	Gross National Product
HIPCS	Heavily Indebted Poor Countries
IDB	Inter-American Development Bank
IFAD	International Fund for Agricultural Development
IDFI	International Development Finance Institution

IIED	International Institute for Environment and Development
IMF	International Monetary Fund
INGO	International Non-governmental Organization
IRIN	Integrated Regional Integrated Networks
IsDB	Islamic Development Bank
LCD	Least Common Denominator
NGO	Non-governmental Organization
ODA	Official Development Assistance
OECD	Organization for Economic Co-operation and Development
OPEC	Organization of the Petroleum Exporting Countries
PRSP	Poverty Reduction Strategy Papers
RSA	Republic of South Africa
SADC	Southern African Development Community
SADPA	South African Development Partnership Agency
SSA	Sub-Saharan Africa
TNGO	Transnational Non-governmental Organization
UNDP	United Nations Development Programme
UNECA	United Nations Economic Commission for Africa
USA	United States of America
USAID	United States Agency for International Development
WTO	World Trade Organization
WB	World Bank

List of Figures

CHAPTER 1

Introduction: A Sense of the Context

International Advocacy Groups are often involved in development efforts in developing countries. One such advocacy group is fighting to stop the construction of the Gibe III dam in Ethiopia (Bosshard and Pottinger, International Rivers). The United Nations Educational, Scientific, and Cultural Organization (UNESCO) is also urging Ethiopia to halt and abandon the construction of the Gibe III dam (nazret.com). In fact, an advocacy organization halted the construction of the Talo dam in Mali (Fink and Meierotto 2002).

Other specific actions in some developed countries as evidenced by some journal and newspaper articles have repercussions on activities in some developing countries. These include the signing of the farm bill by former President George Bush in May 2002. The farm bill was expected to increase the amount of subsidies to farmers by $83 billion spread over ten years. It was estimated that this bill would increase the US subsidies to farmers by about 60% (Mshomba 2002). In a briefing paper by Oxfam, it was indicated that cotton subsidies were destroying the livelihood of farmers in Africa and other developing countries (Watkins, K.—Oxfam 2002; also Oxfam New Zealand).

These are but a few of the international media articles relating to development efforts and farming in Africa. These show just a few of the overt ways external forces try to exercise power over developing countries. There are many other more subtle exercises of power, by these external forces, which are barely visible at a casual glance at development efforts in

C.R. Spencer, *Western Financial Assistance to the Developing World*,
DOI 10.1057/978-1-137-58399-4_1

Africa, especially in the rural areas. External forces are understood to mean all bodies, organizations, notions, concepts, and ideas that may come from outside of the continent. The field is vast and cannot be thoroughly analyzed within this book. I am therefore going to concentrate on development finance generally and mainly to rural areas; more particularly, I shall concentrate mostly on Sub-Saharan Africa. However, I shall refer to other forms of external forces only as they have a bearing on development finance. Why do some of these development efforts generate so much media attention from bodies outside the borders of the countries concerned?

How do the external bodies exercise power or influence over activities being carried out or intending to be carried out by governments in Africa? What powers, seen or unseen, do these bodies have over development efforts in Africa? What perception do the developing countries have of the power and of the wielder of the power? What emotional frames do the people directly concerned with these exercises have before, during, and after the interventions? These perceptions and emotions condition what Scott (1990, pp. 14, 28, 187–190) calls their "hidden transcripts," as well as their "public transcripts." He stated that the "hidden transcripts" (i.e. the private or hidden speech and behavior) are different from the public expression and behavior, which constitute the "public transcript." Can the notions of "public" and "private/hidden" transcripts inform the analysis of the influence of external forces on development finance and rural areas in particular? Do the countries, that are recipients of financial assistance, actually perceive "power play?" These and other questions will be discussed in this chapter and in the chapters which follow.

The need for financial assistance arises because of the gap between financial resources required for development purposes and the amount of financial resources which developing countries possess. This resource gap is the underlying cause of the demand for assistance from external sources and will be discussed in detail in Chap. 3. It is rare that recipients of development finance consciously perceive such financial assistance in terms of power play between two different forces, of which one is external and the other is internal. However, it is not a far stretch to see donors (external) and recipients (internal) in situations of conflict, especially where specific conditions are part of the assistance package. In such situations, the receipt of the assistance by the recipient is dependent on the recipient behaving in a specific way as per the conditions accompanying the package, taking specific actions or carrying out specific activities. Under these circumstances, the donor would have been able to get the recipient to do things, which the recipient may or may not have wanted to do. As we shall see in Chaps. 3 and 4, and in line with the thinking of Lukes (2005, pp. 20, 21, 42–44), Dowding (1996, pp. 4, 5), and Morris (1987, pp. 25, 33, 38), the donors have exercised power over the recipients. This is because they have obtained outcomes of behavior that they expected from the exercise of power.

In addition to the description given above, external forces are further defined as those forces, physical and non-physical, that generally intervene in African development finance and assistance from outside the continent. In short, external forces are all forces exogenous to the continent. This description, though, begs the question as to the category into which we place development finance institutions created by African countries themselves. Internal forces are those forces that are endogenous to the continent. We shall discuss external forces more fully in Chap. 3.

Has any one of the parties concerned been aware of the underlying implications of the act of giving and receiving financial assistance? Invariably, both parties realize that one party has got the other to do things that the other may or may not have wanted to do. But do they feel that power has been exercised? Both parties may consider that a transaction has taken place. One party was selling a good, which we call "development finance" and/or "development assistance," and the other was in the market for development finance and/or development assistance. One party received a good, which we call here "development assistance or development finance," and the other party received, in return, the execution of specific actions or activities. The preceding fact holds true, mainly for grants, but it can also be extended to loans. The recipient of "development finance" uses the funds, equipment, and other materials that accompanied the assistance, or that could be acquired with the funds, to "further" its development agenda. The results of this "furthering" are what are expected to lead to higher social and economic levels in the lives of the population in the recipient country. The "furthering" of development is expected to be the ultimate outcome of the exercise of power by the donor. The recipients thus accept, willingly or reluctantly, for power to be exercised on them, in exchange for the furthering of their development agenda. There is, therefore, a "contract" both literally and metaphorically between the two parties. The motivation of the external party behind this "contract" is varied. The "motivation" of the external force/party could be commercial, economic/financial, strategic, or altruistic/humanitarian.

Does the motivation of the external force influence the perception of the exercise of power by the recipients of development finance?

If there is a "contract," then how can there be a power play between the forces? What are the instruments used to exercise this power? Power play in the field of development finance is a "process," which has prescribed procedures and is generally stretched out over a specific period for any specific package. Each specific package constitutes a building block to strengthen the power of the external force over a much longer period. Thus over the years, the total amount of development finance from any particular donor/external force, as we shall see in Chaps. 3 and 4, helps to give the external force greater "power to" and "power over" recipient countries. Each development finance package contributes to increasing the "strength/magnitude" of the power of the external force. The cumulative strength of the external force helps to ensure that the recipient countries acquiesce to other types of exercises of power, which may not be related to development finance or development assistance. The examples of the Chinese in Zambia and in Nigeria, which will be discussed in Chap. 4, are cases in point. Procedures in development finance start with the official application for assistance and include what is termed the "project/ program cycle."

Targets (people and outcome) of the development finance package are identified, with clear objectives, overall goals, beneficiaries, implementation activities, procurement processes and procedures, and other relevant aspects, such as required resources. In addition, the objectives and other parameters are agreed upon between the donor and the recipient parties prior to project/program start up. These objectives are generally defined, in both the traditional, now less used, "project approach," the sector-wide approach, and the new "budget support approach" as achieving or attaining improvement in conditions of living of the population, or in certain target parameters like income, production, productivity, levels of economic or financial status, money supply, and other agreed-upon goals. Other procedures, which are part of this "process," are preparation and appraisal of the program. Once the program or project has been appraised and the conditions which determine access to the funds are prepared and discussed in the field at appraisal, the whole report embodying the program/project is discussed in detail and agreed upon at negotiations between the two parties. The appraisal report, in the case of development finance institutions, is discussed in a meeting of the approving body, and then theoretically, the funds become available for disbursement. Regular field visits are made by the donor/lender/external force, and desk reviews of the program to ascertain progress, correct any deviation or errors, or redirect the program are also part of this "process." These activities help to strengthen the elements of power and also constitute in themselves exercises of power. In a way, they are means to control the actions and activities related to the development finance package and to ensure that the direction of progress is in accordance with the agreed-upon "contract." In addition, these activities are intended to help lead to the outcomes expected and/or desired by the more dominant force.

During the period of working on the "process," several power sources are called into play. These power sources, which we shall discuss in Chap. 3, become, as it were, fountains from which power flows and is wielded. These sources help to condition the recipients and their perceptions about development finance. They make acceptance by the recipients of the subtle and/or overt exercise of power easier. As we shall see in Chap. 3, these power sources belong to different owners and become the strength by which the donor forces get the results they anticipate as the outcome of the exercise of power. However, are the recipients without strength or power of their own that they accept that behavior patterns or actions are imposed on them? No, they are not without strength of their own. In line with the thinking of Foucault (Foucault—Faubion, ed. 2000, pp. 347) and Scott (1990, pp. 192–197, 199), where power exists, resistance is also present. Foucault recognized that the existence of power does not automatically mean successful exercise of power. A power relationship cannot exist with areas of what Foucault called insubordination. These points or areas of insubordination constitute means of escape.

In all power play, however, "relative strength" is the critical factor, and the party, which possesses the greater strength, is generally the party, which can dictate, to a large degree, the outcome of the power play. As Chap. 3 will show, this party is the dominant party and is generally the donor party. In line with the thinking of Scott (1990, pp. 14, 28, 187–190) and as we shall see in Chaps. 3 and 4, the recipient countries also have tools that they can use to thwart the powers exercised on them by a superior force. I call those times when the power flow is thwarted "breaks in the power flow." These breaks represent gaps in the otherwise seemingly seamless flow of power from the donor countries/external forces to, and over, the recipient countries. Some of the gaps are created by the recipients countries which are the non-dominant parties, whereas others occur as a result of the workings of the "process" as we shall discuss in Chap. 3.

The strength of the powers varies depending on the number of sources of power each party can bring into the power play. In general, in development finance, because of, among other factors, the relatively long duration of the "process" and the often high urgency of the need of the recipient countries for funds, equipment, or other tangible resources to advance their development agenda, the outcomes are often skewed in favor of the donor party. Another factor that comes into play is the alternative sources of funds available to the non-dominant forces. The greater the availability of alternative sources, the lesser the strength of any one source. In addition, the more diverse the sources of funding are, the less the strength of any one source. Efforts have been made, within the past ten years, by the donor group, with strong encouragement from the recipient group to reduce the duration of the "process" of each development finance package. The former group, as we shall see in Chap. 3, comes in the form of and consists of donor countries, donor organizations (governmental or non-governmental), or donor institutions. The donor group is further classified, in terms of traditional and non-traditional. Other classifications include North-South, South-South, North-South-South, and South-South-South. As we shall see in Chaps. 3 and 4, the relative strength of these different combinations also varies, depending on the source of power called upon and the desire and/or the ultimate consideration (i.e. purely humanitarian/altruistic, historical, commercial, economic, political, or strategic) in which the donor party is interested.

The recipient countries are generally the developing countries, and the donor countries are the developed countries. However, in the donor-party category, we now have emerging economies which have resources that they can spare for countries less fortunate than them even though some of them have not yet attained the levels of developed countries and some of them still receive development assistance and development finance from the more developed countries of the North. All these developed and emerging economies constitute the external forces that are part of the focus of the book. Do the emerging economies wield power? Moreover, if they do, do they have the same considerations as the developed countries? These are aspects, which we shall discuss in Chap. 4, and which we hope would help developing African countries to package their development finance ex ante in such a way as to reduce the volume of power exercised on them.

Why do we want to discuss power in development finance? Why do we feel that developing countries would like to reduce the volume of power exercised on them? It is important for the developing countries that they know the different sources of the power that are exercised on them. Knowledge of the relative strength of these sources, and which of these sources the various donor parties can call upon, is very useful. Such knowledge could help developing countries to package their development finance and development assistance to ensure optimum returns from the different transactions involved in the development finance "process." Knowledge of the considerations and interests of the donors is also very useful in the packaging exercise.

If the developing countries are aware of the factors that affect their perception of the exercise of power on them, the packaging exercise could also factor in their perception in a way that would not only ensure optimum returns, but also ensure a package with which they would have the least negative perception and for which they would have greater acceptance. Although this packaging may not always be possible or at times not even possible at all, it would be worthwhile for developing countries to be conversant with these notions and concepts and do the relevant analysis before going into negotiations for "contracts" in development finance.

However, as power is abstract, how can we talk of power seen and unseen? How can we talk of discussing perceptions of power by the recipient countries? If nobody can "see" power, then how can one have a perception of the exercise of power? According to the followers of physicalist, phenomenologists, or haptic theories (Stanford 2011; also Krishnanda 2003), perception is both visual and also involves other senses. These include touch, smell, and hearing and involves memory, past experience, and other factors such as current situation. Though we may not be able to "see" power, some of our other senses may be able to "perceive" power. Objects of power or recipients of development finance and assistance can "feel" the psychological pressures on them to carry out actions, undertake activities, or change ad hoc/specific behavior or modify long-term behavior patterns. We can see the outcome of the exercise of power and "believe" that we have perceived the exercise of power. Many of the authors on "power," such as Lukes (2005, pp. 42, 43), Dowding (1996, pp. 5, 7, 8), and Foucault (Foucault- Faubion 2000b, pp. 340, 341), also assimilate the outcome of the exercise of power to the evidence that power has been, is being, or will be exercised. Some of these theories and points of view will be discussed in Chap. 2.

Power, as Lukes (2005, p. 1) stated, is most effective when it is least observable, in other words, when it is "unseen." Is it possible to have agreement among scholars on the outcome? Can they agree that the outcome that a party anticipated is the outcome that shows power has been exercised? How can we be sure that a donor party exercised power? Donor parties do not generally go about publicizing that they have power or that they can exercise or have exercised power. The exercise of power is even more difficult to discern in the development field, as donor parties often insist that they are only facilitators who provide finance. This, in every way, is a provable fact. The funds donors provide or have provided are visible and can be visible, or the resources acquired with the funds can also be visible. Some donors emphasize that the whole exercise of "development finance and assistance" is more "development cooperation" than development assistance, contending that the "cooperation" is a partnership. Some might go to the extent of stating that the partnership is of equal strength on either side. But is it? As we shall see in Chaps. 3 and 4, the circumstances of the recipient developing countries preclude any possibility of equality in the partnership, especially as far as African countries are concerned.

Power is "seen" in many instances in development finance where transactions are clear and the packages are accompanied by specific conditions—either a few or many, or as in some budget support programs, none at all. In these latter cases, the conditions would have become unnecessary, as during the "process" which we discussed earlier where all the requirements would have been met prior to the finalization of the program document. In many cases, as we shall discuss later, conditions do not exist, or the exercise of power is what could be termed as "exercise behind the scene," or what I call "unseen" power. This "unseen power" occurs when, as Nagel (1975, pp. 15, 16), Morriss (1987, p. 135), and Scott (1990, p. 73) indicated, the non-dominant party anticipates the reaction of the dominant party and behaves in the way the dominant party expects them to, or carries out the action that the dominant party would want them to do. This is because the future expectation of the non-dominant party is such that it "believes" that if it does not carry out what Scott (1990, pp. 13–14, 52–55) calls the "public transcript" expected of them by the dominant party, the latter would use one of the sources of power it possesses to punish them. Another "unseen" exercise of power occurs when critical decision-makers among the dominant party, in order to ensure that the outcome, that they (dominant party) expect should happen, communicate subtly or covertly to the key decision-maker in the recipient party, indicating what they (dominant parties) expect them to do. Very often, because the members of the non-dominant party are aware of the power (reward or punishment) that can be brought on them by the dominant party, it (non-dominant party) is obliged to comply or acquiesce.

Whether the power exercised is seen or unseen, as Lukes (2005, pp. 12, 31, 69, 70, 78) and Morriss (1987, pp. 14, 15, 18, 19) would state, the donor party has and is "believed" by the recipient party to have the "vehicle," the "capacity," and often the "willingness" to exercise power. The recipient/non-dominant party also possesses a large array of sources of power to bring into the power play. How do the recipient countries perceive the outcome of the power play?

How can we perceive power? How can we characterize perception? Perception is a term used in both the behavioral sciences and the biological sciences. However, do these specialist fields have the same meaning of and for perception? What are the differences in meaning? In Chap. 2, we shall discuss the conceptual aspects of "perception" in a bid to understand the outcome of power and its effect on the recipient countries. We shall endeavor to give the term meaning and relevance in the context of development finance and in the specific area of power play. We cannot actually see power or perception and even lessen the perception of the exercise of power. How then can we know that power has been exercised? Authors (Morriss 1987, pp. 156–181; Nagel 1975, pp. 38–48) have discussed and debated on such issues as measurement of power and the indicators of power and tried to furnish methodologies to measure the exercise of power. Very little has been done, however, on the perception of the exercise of power, much less as they relate to recipient countries/non-dominant forces in development finance or development assistance. Social science is not a very exact science, and measurement and methodologies are difficult to establish.

To assist in ascertaining perceptions of power by recipients of development finance and assistance in various scenarios, we shall develop models in Chap. 4. These models will be based on more than three decades of direct engagement, observation, and study of the processes entailed in the "contract." The involvement and participation encompass experience on the side of the recipient country/non-dominant force and experience as part of teams, then head of teams on the side of the dominant external forces engaged in discussion of all aspects of the "contract." This period necessitated discussions; negotiations; and meetings, conferences, seminars, and conversations with various levels of private individuals, such as farmers, taxi drivers, official government drivers, government officials, politicians, ministers, and presidents of countries in Africa. It also included discussions, conferences, meetings, and seminars with other colleagues/peers who are officials of bilateral and multilateral development finance and development assistance agencies, institutions, and governments. The time was spent observing, engaging in, and understanding what Scott24 (1990, pp. 6, 123, 124) called the "private/hidden transcript" and the "public transcript" of officials on both sides of the development perception divide.

This book addresses the issue of what Lukes (2005, pp. 69, 73, 135), Dowding (1996, pp. 3, 8), and Morriss (1987, pp. 32, 34) call "power over" and "power to" as it relates to the financing of development in developing countries, especially those in Africa. This is timely in that Africa is once again the prey of many external forces that are interested in developing its natural resources for their own and seemingly Africa's benefit. We see examples of this in Sierra Leone, where, in "deals," individuals, companies, and external governments purchase large tracts of land to grow food for the population of the external forces (see Tran, The Guardian 2013; also Oakland, Sierra Leone 2011). We see private sector individuals and companies "investing" in diamond mining in Sierra Leone. Other examples include companies from some developed and some emerging nations getting involved in oil extraction in Sierra Leone and Ghana as well as bauxite mining in the Simandou area in Guinea (see Els; Mining.com 2013). These, some would say, are investments that are good for Africa. This is and may be so; however, without discussing the issues relating to the best means of reducing poverty, investments, which bring growth, provide jobs, and contribute to poverty reduction, are good for Africa.

Nevertheless, it could be argued that some of Africa's leaders and their officials do not seem to have the necessary skills to negotiate "contracts" that will benefit the continent's people in the short, medium, and long term. The comments by Mo Ibrahim (2013; World Economic Forum on Africa, Cape Town 2007), the African Telecom billionaire, give credence to this belief, as does the study on three projects in Sierra Leone, by Joan Baxter for Action for Large-scale Land Acquisition Transparency (ALLAT) (Oakland Institute, Sierra Leone 2011). The preceding statement that African leaders do not have the required skills assumes that the leaders are really interested in poverty reduction and not in other goals, objectives, and agenda. The article by Cobain and Hirsch (2013) about mining in Guinea gives weight to such a contrary hypothesis.

When we reflect on the brains, both in terms of quantity and quality, that Africa can call upon within the continent and in the diaspora, it is deplorable to observe how these "deals" seem to lack coherence when one considers the interest of the peoples of the continent. They also tend to be opaque; details are very scarce. We can see this lack of "coherence" as in the case of the Addax Bioenergy deal in Sierra Leone (Anane and Abiwu 2011) or the electricity deal with an Italian firm, also in Sierra Leone. According to the Oakland Institute (Baxter; Oakland Institute; also Hurd, Oakland Institute, Ethiopia 2013; Oakland Africa), there are also instances in Mali (see Oakland Institute, Mali 2011) and other countries in Africa. Under such a situation, the agreements between the governments and the "investors" have a tendency to lock future governments into deals, which make it difficult for them to review when they take over the reins of government much to the advantage of the external companies.

Not being able to review past "contracts" and "deals" becomes a painful reality, even if the interest of the people of the country dictated such a review. It is a painful reality, because it robs the country of leverage and added resources for its development agenda. The reports by the Oakland Institute discuss some of the contradictions, discrepancies, and concerns relating to some of the land deals in Sierra Leone, Mali, and Ethiopia. The study (Cotula et al. 2009) by the consortium of Food and Agriculture Organization (FAO), International Institute for Environment and Development (IIED), and International Fund for Agricultural Development (IFAD) also highlights issues that require revisiting some of these land deals in the interest of the African countries. In some cases, there is a great disconnect between poverty reduction, development, and what actually happens several years after the "deals" have been implemented. The African countries seem to end up with the short end of the stick, as we shall see in the economic statistics provided in Chap. 3. Although the cases mentioned are purely investment deals, development finance and development assistance "contracts" are not exempt from issues of coherence.

In a June 2014 development, apparently as a result of pressure from the media through newspaper articles, blogs, and other media activities, the government of Sierra Leone published on the website of the National Minerals Agency the actual agreements it had signed with five companies for mining operations in the country. This is a manifestation of the "connections power," which I shall discuss in Chap. 3.

By looking at power in relation to development finance, specifically from the perspective of the recipient countries, this book will provide concepts and analytical tools, which will contribute toward deciphering some of the issues involved in investment deals and development finance contracts. It will add to the literature and to the debate on perceptions in relationships of power in development finance, especially in Africa. It will also contribute to a better understanding by officials and practitioners in the developing countries of the "process of power play." Readers will have a better understanding, especially with regard to the perception of the people: ordinary citizens, farmers, government and public officials, politicians, ministers, and presidents of the continent.

It is a contribution to the debate and an effort to kindle discussion on the power wielded by external forces through development finance in developing countries, especially in African countries. It is an unconventional look at issues relating to power, as they relate to development and rural development in particular. It discusses power as governments, and people in Africa perceive it, that is, in terms of positive and favorable or negative and overbearing. We could link this latter term with how it affects their self-esteem or ego. This is linked to what MacLachlan et al. (2010, pp. 64, 65, 66) called "interactional justice" and "interpersonal justice," on which we shall elaborate later.

The book and the analysis it contains would be worthwhile to policy makers and government officials in developing countries, as they would better understand some of the factors, which come into play in development finance and development assistance. The "process" mentioned earlier, involved in development finance discussions, would benefit from an understanding of the strength of the various donors in the power play, leading up to the negotiations of the "contract" binding the parties. These would help them to ensure that the finance package they put together would be the most beneficial for their populations, and one in which the least power if any at all has been exercised.

We trust that university lecturers, senior undergraduate and graduate students, and the informed public, interested in the development of African and other developing countries, would find the analysis helpful and discover useful themes to animate their lectures and discussions. We also expect that it will help them to understand better the situation of many African countries in their drive to develop their countries and reduce poverty. The perceptions and emotions of the people in the recipient countries in relation to development finance will become clearer, through reading this book. The book will add to the knowledge bank of development practitioners in their analysis of contracts and programs. Theoreticians could use some of the models and examples to develop paradigms concerning perception of power in development finance. Researchers would find the line of reasoning provocative enough to take up the subject and do further research, and that the research will look into the relational and dispositional aspects of power seen and unseen and the roles which it plays in development especially in Africa.

Organization of the Book

Chapter 1 (A Sense of the Context) introduces development finance as a contract in which the dominant and the non-dominant forces enter into a contract very much like a trading contract, where one party is selling a good and the other is purchasing the same good. It looks at financial assistance in the context of the traditional providers of financial assistance. It initiates the notion of alternatives to these traditional financiers. It presents development finance as a process akin to a "conflict of wills" between recipient countries/internal forces and those from outside Africa who provide the financial assistance as external forces. It introduces the concept of unequal relationship among the development finance parties and starts the reader thinking in terms of power play among these unequal parties. It asks questions as to why, if there is a contract, can there be issues of unequal power among the parties and why this is important. It opens the discussion, which shall be further developed in later chapters, on the concepts of perceptions of the population in the recipient countries and of the motivations of those who provide the financial assistance.

With regard to the perceptions of the population in the recipient countries, using theories of such authors as Berger (2008, pp. 136, 137, 162), Axelrod (1973, pp. 1248–1266), Gibson (1986, pp. 36, 40, 41, 130–135), Berk (2012, pp. 192, 193, 197–199), Powers (2005, pp. 34–37, 96, 129,165; also 1998, pp. 6–9, 78, 79), and Ballesteros (1994, pp. 9–15), it brings forth the factors that could influence their perceptions as well as the need to differentiate the perceptions of the various segments of the population in the recipient countries. Notions that would improve our understanding of the power play in development finance, such as the notion of "affordance" which was introduced by the Gibsons (1986, pp. 36, 40, 41, 130–135) and the notion of intentional and unintentional blindness to stimuli, are briefly discussed with full discussion, elaboration, and illustration as to their relevance to development finance in Chaps. 2–4. It initiates the concept of power as discussed by authors including Lukes (2005, pp. 20, 21, 22), Dowding (1996, pp. 4, 5), Foucault (Foucault-Fabion 2000, p. 347), Nagel (1975, pp. 15, 16), Scott (1990, pp. 6, 123, 124), and Morris (1987, pp. 14, 15, 18, 19). It brings in the notion of "power over" and "power to," all of which are useful in understanding the exercise of the power play in development finance. All of these are fully discussed in Chaps. 2–4. Finally, it asks the questions of why discuss power and perception in the context of development finance and development assistance to developing countries and to African countries in particular. It shows the need to discuss the perceptions of the peoples in the recipient countries.

Chapter 2 (Conceptual and Key Issues) discusses conceptual issues relating to power, perception, development finance, accountability, legitimacy, and globalization. It presents some of the various theories and authors who have written on these concepts, discussing the advantages and disadvantages and trying to see whether they have any relevance to development finance, especially as it is practiced in Africa. It underscores the discussion of each concept with examples that can demonstrate their relevance to development finance and more particularly to perceptions of power play among the parties involved with and in development finance. Development finance is reviewed as is the reason I use development finance and not development assistance, because development assistance is part of the broader term of development finance or development financial assistance. The relevance of these terms with regard to the notion of power play is highlighted. In Chap. 2, I discuss how some authors define globalization, and I provide attributes and indicators as well as effects, side effects, consequences, and by-products of globalization. I also provide an appreciation of the critical role globalization played in the start of development finance and how globalization enhances the continued practice and operation of development finance; the influence of globalization on perception, power play, and the perception of power play is underlined. The thinking of such authors as Bhagwati (2004, pp. 3–4, 6–7) and Stiglitz (2003, pp. 5, 6–7 and also 2007, pp. 67–74) is brought to bear on the discussion to elaborate specific points in the discussion. The relationship between legitimacy and power play is discussed along with whether compliance to rules and conditions is influenced by legitimacy. The role of the dominant force in setting standards and the influence of this in establishing legitimacy is discussed. The case for accountability and the notion of transparency as presented by different authors are argued in Chap. 2. This will help readers better understand the concepts, notions, and examples given in the chapters, which follow. Chapter 2 also discusses some legal, administrative, and other issues as they relate to the external forces and development finance.

Chapter 3 (Understanding the Exercise of Power) discusses the various sources of power and how they relate to and are used in development finance. Chapter 3 continues by examining the economic situation of the African countries and the problems they encounter in their drive to reduce poverty in their countries. These problems provide the background, which, in turn, facilitates the exercise of power by the dominant forces and the acceptance of such exercise of power by the non-dominant forces. It provides figures from known and reliable sources to demonstrate the strength of the influence of the dominant external forces in the economies and the economic structure of African countries. It also discusses the exercise of power in the context of development finance, with concrete real-life examples drawn from experience over a long period of time. These examples are used to illustrate the various concepts of the authors discussed in Chap. 2. The perception of the population in the recipient countries receives due attention in illustrating how power can be and is being exercised in the context of development finance to African countries.

Chapter 4 (Appreciating Perception and Power) examines, with salient examples, the strength of power, what factors could and do influence the exercise or exertion of power. It looks at the exercise of power by external forces from the point of view of what Simensen (Simensen-Utenriksdepartementet), Kragelund (2010), and Burgess (2012- also Administrator-v-2006-Special Unit New York-2009 and Kilimani, UNECA, pp. 14, 16, 19) call traditional and non-traditional donors and Northern and Southern donors. It continues with examples of such exercise of power. It discusses the frames of the recipients, their perception of the power exerted or exercised over them, and the possible action and reaction open to them. In Chap. 4, I discuss power and the perceptions of various groups in the countries recipient of development finance. These include politicians, government officials generally, and government officials who depend on patronage from the politicians and those who do not. I discuss the perceptions of the ultimate beneficiaries of development finance in the rural areas, that is, the farmers, fisherfolk, and so on. What factors influence their perceptions? Using the discussion in Chap. 3 of the sources of power used by the external forces to obtain compliance with rules and conditions, Chap. 4 discusses different situations where power has been or was exercised and shows the source(s) from which the power was drawn. It gives the different permutations that were used in the various stages of the process of power play in the context of providing development finance. It discusses breaks in the flow of power and the influence of the media and "conveyed concepts" on the perception of the peoples in the African countries, recipients of development financial assistance.

Chapter 5 (Perceptions, Outcomes, and Power: Positives and Negatives) reviews the positive and negative aspects of both power and perception. It discusses the outcomes of power as was examined in Chaps. 2 and 3. It analyzes the conditions, identifying some of the positive and not so positive outcomes in which the power play can result and in which it has resulted. In this regard, as conditions are the manifestations of the exercise of power in development finance, Chap. 5 analyzes various categories of the conditions that accompany development finance packages. It discusses outcomes and whether these outcomes can be directly or indirectly linked to the power play or just to the result of the action and activities of the development finance package. The conditions, grouped into such categories as those requiring reduction in government expenditure; those demanding the enactment of laws, the adoption of policies, and appointments to key institutions or departments; and those concerning governance are discussed.

The outcomes are examined in terms of their impact on the economies of the recipient countries and on the individuals and groups of individuals. We discuss factors that are considered in the perception concerning the outcomes. These are scrutinized to see whether they are the results of the activities of the development finance package or of the exercise of power. The question is whether we could perceive any element of positiveness if there was no exercise of power. Some of the answers are discussed in the context of real-life examples of conditions accompanying development finance packages. In addition to the preceding categories, conditions that concern program management, establishing and reforming institutions, and liberalizing imports are analyzed to determine possible power play. The outcomes are then classified as positive and negative. They are also organized in terms of perceptions; in whose perception, are the outcome considered as positive? The compliance with these conditions is expected to contribute to the improvement of the economies of the countries concerned. It is logical to ask whether the earlier compliance with conditionalities of the interventions of the traditional North-South donors facilitated or in any way helped in the later interventions of the South-South as Amanor (2013, pp. 20–30) stated. What are the negatives and how can they be attributed to the power play inherent in development finance? Can they be considered as a by-product of the power play or simply a side effect of globalization? These aspects and issues are the contents of Chap. 5.

Chapter 6 (Conclusions) summarizes the major arguments of the book. It reviews very succinctly the earlier chapters and draws conclusions as to the perceptions of the recipient countries/non-dominant forces concerning the exercise of power in the specific context of development finance, especially of the rural areas.

This final chapter also looks at how recipient countries can package their development assistance to ensure optimum returns. It also looks at whether such a packaging is possible. The final chapter also addresses the issue of strategy, which could be developed ex ante by the object of the exercise of power, using lessons learned as guiding principles.

Notes and References

Administrator_v. (2006). South-South cooperation defies the North. In *Global envision, exploring market-driven solutions to poverty*, December 6, 2006.

Amanor, K. S. (2013, July). South–South cooperation in Africa: Historical, geopolitical and political economy dimensions of international development. *IDS Bulletin, 44*(4), 20–30 (published by John Wiley and Sons, Oxford).

Anane, M. C., & Abiwu, C. Y. (2011, June). Independent study report of the Addax bioenergy sugarcane to ethanol project in the Makeni region in Sierra Leone. http://www.brotfueralle.ch/fileadmin/deutsch/01_Service/Medien_Texte/Mediencommuniques/Independent%20Study%20Report%20Addax%20Final.pdf

Axelrod, R. (1973, December). Schema theory: An information processing model of perception and cognition. *The American Political Science Review, 67*(4), 1248–1266. American Political Association. http://www.jstor.org/stable/1956546, pp. 1249–1250.

Ballesteros, S. (1994). Cognitive approaches to human perception: Introduction. In S. Ballesteros (Ed.), *Cognitive approaches to human perception* (pp. 9–15). New Jersey/Hove/London: Lawrence Erlbaum Associates/Publishers Hillsdale.

Baxter, J., & Oakland Institute. *Understanding land investment deals in Africa*. Country report: Mali. http://www.oaklandinstitute.org/understanding-land-investment-deals-africa-mali

Berger, K. S. (2008). *The developing person through the life span* (pp. 136–137, 162). New York: Worth Publishers.

Berk, L. (2012). *Infants and children: Prenatal through middle childhood* (pp. 192–193, 197, 198, 199). Boston/Columbus/New York: Allyn and Bacon.

Bhagwati, J. (2004). *In defense of globalization* (pp. 3–4, 6–7). New York: Oxford University Press.

Bosshard, P., & Pottinger, L. *International rivers–Protecting people-water-life*. Petition to Stop Gibe III Dam. http://www.internationalrivers.org/resources/petition-to-stop-gibe-3-dam-3487

Burgess, S. (2012, July–December). Developing from the South: South-South cooperation in the global development game. *Austral: Brazilian Journal of Strategy & International Relations, 1*(2). e-ISSN 2238-6912. ISSN2238-6262.

Cobain, I., & Hirsch, A. (2013). The tycoon, the dictator's wife and the $2.5 billion Guinea mining deal. *The Guardian*. FBI investigating Beny Steinmetz's company BSGR after the lucrative deal to extract iron ore from Simandou mountain range. http://www.theguardian.com/world/2013/jul/30/africa-guinea-mining-bsgr-steinmetz

Cotula, L., Vermeulen, S., Leonard, R., & Keel, J. (2009). *Land grab or development opportunity? Agricultural investment and international land deals in Africa*. IIED/FAO/IFAD. http://www.ifad.org/pub/land/land_grab.pdf

Dowding, K. (1996a). *Power concepts in social thought* (p. 45). Minneapolis: University of Minnesota Press.

Dowding, K. (1996b). *Power. Concepts in social thought* (p. 5, 7, 8). Minneapolis: University of Minnesota Press.

Dowding, K. (1996c). *Power. Concepts in social thought* (p. 3, 8). Minneapolis: University of Minnesota Press.

Dowding, K. (1996d). *Power. Concepts in social thought* (p. 4, 5). Minneapolis: University of Minnesota Press.

Els, F. Mining.com. (2013). UPDATE: Court win for Israeli billionaire in fight over $50 billion African mining prize, 10 June 2013. http://www.mining.com/simandou-the-greatest-mine-ever-sold-36183/

Fink, R., & Meierotto, L. (2002, Winter). *Cultural survival* CSQ issue 26.4. http://www.culturalsurvival.org/publications/cultural-survival-quarterly/mali/moratorium-talo-dam-construction-still-holding

Foucault, M. (2000a). Power. Volume 3. In J. D. Faubion (Ed.), *Essential works of Foucault* (p. 347). Rainbow, P. Series Editor. New York: The New Press.

Foucault, M. (2000b). Power. Volume 3. In J. D. Faubion (Ed.), *Essential works of Foucault* (pp. 340, 341). Rainbow, P. Series Editor. New York: The New Press.

Gibson, J. J. (1986). *The ecological approach to visual perception* (p. 36, 40, 41, 130–135). Hillsdale/New Jersey/London: Lawrence Erlbaum Associates Publishers.

Hurd, W., & Oakland Institute, Ethiopia. (2013, July). Understanding land investment deals in Africa. Country report: Ethiopia "ignoring abuse in Ethiopia. DFID and USAID in the Lower Omo Valley". http://www.oaklandinstitute.org/land-deals-africa-ethiopia

Ibrahim, M. (2013). Skoll world forum. *The Christian Science Monitor*. http://www.csmonitor.com/World/Making-a-difference/Change-Agent/2013/0724/How-and-why-Africa-should-solve-its-own-problems

Kilimani, N. Study on the impact of official development assistance (ODA) flows to Africa: The case of China. *Report for the Economic Development and NEPAD Division (EDND) of the United Nations Economic Commission for Africa (UNECA)*, pp. 14, 16, 19.

Kragelund, P. (2010, February). The potential role of non-traditional donor's aid in Africa. ICTSD Programme on Competitiveness and Sustainable Development. Issue Paper No.11. Geneva, Switzerland.

Krishnanda, S. (2003). The philosophy of life. *PART I*: The foundations of philosophy. Chapter 5: The theory of perception. The perceptive apparatus. Himalayas: The Divine Life Society Press. http://www.swami-krishnananda.org/phil/phil_05.html

Lukes, S. (2005a). *Power. A radical view* (The original with two major new chapters 2nd ed., p. 20, 21, 22, 42–44). Basingstoke: Palgrave Macmillan in association with the British Sociological Association.

Lukes, S. (2005b). *Power. A radical view* (The original with two major new chapters 2nd ed., p. 42, 43). Basingstoke: Palgrave Macmillan in association with the British Sociological Association.

Lukes, S. (2005c). *Power. A radical view* (The original with two major new chapters 2nd ed., p. 1). Basingstoke: Palgrave Macmillan in association with the British Sociological Association.

Lukes, S. (2005d). *Power. A radical view* (The original with two major new chapters 2nd ed., p. 12, 31, 69, 70, 78). Basingstoke: Palgrave Macmillan in association with the British Sociological Association.

Lukes, S. (2005e). *Power. A radical view* (The original with two major new chapters 2nd ed., p. 69, 73, 135). Basingstoke: Palgrave Macmillan in association with the British Sociological Association.

Lukes, S. (2005f). *Power. A radical view* (The original with two major new chapters 2nd ed., p. 20, 21, 22). Basingstoke: Palgrave Macmillan in association with the British Sociological Association.

MacLachlan, M., Carr, S. C., & McAuliffe, E. (2010). *The Aid triangle: Recognizing the human dynamics of dominance* (p. 64, 65, 66). London/New York: Justice and Identity/Fernwood Publishing/Halifax and Winnipeg/Zed Books.

Morriss, P. (1987a). *Power: A philosophical analysis* (p. 253, 338). Manchester: Manchester University Press.

Morriss, P. (1987b). *Power: A philosophical analysis* (p. 135). Manchester: Manchester University Press.

Morriss, P. (1987c). *Power: A philosophical analysis* (p. 14, 15, 18, 19). Manchester: Manchester University Press.

Morriss, P. (1987d). *Power: A philosophical analysis* (pp. 156–181). Manchester: Manchester University Press.

Morriss, P. (1987e). *Power: A philosophical analysis* (p. 32, 34). Manchester: Manchester University Press.

Mshomba, R. (2002, September). Northern subsidies hurt Africa. *Africa Recovery-Now Called Africa Renewal, 16*(2–3), 29 http://www.un.org/en/africarenewal/vol16no2/162agric.htm

Nagel, J. H. (1975a). *The descriptive analysis of power* (p. 15, 16). New Haven/London: Yale University Press.

Nagel, J. H. (1975b). *The descriptive analysis of power* (pp. 38–48). New Haven/London: Yale University Press.

Nagel, J. H. (1975c). *The descriptive analysis of power* (p. 1516). New Haven/London: Yale University Press.

Naret-Nazret.com. The first Ethiopian blog. Current affairs, business, sports, and style. http://nazret.com/blog/index.php/2011/07/29/unesco-world-heritage-committee-urges-ethiopia-to-halt-gibe-iii-dam

Oakland Institute, Sierra Leone. (2011, January). Land deals in Africa: Sierra Leone. http://www.oaklandinstitute.org/sites/oaklandinstitute.org/files/OI_SierraLeone_Land_Investment_report_0.pdf

Oakland Institute, Africa. Understanding land investment deals in Africa. http://www.oaklandinstitute.org/land-deals-africa

Oakland Institute, Mali. (2011). Understanding land deals in Africa. Country report. http://www.oaklandinstitute.org/sites/oaklandinstitute.org/files/OI_Mali_Land_Investment_report.pdf

OXFAM, New Zealand. http://www.oxfam.org.nz/report/cultivating-poverty-the-impact-of-us-cotton-subsidies-on-africa#sthash.G53AH2vZ.dpuf

Powers, W. T. (1998). *Making sense of behavior: The meaning of control* (pp. 6–97879). New Canaan: Benchmark Publications.

Powers, W. T. (2005). *Behavior: The control of perception* (pp. 34–37, 96, 129, 165). New Canaan: Benchmark Publications.

Scott, J. C. (1990a). *Domination and the arts of resistance: Hidden transcripts* (p. 14, 28, 187–190). New Haven/London: Yale University Press.

Scott, J. C. (1990b). *Domination and the arts of resistance: Hidden transcripts* (pp. 192–197, 199). New Haven/London: Yale University Press.

Scott, J. C. (1990c). *Domination and the arts of resistance: Hidden transcripts* (p. 73). New Haven/London: Yale University Press.

Scott, J. C. (1990d). *Domination and the arts of resistance: Hidden transcripts* (pp. 13–14, 52–55). New Haven/London: Yale University Press.

Scott, J. C. (1990e). *Domination and the arts of resistance: Hidden transcripts* (p. 6, 123, 124). New Haven/London: Yale University Press.

Simensen, J. Africa: The causes of underdevelopment and the challenges of globalization. In *UTENRIKSDEPARTMENTET.* Regierengen.no/Utenriksdepartementet/Refleks-utenrikspolitisk.../Serien "Globale Norge-hva.../Afrika/

Special Unit for South-South Cooperation. (2009). *Enhancing South-South and triangular cooperation*. New York: UNDP.

Stanford. (2011). The problem of perception. *Stanford Encyclopaedia of Philosophy*. First published Tue 8 Mar 2005; substantive revision Fri 4 Feb 2011. http://plato.stanford.edu/entries/perception-problem/

Stiglitz, J. E. (2003). *Globalization and its discontent* (p. 5, 6–7, 9). New Haven/London: W.W. Norton and Company.

Stiglitz, J. E. (2007). *Making globalization work* (pp. 67–74). New Haven/London: W.W. Norton and Company.

Tran, M. (2013). Sierra Leone's smallholder farmers 'worse off' after large land deals. *The Guardian*. Push to lure foreign investors has led to a rise in social problems, sparking fears of a return to conflict, warns NGO, 26 July 2013. http://www.theguardian.com/global-development/2013/jul/26/sierra-leone-farmers-land-deals

Watkins, K. (2002). Cultivating poverty: The impact of US cotton subsidies on Africa. *Oxfam New Zealand*. Briefing Paper–No. 30. http://www.oxfamamerica.org/static/oa3/files/cultivating-poverty.pdf

World Economic Forum on Africa. Cape Town, 13–15 June 2007. http://www.weforum.org/pdf/SummitReports/africa07/building_capacity.htm

CHAPTER 2

Conceptual and Key Issues

In this chapter, I shall discuss some of the concepts, terms, and notions which we find in the book. This will help us understand the different meanings ascribed to them. An understanding of these concepts will assist the readers to appreciate the various factors which come into play in the perception of power in development finance. In trying to conceptualize them, I shall discuss what some of the scholars and authors state that the words or terms should encompass and relate them to the context of development finance.

Power

One of the most difficult aspects of power is to define what power actually is. It is much easier to explain consequences, results, or outcomes of power than to define it. However, why should we want to define power? We want to define power because a definition will help us know specifically that what we are dealing with is the outcome of power, not that of any other phenomenon. Power is often discussed in the context of politics and political relationships, sociology and social sciences, philosophy, public/development administration, and psychology. This may be one of the reasons why it is difficult to define power and capture the exact nature of the concept of power. It is possible that each specialist knows what he or she perceives to be the manifestations of power in his or her specialist field. However, is there a unique concept of power around which all specialities

C.R. Spencer, *Western Financial Assistance to the Developing World*,
DOI 10.1057/978-1-137-58399-4_2

can find a common ground or a common understanding? Is there, as mathematicians would say, a "least common denominator" (LCD) when it comes to defining and understanding power? The field of "development studies" is one of the few fields of study that both transcend and encompass some of the specialities mentioned earlier, such as politics and political relationships, sociology and social sciences, public/development administration, and psychology. Development studies examine individual and collective behavior and power relationships in organizations, society, and their effects on national socioeconomic growth and development.

In development studies, power can be understood better when the context is clearly defined as in the case of international aid, development finance, development assistance, and more specifically in project or program implementation or other economic development activities. Some will argue that this can also be said for most areas of the social sciences. True, but in development studies, each of the preceding specialities can influence either individually or collectively, positively or negatively, the way we go about carrying out actions relating to growth and poverty reduction. Understanding the concept of power as it relates to development finance can help structure efforts to reduce poverty using the resources provided by external forces.

In this section, I shall look for the possible LCD and put this in the context of development finance in general and rural development finance in particular. I shall discuss a few of the authors, whose views can help us in this exercise. Max Weber (see Shortell) and Foucault (see Faubion 2000, pp. 41, 51, 52) discuss power in the context of conflict and struggle. The fight is between parties who are trying to garner "power" to their side. Why would any party want to garner "power" to its side? In this case, "power" becomes a resource, which can be utilized to obtain the outcome, which the party who possesses it desires. This has to do with the desire to control actions and behavior of the other party. This is relevant in the context of development finance, when we think of donors or external forces, as I call them in this book, seeking to control actions and activities of those receiving their assistance. They would like such control to yield fruits. In other words, like Foucault stated, the control or the power should produce an outcome.

Foucault (see Gordon 1980) talks of the productivity of power. For one to say something is productive, it first must produce. If we talk of productivity, as an economist, then the notions of cost and of returns spring to mind. In other words, the efforts, which are expended for a given amount of dollar (i.e. the "productivity"), are calculated and assessed and then compared with the returns obtained. Foucault (see Gordon 1980) states that power produces things, forms knowledge, and produces, among others, discourse. In addition, what is produced should be useful for something or to somebody and thus becomes a worthwhile production. What can we then say that power produces? Earlier, we have seen that power produces outcomes. So can we say that "outcomes" are all power can produce? Briefly, yes. Outcomes, however, are very powerful. In the case of power, outcomes could be a manifestation of changes. In the context of development finance, power can reflect action and activities. These lead to tangible products, as in agriculture, industry, and services; they lead to, or should lead to, growth, development, and income. However, power can also produce a feeling of dependency, as in the case of continued dependency by many African countries on development finance and assistance. Dependency begets dominance of the party on which one is dependent.

Moreover, dominance and domination are a major issue discussed by Lukes (2005a, pp. 85, 86, 115, 118–119). How does Lukes see power? What is Lukes' main theme with regard to power? Is his viewpoint relevant to development assistance and development finance? Can it help us to better understand the power play taking place in the financing of development? Lukes (2005b, pp. 20–28) discusses power in terms of dimensions. He saw power, which at some point, one feels that he equates to control, as having different dimensions, three in all. Though his works discuss power mostly in the political arena, the issue of getting others to carry out one's bidding against the person's will is the major thrust of his discussion. In his words, that person who carries out another's bidding is "less free to do things according to his nature and judgment." In fact, he cites examples where the non-dominant individual internalizes the dominance to the extent that he or she accepts dominance as being a natural situation. As part of this discussion on dominance, Lukes (2005c, pp. 118–119) believes that identity recognition is an important aspect of being free to "live as nature and judgement dictates."

Withholding of recognition or denying recognition can be confining and can reflect a "power over" the one whose identity is withheld. Domination, he went on "occurs where the power of some affects the interests of others by restricting their capabilities for truly human functioning" (Lukes 2005e, p. 119). He quotes Charles Taylor saying that such withholding of recognition could be considered a "form of oppression." Of all the themes discussed by Lukes (2005e, p. 119), "regional domination" is the most relevant to our discussion on power and perceptions of power by developing countries.

He defined "regional domination" as a situation where the dominant force controls the means of interpretation and communication. With this control, the dominant group projects its own experience and culture and *imposes* it as the norm. In this way, as Lukes continued, the perspective of the non-dominant or, in this case, the dominated is rendered invisible. In a way, this negatively affects the confidence of the dominated. Is there any parallel of this to what we see in the field of development finance and assistance? Is it possible that the developing/recipient countries have both internalized an inferior status and accepted external "experience and culture" as the norm?

We may need to refer to Dowding (1996a, pp. 4–6, 8) and his concepts of "power to" and "power over," with the former being subsumed in the latter, to answer these questions. This implies that the "capacity" is within a person to get another person to do something against his/her will if the former has "power over" the latter. To a large extent, external forces have different sources of power, which we shall see in Chap. 3. The sources of power that external forces can call upon have made it such that these external forces can be said to have both "power to" and "power over." We shall elaborate further in Chaps. 3 and 4 on these powers and the outcomes. Another aspect of Dowding's (1996c, p. 38) view on power, which I find relevant to our discussion on power and development finance and assistance, is his view that the characteristics of a group can affect "its ability to mobilize its members to secure common aims." This is important when we discuss the perceptions of recipient/non-dominant forces concerning power play in development finance in Chaps. 3 and 4.

In Chap. 3, I mention economic/financial power as one of the sources of power. This is in line with Dowding (1996d, p. 3), when he stated that elites and business people often dominate through their power. In his analysis, he indicated that power is closely related to cause. This means that to show power, the actor must cause another to do something. However, unlike Simon (1969), Nagel (1975a, pp. 9, 10, 11, 20), and Dahl (1968), Dowding (1996e, p. 3) states that causation and power are not the same. He considers power to be a dispositional concept, from which I would like to infer that it is a "capacity" to do things and the capacity to exercise power. In his view, power consists of two concepts: "outcome power" and "social power." The former is the ability to bring about outcomes using another person, and the latter is the ability to change the incentive structure of another person or persons. Here, I would draw a parallel to "power to" and "power over," respectively, which I had explained earlier.

Other authors such as Dahl (1968, pp. 91–96) and Nagel (1975b, pp. 36, 72, 73, 83–91) have made efforts to measure power. As part of the effort to measure power, Nagel discusses direct and indirect influences and the relationship of power with causation. Nagel (1975c, p. 24) indicated that power is a causation of preferences. He brought in the concepts of attenuation and obsolescence of influences. Attenuation relates to the number of "links" between what he calls "ultimate" cause and the outcome. If the number of links is high, the lower would be the direct effect of the cause on the outcome. Obsolescence refers to the time taken for the cause to take effect. In other words, if the time taken from cause to outcome is long, other influences could have made the person change his preferences, and therefore, one cannot attribute the outcome directly to the cause. These concepts can help to improve our understanding of the discussion in Chap. 4 relating to the way the source of information can influence the perception of the person receiving the information concerning development finance package. Whether the information is received, first, second, or third hand could influence the way the perceiver regards any power play involved with providing development finance. It is possible that information received a long period after the initial/original information is diffused could have been influenced, as we shall develop in Chap. 4, by other factors and even by the perception of the person conveying the information; this combines, in a sense, both the attenuation and the obsolescence factors.

Nagel, like Weber (1947), Bierstedt (1950) before him, and also Axelrod (1970, p. 154) discusses the effect of conflict and power. He believed that the relationship between the two is complex. Weber, Bierstedt, and Axelrod feel that the conflict is a necessary condition of power. In development finance, it would seem as if there is perpetual conflict, especially in the context of the conditions required by the dominant forces/donors before the assistance package is disbursed. However, as we saw in Chap. 1, if we consider development finance as a "commercial" good and the non-dominant force is buying, the "contract," as we saw, is the document binding the two parties together, and the conditions are thus the part of the "contract." There does not then seem to be conflict as a *condition* of power in the context of development finance and development assistance. Even if we accept Axelrod's (1970, p. 154) "conflict of interest" which Nagel (1975d, p. 154) called "conflict of preferences," and for which he states that the relation of power to conflict of interest is complicated, I do not see, a priori, conflict as being a condition of power in the context of development finance and development assistance. As we shall see in Chap. 3, the dominant forces have many sources of power that they call upon depending on the circumstances. These have ensured that any possible "thought" of conflict would have been eliminated well before. I shall discuss the issue of conflict in development finance later.

If we go back into the history of African countries, as we do in Chaps. 3 and 4, we can see that some of the power sources existed even before development finance and development assistance as such existed. There was thus a situation of an unequal relationship during the colonial period. This unequal relationship carried on into the independence and the post-independence periods. Moreover, as we shall see in Chap. 3, there may not necessarily be a conflict of interest or of preferences, because as we shall see again in Chap. 3, the dominant forces and the non-dominant forces in the context of development finance have one objective in mind. This objective is *development*, and hence, the development finance package. In those cases, when the dominant and non-dominant forces focus on the same objective, we shall call these times situations of "constellation of interests." However, I can see circumstances where one can envisage conflict, especially where there is conflict of "preferences," not necessarily of "interest," as I shall show in Chap. 3. This is when the non-dominant force would prefer certain types of conditions—say for example, conditions which they do not have to fulfill before disbursement or conditions that are easy to fulfill—and the dominant force prefers more stringent conditions or condition precedent to first disbursement.

Another aspect of power often discussed is whether power is fixed or variable. Nagel (1975e, pp. 158–159) discusses the positions of Parsons, Tannenbaum, Pye, and Huntington and discussed issues relating to total power as being fixed. He provides equations as to how to measure total power. However, in the context of development finance, and as we shall see in Chaps. 3 and 4, total power increases with time and with any addition to the development finance amount. We shall see this in Chap. 4 in the case of Chinese financial assistance in Zambia (Mining Review 2011; also Amanor-WP-054) and Nigeria (see Falk 2013). Nevertheless, this increase, though it is dynamic, has to continue over time for the total power to be of a level that would acquire both "power to" *and* "power over." If the development finance amount does not continue to increase cumulatively, and the "contracts," which we discussed in Chap. 1, are finalized, the flow of funds will be reduced, and the flow of power, or as some would say the flow of influence, would wane and disappear. Such a situation could happen in the case of loans, and debt servicing would continue over time. Where we are dealing with grants, there would be no debt servicing payments due.

As loans were the order of the day in the past, however, and where the debts had not been canceled, the payment of debt services to the dominant forces would continue over decades. As such, the "capacity" and the "vehicle" would still exist for power to be exercised, and for the dominant forces to "cause" the non-dominant forces to carry out actions or activities which could be considered "outcomes" of the actions of the dominant forces. In fact, as we shall see in Chap. 3, the new budget support approach to development finance and the continuous flow of development finance continually increases the total amount of the funds disbursed from a large number of donors/dominant forces. The continual increases, and the cumulative amount of funds from all the dominant forces participating in the package, tend to lock the non-dominant force into a gridlock-type situation, from which it would be difficult for power not to be exercised on it.

In the context of development finance, the question by Nagel (1975f, p. 158) concerning absoluteness, that is, fixed or variability, of power remains a moot question. The common denominator, I can find from the different authors discussed earlier and those we reviewed, is that power makes another person do something. It is, as Domhoff (2005, p. 1) would say, "the ability to produce effect." This act of producing effect is similar to Foucault's (see Gordon 1980, p. 119) view that power is productive, which we saw earlier. Domhoff (2005, p. 1) went on to talk of collective and distributive power. These are facets of the same concept of power, which in the final analysis is a relational phenomenon; power always concerns the relationship of one person or group of persons with another person or another group of persons. These relationships lead to outcomes. The outcome is caused by the act of one person "exercising power."

In the context of climate finance and the choice of the institution to manage the funds that would become available, Ballesteros et al. (2010a, pp. viii, ix, 2, 4) discuss three crucial dimensions one of which is power. The power the institution will have over the funds and, both directly and indirectly, over the recipients of the funds. However, Ballesteros et al. stated that power goes with responsibility and accountability. In fact, these last two aspects are relevant to the discussion that we will have later in this chapter and also in Chap. 4 concerning "breaks in power" flow. Still in the context of development finance for climate change, Ballesteros et al. emphasize the issue of how perception of an institution's legitimacy can be influenced by design choices. These include how transparent it is in its operations, how participatory it is perceived, and how the contributors and recipients perceive it as accountable for its actions. These factors thus demonstrate the critical nature of perception in the field of development finance.

Perception

The purpose of this section is to explore which of the many theories or models of perception would best help us understand the perceptions of the recipients of development finance (i.e. the perception of the non-dominant force), as it relates to power play between the external and internal forces. To help us in this respect, it would be appropriate to understand what we mean by "perception." Bustos Farias (University of London) gives a good definition of perception by stating, "perception is a process by which individuals organize and interpret their sensory impressions in order to give meaning to their environment." Perception then is a response to stimuli. Authors, including Rock and Mack (1994a, pp. 23–24), Ballesteros (1994a, pp. 1, 3–6), and Robinson (2001a, pp. 2, 3, 4, 8–9), deal with perception in terms of response to visual stimuli, emphasizing such aspects as the degree of attention to the specific stimuli and possible surrounding geographic areas relating to the specific stimuli. In his discussion on behavior, control, and perception, Powers (1998a, pp. 6, 7, 9 24) links perception with control. He feels that perception is important for control, believing that perception is what our brains through our senses tell us about the world. In his schema theory as an information processing model, Axelrod (1973a, pp. 1248–1266) talks of perception as "how a single person observes and makes sense out of a complex environment." This is similar to the Bustos Farias' (University of London) definition indicated earlier. In the viewpoint of Powers (2005b, pp. 3, 106, 252), we see the use of the plural "senses." This means that it is not just a visual sense as some of the previously mentioned authors state. Powers (2005c, pp. 7, 10) puts emphasis on controlling; he feels that the general rule about control is that perception precedes control. So far, we note that the authors dealt with single individuals. In our discussion in this book, we need to move from the perception of the single person to the perception of group(s) of persons. In fact, we need to see how different groups, both homogeneous and heterogeneous, perceive the exercise of power on their countries and on themselves.

In all of the authors' (Powers 1998e, 2005; Ballesteros 1994a) viewpoints, the common denominator is the brain. The cognitive process plays an important role in perception. Most of the authors in their discussions give importance to memory, both short and long term. However, as Schacter and Badgaiyan (1992) indicated, "memory is not a unitary or monolithic entity." Berger (2008a, p. 166) indicated that brain-imaging techniques show that there are distinct sections of the brain concerned with specific aspects of memory. All of the authors mentioned have subsumed the notions of storage and retrieval of stored material from the brain in their discussions. This is similar to Berger's (2008a, p. 166) explicit and implicit memory, where explicit memory is one that can be recalled as needed and implicit memory is for, as Berk puts it, "routines" that stay concealed until "a particular stimulus brings them to mind." In Robinson's (2001b, pp. 1, 4, 29, 30) book discussing the various theories of perception, the underlying theme throughout the discussion relates to sense data; in other sections of his book, some theories question the actuality of sense data as opposed to illusory nature of the stimuli, whether the perceiver is not hallucinating and whether the perceiver has an actual physical experience.

Unlike some of the other authors such as Ballesteros, Rock and Mack (1994b, pp. 24–32) whose laboratory tests relate to vision and what is seen by the "perceiver," over a specific, generally short period of time, Powers' (1998b, pp. 8–10) examples/models are drawn from the motoring world, and the "experience" lasts for a much longer period. In this context, Powers (2005d, pp. 148–153) believes that control and perception work at various levels and that the brain is the uppermost level in determining the action. How a person deals with the new information in the Axelrod (1973a, pp. 1248–1266) model of perception and cognition is by checking to see if the new information or stimuli fits well with interpretations, that is, information already stored in the brain. An example is drawn from the motoring world, when we stand in the street and watch vehicles go by. When we see a vehicle with the insignia "H" go by, and on the assumption that we have stored various vehicle insignias in our memory, we go to our memory bank to see if it is the "H" of the Honda or slightly different "*H*" of the Hyundai. This has some similarities with some of the other authors, for example, Ballesteros (1994b, p. 9), who talk of intentional/unintentional retrieval of previous experience.

All of the authors cited agree tacitly that information processing subsumes all their thinking about perception. The perceiver gathers information during the experiments in the laboratory, by such authors as Rock and Mack (1994b, pp. 24–32), Robinson (2001b, pp. 1, 4, 29), and Ballesteros (1994b, p. 9), or observed in real life or presumed in the models as in the case of Powers. In a review of the book by Mack and Rock (1998, pp. 24–32), Cathleen Moore (2001, p. 3) discusses "conscious and unconscious" perception, meaning when a perceiver deliberately reacts to the specific stimuli and/or reacts without actually realizing it, to visual stimuli within the geographic area of the specific stimuli. All of these authors, including Powers (2005e, pp. 37, 38, 39), agree that information is received by the brain. How the brain stores the information is often a cause for discussion among psychologists. In addition, the different psychologists have different and varied models of memory and what information is stored and/or recalled.

However, each individual uses the information in his or her own way, remembering some and forgetting others, either deliberately or unintentionally. This last adverb has spurned debates among psychologists as to intentionality and unintentionality. This aspect of unintentionality is similar to what some authors and reviewers, such as Mack and Rock (1998), Rock and Mack (1994c, p. 35), and Moore (2001, p. 3), refer to as "inattentional blindness," that is being unintentionally "blind" to some aspects within the geographic area of the stimuli of the senses, generally visual stimuli. Some authors (see Rock and Mack 1998) believe that such "blindness" may be a limitation of the memory or of the perception itself. There is also not much of an agreement concerning whether to attribute the "blindness" to memorial limitation or perceptual limitation of the perceiver. "Unintentional blindness" is similar to what social information processing models of perception call selective attention/comprehension. The perceiver consciously or unconsciously "selects" what he or she would want to recall.

Again, still in the arena of information processing, it is possible that the Gibsons' (1986a, p. 36) reference to "affordance" could explain these different concepts. "Affordance," according to Gibson (1986a, pp. 36, 127–134), relates to how one perceiver "perceives" an object, with perceiving here being a conscious "action" oriented concept. One can see but not perceive, with seeing being a "passive" act or a stimulus reaching the eye; seeing is something that we unconsciously do, just like hearing, which is stimulus passively reaching the ear. "Listening," on the other hand, is conscious "action" oriented. It is possible that the perception of the same object by different "perceivers" would be very different. Gibson believes that in such cases, past experience, information already stored in the brain (which, in effect, is a function of past experience), and particular interests, all of which I call outcome of one's socialization process, influence the "affordance" (i.e. the *focus*), given to a particular object or stimuli.

The "socialization process" is embodied in the "schemata" of the individual that he/she calls upon to help analyze any stimuli to the senses. In other words, the interpretations of different perceivers would be different one from another, based on, among others, the factors mentioned earlier. In a way, Chemero (2003, p. 580) confirms this when he stated that "affordances are opportunities for behavior," believing, as it were, that "different animals have different abilities, and therefore, affordances are relative to the behavioral abilities of the animals that perceive them." I find that all of the concepts by the various authors have some relevance to perception as it relates to development finance and development assistance.

How do these authors help us understand how the recipients of development finance "perceive" the assistance? The more important question is how do they help us understand how the recipients "perceive" any power play between the dominant forces, which are giving the assistance, and the non-dominant forces, which are receiving the assistance? In a way, each of the various authors and the theories they espouse contribute to our understanding of how the non-dominant force processes the information received concerning development finance. In fact, the different concepts and notions regarding information received and how it is processed, as brought out by information processing theories, help us look more closely at what is received in terms of information. It also brings us to the notion that is known as "conveyed concepts" (i.e. ideas and concepts transferred from one individual to another) (see Pediaview). The issues relating to "conveyed concept" is important for our analysis, as we shall see later. In fact, as we saw earlier, psychologists have different models, and each of these models has different limitations. These different models with their limitations lead to questions as to whether a perceiver who is receiving the sensory stimuli first hand is actually seeing objects as they really are. For the models explain some behaviors and not others. Because of the limitations of the various models, there is not agreement, though some psychologists would not agree with me.

In "conveyed concept," the problem could be more serious. For the issue of conveyed concept, wherein the perceiver's auditory or visual senses do not receive the stimuli firsthand, could pose significant concerns regarding the physical actuality, or the veracity of what is being conveyed. Here the concepts of "attenuated and obsolescent influences" discussed previously are relevant. In addition, the method or the style of conveying could influence both what is conveyed and how it is received. As with other concepts relating to perception, in conveyed concept, the perceiver has to encode the concept in his or her brain and retrieve stored information that, as Powers (2005e, pp. 37, 38, 39) and also Axelrod (1973a, pp. 1248–1266) noted, will help him or her find the right combination in his or her stored memory. He or she will try first in the short-term memory, which can be understood to refer to Ballesteros (1994b, p. 9) and Berger's (2008a, p. 166) "implicit memory," which is considered as non-declarative. If none can be found there, then he or she will go into the long-term/explicit memory, from which any retrieval has to be consciously done, as opposed to "implicit memory" from which retrieval may be unconsciously done. This information will help him better understand the new stimuli, new situation, or new information. This process will help put the new stimuli/situation in perspective and then take appropriate action. Powers (1998e, pp. 12, 21, 24) believed that the biology of humans plays an important role in this decision-making process and in the subsequent action.

In development finance, the information concerning the details about the finance can be directly obtained as in the case of the government officials or public servants directly involved with the finance package with the lender/donor, either finalizing it, negotiating the terms of the package, or signing the grant/loan agreement. For many others, such as the ultimate recipient/beneficiaries of development funds, they may have been involved, directly or indirectly, in the preparation of the program, but may not be aware of the terms and conditions of the finance package. There is a third category of persons or groups of persons who may not be aware of the package and who learn about it through a third party. They may not also be aware of the terms and conditions of the package. Very often, the terms and conditions influence the perception of power play in the context of development finance. The source of information about the package and the knowledge of the terms and conditions in turn influence the perception of the person receiving the information.

From where do the ultimate recipients of development finance (e.g. the farmers, and the ordinary citizens) get their information, if they are not privy to, or aware of the detailed conditions of the finance package? Do they get the information from newspapers, the radio, or other media instruments? Perhaps they get their information by word of mouth from people who have read newspapers, listened to the radio, or received from other media outlets. How reliable is the information from the different sources? The source or sources of their information are very important. The source would influence their perception of, first, the development finance package, negatively or positively. Secondly, it would also influence their perception of the power play between the different forces: their country (the non-dominant force) as represented by their government and the external force (the dominant force) which is the lender/donor. If the source has a negative view of the donor/lender, the information that is given about the development package would tend to be "colored" and very judgmental in a negative way. "Colored" information is understood to mean, information that has been influenced by the perception (i.e. past experience, information stored in long- and short-term memories, etc.) of the person conveying the information. Therefore, the information that the farmer, fishermen, traders, and others receive would be colored by the perception of the party giving them the information. The information then would be put in a negative perspective. As Eleanor and James Gibson (1986b, pp. 138, 139) would say, this is because of the "affordance," with which the person or persons perceived the information.

In general, Gibson (1986b, pp. 138, 139) believes that in response to stimuli of the five senses by an object, each individual focuses on aspects/affordances that concern them directly. He cites Koffka that a "postbox has a demand character only when the observer needs to mail a letter." However, he stated that the object, in this case the postbox, is not dependent on the need of the perceiver, but the affordance of the postbox is invariant and exists, whether the perceiver has a need to post a letter or not. This could be considered similar to what Rock and Mack (1994c, p. 35) called "in-attentional blindness," in the sense that one can be "blind" to things to which one does not pay attention.

With the preceding discussion in mind, how can we perceive power? Is it possible to describe how people perceive power? What are the sociolinguistic adjectives that we can use to describe perceptions of power? Human information processing begins with input picked up by the five senses; then proceeds to brain reactions, connections, and stored memories; and concludes with some action such as a word or a gesture. Can we find a way of understanding the perception of power in the information processing theory? Can we say our perception is favorable, unfavorable, positive, or negative? Power on those whom it is exercised can be described as overwhelming, overbearing, and oppressive; they perceive power as oppressive, overwhelming, or overbearing. Power is abstract and cannot therefore be physically seen. What sensory organ do we use to perceive power? We can therefore say that power does not respond to any stimulus of our sensory organ. Can we use the sense-datum concept (see Robinson 2001c, pp. 1–2, 188) to describe how we perceive power? Although it may not be possible to use our sensory organs to perceive power, we can "feel" (in our mind) power when it is exercised. In that case, we can perceive what the power has made us to do.

As we shall see in Chaps. 3 and 4, such authors as Dowding (1996b, pp. 4–7), Lukes (2005g, pp. 26–30), and Morris, (1987, pp. 30–34) among others, have shown the "force" that "power" can exert or exercise on people, and which can provide expected or unexpected outcome. In general, the exercise of power by someone on another person produces expected outcome, which we earlier called, the product of power. However, there are many questions that arise when discussing perceptions of power in the context of development finance. Does the outcome of the exercise of power have any influence on how we perceive power? Can the way power is exercised influence our perception? Does the objective of the intervention influence our perception of power? Does the source of power influence our perception?

Like power, perception is a vast area of study. Philosophers, psychologists, psychiatrists, neurologists, and computer scientists have written many papers and books trying to get the exact nature of perception and what influences or could influence it. As we saw earlier, there are many theories which seek to help us better understand perception. These theories will help us evaluate what the recipients of development finance feel about power that is exercised on them. In his discussion of models and generalizations, Powers (1998f, pp. 19, 21, 22, 24) reviews the behaviorists' theory of behavior. In this model, the environment and the biological makeup have an important influence on behavior, which is, in turn, influenced by perception.

The information they receive from the media or other parties are akin to "conveyed concepts," as they receive it secondhand, as it were. First, second, or thirdhand, do we know whether these recipients are concerned about the conditions of the assistance? If they received their information about the development finance package from the media or another person, or are themselves directly concerned and are privy to the negotiations or agreement concerning the package, we can ask, as with James Gibson (1986c, pp. 130–136) which of the many affordances did they perceive? In general, each individual or group of individuals will focus on that aspect or those aspects (i.e. the "affordance"), which concern them directly. As we shall see in Chap. 4, the civil servant will want to focus on those aspects of the development finance package, which he or she thinks will further his or her career, that is his or her chances for promotion or for an increase in income. For politicians in government, their affordance will be those aspects of the program that will help them stay in office. However, if they are corrupt politicians, their affordance may not be the program or its outcome, or the conditions, which the country had to fulfill before accessing the package. Their "affordance" will be the possibility it affords to them, through various means to siphon some of the funds to their private use. This latter statement receives corroboration from the many cases of fund diversion reported in the media (see Faul 2014; also United States House of Representative 2002) and the arrest made of the former governor of Delta state in Nigeria, Iboris, and the jail term of 13 years he got for fraud totaling US$50 million. This type of affordance will also be that of the less-than-honest civil servant in the ministry concerned with the implementation of the program.

Thus, as the Gibsons (1986c, pp. 130–136) stated, "perception is not automatic." I stated earlier in this chapter that perceiving is an active process that occupies our senses. The particular affordance we choose is influenced by what Ballesteros (1994c, pp. 9–13) called "priming." This is the prior attention paid to the object or the stimuli. The key word is "attention." This is because "to perceive," we need to pay attention; however, attention is not the only factor that influences the affordance we choose to perceive. Berger (2008b, p. 162) listed four factors which contribute to the choice of affordance we perceive. These include sensory awareness, immediate motivation, current development, and past experience. She gave the example of a lemon, which she stated gives "affordances" of smelling, tasting, viewing, squeezing, biting, and throwing. The specific affordance selected will vary depending on the four factors listed earlier. In other words, the interest and/or the specialty of the person(s) will influence the particular affordance selected. I would add that the interest is dynamic and could vary with time or even change in circumstances. In the preceding example of Berger, (2008b, p. 162) if the object is changed to an orange and the perceiver becomes thirsty, he or she would be more interested in using the orange to partially assuage his or her thirst.

In the same vein, as we saw earlier and as will be elaborated in Chap. 4, the development finance package provides different "affordances" to the people and the governments of the recipient countries. However, affordance does not explain all aspects of perception as regards the power play in development finance. The various concepts discussed so far relating to perception (e.g. the response to visual stimuli) are appropriate when considering the reception of information through the written, audio, and visual press.

The people of the recipient countries first have a perception of development finance package directly through the media. Given the preceding discussion, the issue at hand would be which aspect of the information received was actually perceived by those who received the information about the package. With news in the written press, it is possible to go back and read the relevant sections in detail, and then those aspects, which were not perceived at the first reading, could be better understood at the second or third reading. The first reading of the article could be related to Ballesteros' (1994c, pp. 9–13) "priming," with the second reading influenced by the prior priming through the first reading. In the case of perception through the radio, the means through which many people in Africa receive information, the possibility of relistening is negligible to non-existent. With television, the possibility exists for one both to listen and to see the information and the issues involved. The act of perceiving would then be stimuli to at least two of the sensory organs. With the stimuli now directed to/on two sensory organs, the question then arises as to whether the perception would be stronger, eliminating in a way some of the aspects of "inattentional blindness," which we discussed earlier. Would the perceiver then become aware of more areas surrounding the stimuli than if it were just one sensory organ? In some rare cases, and in both radio and television, an added aspect is the possibility of recording the item. This situation is not common in the African context.

It exists as a possibility, however, that can influence the perception. On the assumption that all the details concerning the development finance package were made known to the people in the recipient countries through one of the media facilities available to the perceiver, would he be able to perceive that there was and is power play involved in the development finance package? In most of the information relating to reporting of development finance packages on a sample of current and archival newspaper coverage of development finance packages, for Ghana (GhanaWeb 2012; also GhanaWeb 2006) Mali (Malikounda 2014), Malawi (allAfrica 2008; also MACAUHUB 2009), Kenya (Sang 2014), Zambia (Lusaka Times 2013), and Sierra Leone (Awareness Times 2014), which I reviewed, the conditions of the finance packages were not divulged. The information generally stated that *country X, or group of countries C, or institution Y gave a grant or a loan to the country for purpose D.* In general, the donor country is a developed country, a development finance institution in a developed country or in a developing country, or an emerging power.

As we shall see in Chap. 3, we have situations where developing countries well-endowed with financial and economic resources are also providing development assistance to less-endowed countries. Even if the conditions of the grant or loan had been divulged in the reports in the media, would the ordinary citizen or farmer recognize the full impact and implications of the conditions, which the government had to fulfill before receiving the funds? As we shall note in Chap. 4, strong influences on the affordance of any perceiver or group of perceivers will be the current situation and their past experience. This is the aspect some psychologists, like Powers (1998g, pp. 9, 10, 11), refer to as checking with the "reference position" and what I will call "going back to memory." It means checking in one's short-term memory to see how the particular stimulus (i.e. the information) was dealt with in the past. Although not directly related, I see some connection with Wilson and Sperber's (2004, pp. 607–632) notions of relevance and cognition. This is the notion that an input captured by one of the senses or even one captured earlier and stored in the memory becomes relevant when this input connects positively in the "perceiver's cognitive processing." Here the connection, which I see, is not in the theory (relevance theory) proffered by Wilson and Sperber (2004, pp. 607–632), but in the role played by the cognitive function embodied in the brain. The main point to note and the connection with the other authors, which I see, is that the "perceiving," even though it is carried out as a reaction to the stimulus by the sensory organs, is processed by the brain (i.e. a cognitive function) and is done individually.

These two facts, "processing by the brain" and "done individually," make it difficult to ascertain the perceptions of the individual who perceives. As I explained earlier, many factors influence the perception of which two of the key ones are "past experience and current situation." Braman (2009, pp. 20–24, 120–123) infers this when she talks about attitudinal and policy preferences which influence judicial decision-makers. These two factors (attitudinal and policy preferences) are in turn influenced by past experience and current situation. As a result, like Braman, I agree that it is hard to know what is in the minds of the perceivers, who in our discussion are the population of the countries recipient of development finance, and in the case of Braman, the Supreme Court judges in the USA. I have therefore used examples and models in Chaps.3 and 4, to help understand the perceptions of the various segments of the population in the recipient countries. The use of their private/hidden transcripts, reserved only for persons who are family members, close friends, or close group members, contributes to "getting into their minds." This gives us, as it were, more precise ideas about how they felt with regard to the development finance packages and the possible exercise of power in their countries.

Development Finance

In this section, we shall try to circumscribe development finance as the word is used in the book. We make a distinction between development finance and other forms of assistance which constitute foreign assistance/aid. These other forms include emergency relief, humanitarian aid, and military assistance. Development finance and development assistance are also known as "foreign aid." Sumner and Mallet (2013a, p. 12) cite some of the authors who have proposed what they call normative definitions of development assistance. They believe that these definitions are conventional and have remained so despite the fact that the world is changing. These authors consider the definition proposed by the Development Assistance Committee (DAC) of the Organization for Economic Cooperation and Development (OECD) (Sumner and Mallet 2013b, pp. 13–16) as the standard and conventional definition of foreign aid/assistance. This relates to providing financial resources, technical experts, or in-kind goods to developing countries. Such resources are intended to stimulate socioeconomic development and growth and are to be provided as grants or loans with concessional financing of 25%. Lancaster (2007a, pp. 9–11) uses the conventional definition of foreign aid, and she includes official assistance to countries including Russia, Israel, Ukraine, and Korea, which have per capita incomes of $US9200 (see Lancaster 2007a, pp. 9–11). The DAC's definition refers only to low-income countries.

In this book, our analysis refers to development finance. This includes all transfers intended to promote, foster, or stimulate economic and social development and growth. It also includes provision of funds for the encouragement or the establishment of growth- or development-enabling environment, such as funds relating to the improvement of the judiciary, parliament, financial, and other governmental services. It could be argued that concessionality can increase the "capacity" of the external donor to exercise power, especially if the amount of the financial assistance is substantial and very important to the recipient country. The recipient country would not be inclined to lose such an important amount that has a reduced transaction cost. Our theme is power and perception and "concessionality" of the financing neither adds nor subtracts from the power the external forces exercise over the recipient countries. However, the "concessionality" of the financing can influence the perception of the population of the recipient countries if and when they are made aware of it. It will suffice for our purpose in this book to agree that there are various views concerning the meaning of development finance and development assistance; often the differences are nuances. All the authors agree that development assistance is virtually synonymous with concessionality. The nuances are often in the terms used. For example, for the DAC, the objective is to improve "development," whereas Lancaster (2007b, p. 10) prefers "to improve human condition."

In the context of analyzing power and the capacity to exercise power, the issue of concessionality is not very relevant. I am interested in observing and analyzing the instruments that give donors, lenders, and others, whom I group together as external forces the power to influence, control, or change behaviors. I would like to focus on that factor or those factors which get countries and their people to accept things they might not otherwise accept or to do things they might not otherwise do. In other words, I would like to direct attention to the "vehicle" of power. We have chosen to look at this issue of power within the field of financial, economic, and social assistance. I therefore refer to "development finance" as assistance, which enhances the economic and social well-being of the people and promotes growth and development in the recipient countries.

A major aspect discussed concerning development finance is the motivation for the financing. Some authors, quoted by Lancaster (2007c, p. 3), based on the premise that states operate in a chaotic environment, believe that power, security, and survival are the overarching objectives of countries that provide development finance, especially development assistance. Alesina and Dollar (2000, pp. 33, 34) and Martens (2002, pp. 15, 23), among others, believe that development finance is influenced by political, commercial, economic, and strategic considerations. They are actually echoing Morgenthau and Liska, quoted by Lancaster (2007d, pp. 3, 64), who stated that foreign aid is an instrument of political power. Some authors (Lancaster 2007d, pp. 3, 64) see foreign aid as being driven by self-interest. There are others (Lancaster 2007c, pp. 3) with socialist inclinations who believe that foreign aid is a tool used by some countries to dominate and subjugate the people of other countries. Development finance/foreign aid is indeed a tool for foreign policy or diplomacy. Lancaster (2007e, pp. 43–50) demonstrated that foreign aid is used by different countries for different purposes at different times in the evolution of time. In Chap. 3, we shall see that the motivation for foreign aid/development assistance is not static. I agree with Lancaster that the motivation is dynamic and is to some extent influenced by the intrinsic value put on the recipient country by the specific donor at any particular time. As Lancaster puts it, aid helps the recipient countries to use their own resources for other activities, stretching, as it were, the disposable resources of the recipient government.

Nevertheless, Lancaster states, though, that aid can be used as an inducement and a compensation for recipients to act in "ways favoured by the donor." This is linked to the "reward and punishment" power which is possessed by the external forces which we shall discuss in Chap. 3. This is in fact the power to reward and to punish that is "owned" by the dominant forces and which we discussed earlier in this chapter. In fact, as Sumner and Mallet (2013c, pp. 14–17) stated and as we shall see in Chap. 3, donors/external forces use different instruments. These instruments are a function of the motivation of the external forces. Chapter 4 discusses how the different motivations influence the source of power called upon by the external/dominant forces and the instrument used is, in turn, varied according to the desired objective of the moment. Thus, the motivation or purpose of giving assistance varies from strategic to economic, and commercial to humanitarian. This last is related to the moral aspect of what Najam (2002a, pp. 153–160) termed "charity." The motivation or purpose of giving development finance and development assistance, as we shall see in Chaps. 3 and 4, does not annul the fact that donors acquire both the vehicle and the capacity to exercise power with such assistance.

Lancaster (2007f, pp. 4, 6) argues that the motivation or purpose of the assistance is significantly influenced by domestic politics. This tandem motivation/domestic politics also affects the organizational arrangements put in place to manage the transfer of funds. Domestic politics, especially domestic political institutions, influences many aspects of the country's aid-giving structure. This includes the list of countries to receive assistance, the specific ultimate recipients or beneficiaries, the type and volume of the assistance received by each country in the list, the terms of the assistance, and the institutions to manage the assistance from the donor perspective. Lancaster (2007g, p. 6) goes even further by stating that the "structure of government" also has a significant role to play in the area of motivation, aid policies, and how the issue of assistance is handled. These policies reflect the financial situation of the government and the political situation within the country. The structure of government also assists in fostering interest groups including non-governmental organizations (NGOs) involved in managing aid funds and implementing programs and projects. These interest groups take various forms. Some of them are humanitarian and/or philanthropic societies, whereas others are region-specific from within the donor countries as well as from the developing countries. Others try to promote their specific causes. These groups become part of the domestic political pressure groups, fighting for one cause or the other. They would be lobbying to obtain more government funds for foreign aid geared toward promoting their specific causes, whether these relate to poverty reduction, women and gender issues, transparency and accountability in the recipient countries, or judicial uprightness throughout the economy in the recipient countries.

The interest groups in the developed countries and the general public in the developing countries are part of the political arena and are stakeholders in any development agenda. Kindornay et al. (2012, pp. v, 6) consider that the "development cooperation architecture" is presently dominated by what they call Northern countries and that this architecture needs to be broadened to include more South-South actors into the development architecture. In that regard, the interest groups discussed in the preceding paragraph would monitor, some closely and regularly and others periodically, the use of the funds by the recipient countries, trying to ensure that the funds are used for the intended purposes and that they are not wasted or go into private pockets of leaders in the recipient countries. Najam (2002b, p. 156) indicated that development assistance funds should be used to foster sustainable development in the recipient countries. Fostering development is not always achieved, and the effectiveness of the operation and the transfer of the funds are inadequate. This is discussed in Chap. 3.

Development finance is an integral part of development cooperation. However development cooperation implies an overt acceptance of the existence and the participation of the recipient countries, much more so than the term development finance. I consider development finance more neutral, wherein the recipient is less "visible" but the tendency is more toward thinking of the financier than the financed. Thus, cooperation, to some extent, takes care of Najam's (2002c, p. 155) criticism that too much emphasis is placed on the supply side, with efforts being placed more on increasing the supply of the flow of funds. The demand side tends to be neglected. Kindornay et al. (2012b, p. 5) seem to agree, especially with regard to the governance mechanism for managing funds relating to climate finance, which is part of development finance as is discussed in this book. Kindornay et al. believe that the balance of power with regard to the governance mechanism for climate finance should be such as to make decision-making less unequal and more balanced. Recipient countries should perceive less domination in the mechanism.

Can a more balanced cooperation architecture be generalized for all organizations involved in managing and/or transferring funds to developing countries? Is it possible to have an architecture where "more power is released to those further down the food chain of development cooperation?" Given the fact that donors often use funds obtained from and approved by their taxpayers for the purpose of "assisting the less fortunate" recipient countries, donor governments and institutions have to account for the use of the funds. Therefore, releasing more "power to decide on" to the recipient countries would seem difficult, if not impossible. However, development finance/cooperation has evolved to the extent that the "power to decide on" in many ways and in many aspects now rests with the recipient countries. Decisions about priorities and other aspects now seemingly rest with recipient countries. However, these priorities tend to be guided by what the donors consider as important for the economies of the recipient countries and where they would be prepared to put their funds. As we shall see in Chaps. 3 and 4, with the present architecture surrounding the new instrument of budgetary support financing, choices for the developing countries in terms of sources of funds seem to be limited.

Nevertheless, in the case of international development finance institutions, there seems to be a gradual "release of power." Nonetheless, in some institutions, where the developed countries still hold the balance of power, it would be worthwhile to revisit the architecture of the governance mechanism. A possible candidate could be the African Development Fund (AfDF), where the participating states (which are non-African countries with the exception of Libya and the Republic of South Africa) contribute a very substantial proportion of the total resources (African Development Bank 2014). As a result, the decision-making mechanism concerning operations or programs to approve is very heavily skewed in their favor. Given the shareholding structure, this imbalance can only be modified if and when more African countries become financially strong to take up shareholding participation in the AfDF. Another possibility would be when all of the countries in Africa become developed to the extent that they have graduated to a higher income level where they do not need a grant or concessional financing.

Legitimacy

Legitimacy is derived from the Latin "to make lawful." But what actually is "legitimacy?" Why is a discussion on it relevant in an analysis of power, perceptions, and development finance? In general, legitimacy, used with reference to governments, organizations, and institutions, is very much related to the perception of society, in the broad sense of the word, with regard to the lawfulness of the government or organization to carry out its operations or some aspects of its operations. There are various types of legitimacy. In fact, Brinkerhoff (2005a, pp. 3–6) identifies four meanings of legitimacy: normative, legal, sociological, and cultural. In addition to these, Brinkerhoff focussed in his paper on what he called "organizational legitimacy." In this regard, normative legitimacy concerns the reflection of norms accepted and/or desired by society and which the organization reflects. There is also pragmatic legitimacy, which is the value of the organization to the members and others to whom the organization relates and/or with whom it interacts. Other types of legitimacy include cognitive legitimacy, which is accorded when societally and appropriately accepted values are part of the objectives and activities of an organization. Apart from "organizational legitimacy," which Brinkerhoff (2005b, p. 3) discussed in his paper, Najam (2002d, pp. 154–155) discussed issues of legitimacy and its relations with the effectiveness of resource utilization, believing that these two aspects are important and have a direct influence on questions of fund mobilization for development. Najam focussed more on utilization of development funds and the challenges it has on legitimacy and effectiveness in the field of financing for sustainable development. In this regard, Najam (2002c, p. 155) discussed what he calls three inter-related levels. These are the "legitimacy of goals of financing, legitimacy of the actors involved, and the legitimacy of the measures by which success or failure is estimated." In his discussion, he linked legitimacy to accountability.

In fact, Najam's (2002c, p. 155) three levels of "legitimacy" are all concerned with the institution, that is, all three are components of what Brinkerhoff (2005c, p. 3) calls "organizational legitimacy." The linking of the institutional or organizational legitimacy with "accountability" and in Najam's case with institutional transparency brings the issue of legitimacy closer to the subject of development finance. The institutions or organizations concerned with transferring funds, capital equipment, and technical assistance have to be seen as possessing legitimacy for them to operate. In fact, Najam (2002e, p. 156, 158) stated that institutions, which are involved in development finance, see themselves more as "financial institutions" than as "development institutions." He believes that this contributes considerably to what he called the "deepening crisis of legitimacy of development finance." In his thinking, financial norms and ratios of sustainability of the institution as a "financial" institution should be seconded, in a way, to norms of development effectiveness and sustainability of the development activities and actions, building up to the paradigm for "sustainable development." Thus, those who transfer funds should be held accountable for actual sustainable development in the areas of their interventions in the recipient countries. With both the accountability criterion and the transparency criterion satisfied and the institutions doing what is considered "right," according to "acceptable and desirable standards and norms," society, that is, its constituents—both the national/recipient countries and the international/external forces—would perceive the institution as having acquired what Brinkerhoff (2005d, pp. 4, 5) considers as normative, pragmatic, and cognitive legitimacy.

The notion of perception is also important in the discussion of legitimacy. Franck (1990a, pp. 16, 19) observed this, and he believes that it is relevant to the power relationship among nations. He considers legitimacy as "the perception of those addressed by a rule or a rule-making institution that the rule or institution has come into being and operates in accordance with generally accepted principles." Here we see that legitimacy is not only concerned with institutions, it is also important that the "constituents" of the institution have the perception of it having been established under acceptable rules and is operating using generally acceptable principles. This issue of the perception of the constituents ties in with Brinkerhoff's (2005d, pp. 4, 5) normative and cognitive legitimacy. Franck is more concerned with the international arena, mainly legal and political. He is more interested in rules and rule-making institutions, especially with the compliance of the "constituents" with the rules that the institution which has acquired "legitimacy" has formulated. His concern with compliance contributes to his quest for the components which influence legitimacy of the rules and the institution. His quest takes him into the literary domain, and he believes that the clarity of the rule or what he calls the "determinacy" of the rule is a significant contributor to compliance with the rule. This compliance in turn contributes to the "legitimacy" of the rule and the rulemaking institution. One of the attributes of such clarity is that it is unlikely to be misunderstood by any "reasonable" constituent. Clark (2005a, pp. 3, 4, 5, 12) is also concerned with the "international society" as well as with rules. He believes that international stability results from international legitimacy. But is there an intrinsic evidence of legitimacy? Hurd (2007, pp. 3, 4) is also concerned with legitimacy and power. He concentrates on the issue of legitimacy among states in the United Nations Security Council. He stated that "legitimacy is a quality that might become attached to a formal organization, an informal institution or practice, or a particular rule or individual." He indicated that international lawyers have displayed an interest in what legitimacy might add to legality when considering the compliance pull of rules and institutions. Non-coercive compliance to a rule could be considered an important evidence of legitimacy.

A major aspect of legitimacy in all the different authors, whom we have discussed, is the notion of "acceptability." All the authors put emphasis on "acceptability" as a key to "legitimacy." Another aspect is the notion of "who?" In other words, who accepts the rule or the institution or organization? Here I would answer the "who?" by stating that the "constituents" or the "stakeholders" or those who come regularly in contact with the rule or the institution are the ones, who, in the discussion of all the authors, have to assess the rule or the institution and accept to be bound by the rule or the operations of the institution. How do these different concepts and notions link with development finance generally and the operations of the institutions set up to administer the funds by the external forces in particular?

Can there be, as Najam (2002f, p. 158) stated, a legitimacy of development finance?" In fact, are there "sources of legitimacy" as Brinkerhoff stated? Can "legitimacy" be managed as he thinks? Brinkerhoff (2005e, pp. 6, 7) discusses the "process of legitimation." Franck (1990b, pp. 51, 52) states that "the role of community in validating rules is at the very core of the notion of legitimacy." In this context, Clark[128] (2005b, p. 13) discusses international history and how it can affect legitimacy. The principles of legitimacy he stated evolve historically. Thus, it could be inferred that the principles of legitimacy are not static and that there are procedures and process that can be followed to make a rule or institution "acquire" legitimacy. This is similar to Franck's "indicators of rule legitimacy." There are ways through which a rule or a rule-making institution acquires "legitimacy," through these procedures and processes. This is done by aligning the operations, values, beliefs, practices, and other essential aspects of the institution with established and "accepted" practices and values. Such alignment would contribute to the "constituents/stakeholders" *perceiving* the institution as doing the right things and putting value to the institution as pursuing beneficial objectives. The institution thus acquires "legitimation" which contributes to its "normative legitimacy." In line with this thinking, the government of donor countries and the institutions they set up to manage the transfer of funds are often seen by recipient countries to be doing the right thing, thus acquiring a "legitimacy," which is separate from that bestowed on them through their constitution and the laws of their lands. In addition to the recipient countries acceptance of them doing the right thing, constituents in the donor countries also accept that they are doing the "right thing" and following acceptable decision-making procedures. This further strengthens the legitimacy of the governments and the institutions through "acceptance by a 'tolerable' consensus."

We saw earlier that "acceptability" is a key factor in the acquisition of legitimacy. We saw also that "the constituents/stakeholders" are, in a way, the assessors, because they determine what is and/or is not "acceptable." Clark (2005c, p. 3) introduces what he calls a "procedural dimension" into the debate about legitimacy. In the context of international relationship, which Franck calls relationship among nations, Clark questions what can be reasonably accepted or what is considered "acceptable." He also poses questions about what is the critical number of constituents/stakeholders who have to accept the rule or the institution for it to acquire legitimacy; this is what Clark calls "tolerable consensus." These are fundamental questions, which link "legitimacy" to consensus." In other words, does consensus contribute to legitimacy or does legitimacy give credence to consensus? How do these relate or link up with development finance?

We have over the years unequivocally accepted the legitimacy of external forces that provide development finance to less fortunate recipient countries. This legitimacy rides on aspects of legitimacy such as constitutionality, and legality of the establishment of the governments and the institutions they set up to organize the transfers. Over the years, as we saw earlier, these institutions have acquired "consensus." This consensus provides them with legitimacy. However, Clark (2005d, p. 4) quoted Bukovansky (see Clark 2005d, p. 4) and Dunne (see Clark 2005d, p. 4) as stating that legitimacy is greatly influenced by the balance of power. Bukovansky indicated that the dominant conception of legitimacy, especially after the great wars, tended to reflect the views of the victorious and powerful states. From Bukovansky's analysis, we are "compelled to acknowledge the existence of an important relationship between power and legitimacy." Both Dunne and Bukovansky argue that what is "true or right is entirely contingent on the play of power and domination." This is a position that is amply discussed in Chaps. 3 and 4 in relation to development finance, especially as regards the conditions imposed by the dominant forces on the less-dominant or non-dominant forces. In fact, Lukes (2005f, pp. 27, 45, 46) states that in society, whether in a single country or among nations, those who have more "power over" tend to shape the views and needs of those who have less power. Clark (2005e, p. 20), on the other hand, takes a middle position, believing, as it were, that "legitimacy constrains power, but also enables it." In the context of development finance, these constraining influences are discussed in Chap. 4 as part of what I call "breaks in the flow of power."

In line with the thinking of Bukovansky (see Clark 2005d, p. 4) and Dunne (see Clark 2005d, p. 4), the rules and ideas of the stronger power acquire legitimacy, and its norms become the "accepted" norms, and consensus is developed around these norms and rules which are made legitimate. This can be linked to what we discussed earlier under the section on "Power." This is the position of Lukes (2005h, p. 20) that the perspective of the non-dominant force is rendered invisible by the dominance of that of the more-dominant force.

The question to be asked concerns the "legitimacy" of donors imposing conditions, whether mild or stringent, on recipient countries. Legitimacy is relevant to development finance as it situates the authority by which donors impose conditions. What makes it "lawful" for external forces to impose conditions for their assistance, whether as a loan, concessional loan, or grant? Do these conditions, which we shall discuss in Chaps. 3–5, have fundamental/intrinsic "legitimacy" of their own, based on Franck's determinacy and coherence? (Franck 1990c, pp. 47, 49, 52). Why should countries, recipients of funds, comply with these conditions? Is it the intrinsic value based on Franck's "legitimacy" decomposition that ensures compliance? In terms of both determinacy and coherence, do these conditions which accompany the transfer of funds from what I call external forces/dominant forces to non-dominant countries have both? Can we then say that they are complied with only because they have coherence and determinacy which are key components, according to Franck, of legitimacy? As I explain in Chaps. 3 and 4, without the "coercive power" of the external forces, compliance could not be obtained. Can we then say that because these conditions are complied with as a result of the coercive power exerted to achieve compliance they do not possess legitimacy? As we shall see in Chaps. 3 and 4, these conditions are imposed by institutions which, as we saw earlier, have themselves achieved legitimacy.

In addition, in the case of several external forces coming together to provide funds, the conditions have been agreed upon through consensus among the donors, thereby attaining what Clark (2005f, pp. 3, 4, 20) would call "tolerable consensus." In the field of development finance, such "tolerable consensus" can be created, especially in the context of budgetary support program, where several donors come together to provide funds for a country's entire budget or a substantial portion of it. In the present balance of power between donors and recipients, which we discuss in Chap. 3, "consensus" can be dictated by the most powerful of the donor in the support program. This could be the financier who has put in the largest share into the financial basket, or the financier who has acquired the most "expert power" or has acquired "legitimacy" over time, of and for its possession of "expert power." In the field of development finance, the World Bank and the International Monetary Fund (IMF) have acquired "legitimacy" of such level of "expert power," as to be in a position to develop/design the conditions. Such "legitimacy" of "expert power" thus confers on this donor, what I would term as the "first call" on drafting the specific conditions. These conditions, after discussion and/or examination of and by the other donors, would acquire currency, around which the other donors would agree, thus providing, as it were, the quality of "tolerable consensus." In agriculture, the Food and Agricultural

Organization has acquired an expertise, similar to that of the World Bank and the IMF.

Clark (2005g, pp. 16, 17, 18, 27) indicated that there is a "presumption of shared values" in order to achieve such consensus. In this case, the "shared values" are in the norms and standards of what a good economy in a developing country should be. It is also in the assessment by the donors of the economic and social situation of the recipient country, especially the deficiencies. These deficiencies are what the funds provided or will be provided, and the conditions accompanying the finance package are expected to help rectify or remedy. This "tolerable consensus" would be furnished not only by the donors, but also by the recipient country whose economy would be expected to receive a boost by the injection of the funds from the donors, as we shall see in Chap. 3. In Chap. 3, we discuss the sources of power and note the sources of power which the donors use to buttress the compliance with the conditions, thus providing added fillip to the magnitude of "tolerable consensus." Tolerable consensus helps to strengthen the notion of legitimacy of the conditions, when, as Chap. 3 discusses, legitimacy through non-coercive means is actually subsumed in the display of the various sources of power. As such, compliance with the conditions is not a factor intrinsic in the "legitimacy" of the conditions. Compliance, as we shall see in Chaps. 3 and 4, is based on the perception of the recipient countries of the existence of the capacity and the vehicle of power that can be exerted to ensure compliance.

In the context of development finance, Kindornay and Samy (2012c, pp. 1, 8) discuss legitimacy in development cooperation architecture, focussing more on the issue of governance of the architecture. They introduce the concept of legitimacy by bringing in the Busan Global Partnership (the Partnership) (see Kindornay and Samy 2012d, pp. 2, 8, 9, 10–13) and its governing mechanism. They believe that the globalism of the Partnership will depend on the perception of the stakeholders of the mechanism's legitimacy in terms of "inclusivity, representativeness and effectiveness." Here they drew on what Graves and Burall (see Kindornay et al. 2012, pp. v, 2, 9) consider as the "tripartite notion of legitimacy" in development finance and development cooperation. Inclusivity and representativeness are considered as "input legitimacy"; the quality of the decision-making process as being "throughput legitimacy"; and effectiveness in achieving outcomes is considered as "output legitimacy." This is echoed by Ballesteros et al. (2010b, p. 2) when they stated that in the context of climate finance, that any institution, which is set up to manage the flow of funds, should be perceived by both contributors and recipients as legitimate. This is the link with Clark's notion of "tolerable consensus," of the stakeholders/constituents. Ballesteros et al. (2010c, pp. 2, 4) continued to state that legitimacy can be achieved among other things, through assessment by these constituents of the basis of the "procedures by which the institution takes its decision" and the "effectiveness of its investment." The stakeholders' perception would consider it "legitimate" when the institution "operates in a transparent, participatory, and accountable manner," setting and abiding itself by "clearly articulated rules." These latter aspects are similar to the Graves and Burall's (see Clark 2005f, pp. 3, 4, 20) tripartite notion of legitimacy discussed earlier.

Najam (2002g, pp. 154–156) feels that these recipient countries are, as it were, crying for legitimacy, and he sees motivation for the transfer of funds as an important aspect of that cry. He rebukes donor countries for believing that they are providing charity to the recipient countries, stating that the recipient countries are actually providing a universal "public good, among other things, by maintaining climatic stability and biodiversity." They should thus be compensated for such provision rather than being treated with pity and receiving what he calls "crumbs" from the tables of the rich. He, therefore, sees the transfer of funds from rich to poor as a "contract," similar to that which we discussed earlier in Chap. 1. Still with Najam (2002g, pp. 154–156), the recipient receives funds in exchange for the provision of both climatic stability and the maintenance of biodiversity. In line with this thinking, we observe that the importance of perception and also of the motivation behind the transfer of funds, to some extent, dictate how the recipients would perceive the donor, whether exercising power or assisting in its development.

Donor perception and motivation, however, have evolved, and in development finance as opposed to humanitarian/relief assistance, donors' perception of recipient countries has become more sophisticated. The perception tends to have moved away from the overt thinking of "giving charity" and has become a function of the motivation for the transfer of funds, as we shall see in Chap. 3. Aspects such as strategic importance of the country and diplomatic friendship, among other things, have gained currency in development finance and development cooperation. As we have seen in this section, there are several facets and connotations to the concept of legitimacy. The key aspect of all the authors previously discussed is what I call stakeholders/constituents, and their perception of the institution, their rule, and their notion, of what is correct, right, appropriate, and the value they attach to these as well as whether these values are shared or not. These values could be shared or imposed by the dominant party. Whether the values are shared or imposed by the dominant party or force, does legitimacy bestow on these dominant parties the "properties" required for them to impose conditions for their financial assistance? In fact, is legitimacy a critical factor in development finance where, as we shall see in Chaps.3 and 4, "power" by the dominant force is sourced from different areas and a "contract" with conditions is signed between the parties concerned? This "contract" and the "power" it bestows on the donor trump all issues of the legitimacy of the donors' right to impose conditions for the accessibility of their funds. These questions go beyond the scope of this book; nevertheless, they are relevant to further research on the topic of development finance, power, and perception. Another key factor discussed earlier is that of acceptability. The values discussed earlier, as we shall see in the next section on accountability, are indicators of norms for which the stakeholders, especially in the context of development finance, can be held accountable, in a way that Kindornay and Samy (2012e, pp. v, 1, 4, 8) discussed and advocated.

Accountability

The key questions about accountability are: accountable for what and accountable to whom? The question of accountability to whom varies as does the accountability for what. An organization/institution can be accountable to several others for the same thing, as it can be accountable for several things to the same institution/organization. In another variant of the situation, an organization can be accountable for several things to several other organizations. Taking care of these accountability, issues can be time-consuming and/or staff- intensive, that is, requiring several staff members at various levels and at various time. Taking care of the responsibility for "accountability" can be such that some institutions need to have a whole section or department dedicated to taking care of these issues. In the field of development finance, these possibilities and variants operate on a very regular basis.

Donors/external forces are very concerned about accountability. Such concerns about accountability relate mainly to financial accountability. However, there is also accountability relating to the attainment of the objectives set. This latter is often referred to as effectiveness, which I shall discuss in Chap. 3, and is close to what Najam (2002f, p. 158) calls "legitimacy of development finance," which I discussed in the section under Legitimacy. Tandon (1996, pp. 53–55) discussed accountability in relation to NGOs. However, can the same norms that are used for NGOs be used to analyze accountability as it relates to external and internal forces in development finance? In Chap.3, we shall see that the external forces in development finance, especially from the North set out norms by which tacitly or openly, they carry out their business.

These norms have various names including "best practices," "guiding principles," "cutting-edge technology," "standard practice," and many others. These norms differ from the objectives or goals assigned to the operation or intervention. In the case of non-traditional cooperation, such as South-South cooperation, there are also "guiding principles" which inform the actions of the Southern external forces. In fact, this latter cooperation is growing very fast, and the terminology "non-traditional" is no longer helpful in analyzing it. In South-South cooperation, such guiding principles include such notions as "mutual benefit" and "non-interference." These are operating frameworks, or in practical terms, "norms," by which the external forces would like to be, or could be, "judged" for their operating performance. Whatever the actual notion selected for the analysis, the external forces would like to see themselves as either adhering to these "principles" or moving toward the attainment of these abstract goals. Hence, we can say that these are the standards by which their accountability should be discussed. It is similar to what Clark (2005e, p. 20) stated that even though legitimacy enables power, it also constrains power. In many instances, many of the external forces have incorporated these norms into their normal operations. In fact, through the use of "expert power" which we shall discuss in Chap. 3, non-dominant forces have come to use the norms such as "best practices" when evaluating donors operations in their countries. They also use such notions when discussing their own operations, striving for "best practices," which in fact is a dynamic concept that varies over time and can be revised within a very short space of time.

There are, however, other aspects that inform the accountability debate. In discussing NGO governance in China, Xiaoguang and Li (2006a, p. 129) consider accountability as providing a framework of operation for NGO. Accountability also provides indicators for assessing "effectiveness" of the organization or the institution. Xiaoguang and Li (2006b, pp. 129,130) stated that any discussion on accountability should take both internal and external accountability into consideration. Thus, in discussing power imbalances, perception, development finance, and external forces, accountability of both the internal/non-dominant forces and of the external dominant forces need to be considered.

What then are the aspects of accountability for the two sets of forces? What then, as Xiaoguang et al. (2006b, pp. 129, 130) put it, are the "internal and external mechanisms" that provide a framework for the forces? What factors influence them and how do they influence perception and power as these relate to development finance? The internal mechanisms relate to such aspects of internal organizational structure as management systems of the donor/external forces. External mechanisms relate to the external relationships of these forces to other bodies. These latter include oversight agencies and such institutions, as audit agencies, parliaments, regulatory bodies, compliance bureaux, and procurement offices.

This line of thinking on accountability is supported by Edwards and Hulme (1996, p. 8), in their statement that accountability is "a complex and abstract concept." They acknowledged, however, that in general interpretation, it is "the means by which individuals and organizations report to a recognized authority or authorities." Though they were referring to NGOs, the concept and its related components can be used for other agencies and bodies which operate in the field of development finance, including governmental organizations and agencies. Within this context of NGOs, Frit Wils (1996, p. 76) stated that accountability can be vertical, affirming that there is upward and downward accountability. In fact, I would add that there is also horizontal accountability. This last relates to accountability to those within the organizations, institutions, or agencies whether as members, paid staff, or volunteer staff.

As we saw earlier in this section, the components of accountability (i.e. the norms, notions, etc.) are elements for which donors can be and are held accountable. These components are also used to evaluate and hold recipient countries accountable. Thus, with regard to "internal and external mechanisms," governance, both internal and external, has become a very dominant issue. However, governance is just one of the aspects for which both donors and recipient countries can be held accountable. Other aspects include financial management, outcome of the intervention, and impact of short, medium, and long term of the operations. Apart from these aspects mentioned earlier, Bejar and Oakley (1996, pp. 91, 95) discussed, in the context of NGOs, such others as assessment, evaluation, cost-benefit analysis, and sustainability. This last, which is also a concern of Najam (2002b, p. 156), has become a very important and critical concept.

It is concerned with the question whether all necessary and relevant activities/actions have been carried out or put in place to ensure that several years after the donor financing is completed, the operation/intervention will still be running, effectively and efficiently. A successful sustainability example is given by MacLachlan et al. (2010, pp. 100–102). It concerned an intervention in India that was so successful in meeting its objectives that the beneficiaries requested that the financing be discontinued as they had become self-sufficient and were able to ensure sustainability with their own funds. They requested that the funding be transferred to groups in another area of the country.

Another aspect of accountability mentioned earlier relates to vertical and horizontal accountability. Recipient countries (i.e. countries receiving assistance, whether on concessionary or non-concessionary terms) are generally held accountable for the correct use of the assistance. In other words, the recipient countries have to account for the use of the assistance. For the recipient countries, this is upward accountability, and donors often endeavor to provide tools for such accountability assessments. These include logical framework analysis, result-based management, balanced scorecard, and cost effectiveness. These tools are required to be used to assess the performance of the recipient countries and also to provide information and data, that donors can use across different countries to compare and contrast performances. These data would help them develop norms for "best practices," which can be used to improve management and performance. However, it has to be noted that "best practice" is mainly related to certain aspects of operations, which include financial management, reporting procedures, and systems. For the assessment of the other aspects of operation and the management of purely development activities, decision-makers need to take into consideration the specifics of the situation which include sociology, the demography, and the dynamics of the populations. These three factors can affect the attainment of development objectives. Practices and tools that succeed under one set of circumstances in one country may not necessarily give positive results when the parameters differ and vary in both space and time. Nevertheless, such data help researchers to analyze the various aspects of the donor/recipient or external/internal forces tandem.

In addition, such concepts, as result-based management and the indicators for performance, are important for the donors/external forces, as we shall see in Chap. 3. They provide donors with the necessary information and analysis for their own accountability exercise with those to whom they are answerable. These tools are useful for improvement in both donor and recipient countries management of and delivery of development finance. As we shall see in Chaps. 3 and 4, these tools together with the notion of "upward accountability" itself are other manifestations of the exercise of power by external donor forces on non-dominant recipient countries. Nevertheless, one cannot question the legitimacy of this "power to exercise." It is based on the fact that funds for such development finance were appropriated from resources approved by parliament and obtained from taxpayers of the donor countries. The "legitimacy" of the exercise of power is thus rooted in the legitimacy of the donor government. The exercise of power is such that the recipient countries cannot refuse to provide the required information, at risk of the flow of fund being terminated by the donor.

As in the case of NGOs, it would be also worthwhile for donors to show some amount of what some authors (e.g. Jacobs and Wilford; Bejar and Oakley; and Edwards and Hulme) call "downward accountability." Though the concept is more often used in discussions concerning NGOs, it would be useful to borrow this and use it perhaps with some adaptation in development finance, especially in donor–recipient relationship. This "downward accountability" in the case of NGOs is, as Jacobs and Wilford (pp. 3, 5) stated, to "release power to those further down the aid chain." This is in conformity with the organizational pyramid for development finance, which I describe in Chap. 4. In the case of NGOs, downward accountability "goes beyond the ability of beneficiaries to influence NGO actions" by, among others, "participating in decision making" concerning project activities.

The participation of recipient countries in decision-making with regard to development finance, however, may no longer be as relevant as it was in the late twentieth century. The donor countries or the financiers do not now "dictate" the details of the programs for which the financial support is required. Nevertheless, downward accountability can be considered in the context of this book, as "having to do with the unequal distribution of power" which is in place in the overall development finance architecture, especially when those that are meant to "benefit" have a weak political and economic voice. Though the concept is more appropriate in the context of NGOs, the power relations in development finance, and more so in development assistance, would be less frustrating for the non-dominant forces if there was some amount of downward accountability on the part of the dominant forces. It would also be more transparent. What then can we say are the factors that can influence the perception of the donors and the recipient with regard to downward accountability? The motivation of the donor is one of the factors that can influence the perception. As regards the recipient countries, transparency in the operations of the donor in the recipient's country can influence the perception of the recipients significantly.

Transparency in the circumstances of development finance can be influenced by the motivation of the donors in providing development assistance or finance. It can be argued that the more altruistic the motivation, the greater the propensity to be transparent. When such factors as diplomacy and/or acquiring influence are of primordial concern to the dominant force, the desire to be transparent may not have much sway in the perception of the dominant force. Hence, downward accountability may not take place. Transparency, in the context of donor downward accountability that would provide data, give information as to the donor's operation and his governance system, some of which are already available under disclosure policies in some donor countries.

Such information, however, does not furnish details concerning staff attitude and their perceptions of recipient countries' officials and leaders. The perception of the donor staff strongly influences the behavior of the staff and their treatment of recipient countries' officials and leaders. By dint of regular and frequent visits to the recipient countries for preparation, appraisal, supervision, and other field missions, as well as regular correspondence with them, by donor staff examining and analyzing the data which the recipient government staff provide and assessing their performance, staff of institutions of donor governments and of international development finance institutions come to know the government officials and leaders closely. Donor staff tend to categorize them with regard to the attainment of the objectives of the program or project. The attitude and behavior of the personnel of the external forces toward the officials and leaders of the recipient countries are influenced by such categorization. Staff members from both bilateral and multilateral agencies have regular inter-donor meetings, either biannual or annual to discuss and exchange information and data about progress in project/program implementation. One such is the annual meeting of financiers and other agencies intervening in the agricultural economy of countries in west and central Africa (see IFAD 2006). In turn, this categorization, attitude, and behavior, contributes to the perception of the officials and people of the recipient countries concerning the assistance received from the donors/external forces, especially the conditions which often accompany such assistance and the power play which is inherent in the transaction. This will be examined in Chaps. 3 and 4.

Globalization

In discussing globalization, I shall first try to understand what the different scholars and authors consider as the definition or the meaning of the term. This would help us appreciate the use of the term in the book. Another aspect that we shall discuss in this section is what I will call the attributes of globalization or, in other words, the indicators that will help us to note that globalization is taking or has taken place. In this way, we would be able to ensure that what we are "perceiving" and dealing with is actually globalization and not another phenomenon. The phrase "we are perceiving" is a deliberate effort to emphasize the continuous and dynamic nature of globalization. It keeps changing, in both form and attributes, as well as in consequences over the years. Bhagwati (2004a, pp. 10, 11) realized this in discussing aspects of "globalization" and how the different aspects have evolved over the years and the way globalization is evolving since then. In the past, globalization was mainly in transportation and communication. Now it covers such aspects as financial and economic policy, exchange rate policy, and cross-border movement of persons and workers and of capital, goods, and services. All these are made possible because of the rapid advances in transportation and communication.

Finally, I shall briefly discuss what some authors see as the consequences of globalization. These can also be referred to as the effects, side effects, and results of globalization. The main theme of the book is about perceptions of the imbalance of power of the external forces in development finance mainly in Africa; I shall discuss the influence of globalization on such aspects as the exercise of power in the area of development finance, the influence of power in development finance on globalization. In Chaps. 3 and 4, I shall examine how globalization has affected perceptions, especially of the different segments of the population in African countries, and how perceptions of these people affect globalization, building models based on concrete examples to illustrate my points.

Trying to pin a definition to the word "globalization" is very much akin to the three blind men trying to describe an elephant. One was holding an ear, the other was holding a leg, and the third was holding the trunk. Because of their visual challenges, each relied on his tactile sense to describe what each believed an elephant looked like. In the same way, globalization is a different phenomenon depending on the interest, training, and/or speciality of the person analyzing it. This is to some extent similar to the "affordances" presented by James Gibson (1986a, pp. 36, 127–134), which we discussed earlier in this chapter and will again in Chap.3. Each specialty looks at globalization through the lenses of key aspects of their speciality concerns. For example, writing in the Albany Law Review, Harrington (2012, pp. 3, 4, 5) discussed issues relating to labor outsourcing and the challenges it entails in terms of social and legal responsibilities and practices. He saw globalization in terms of whether multinational corporations should adhere to host countries' labor laws and arrangements or to standards accepted in their home base. He saw globalization as bringing both benefits and burdens. Benefits are opportunities for employment in developing countries brought about by labor outsourcing. An example of burden is the temptation for labor exploitation faced by multinational corporations, where host outsourcing countries have weak legal regimes that do not protect labor as well as in their home countries.

In discussing globalization, Sodhi (2011, pp. 562–570) talks about what it meant for the neoclassical economists for whom it meant that rigid policies, and fixed exchange rates have disappeared or are disappearing. Such trade barriers, as import tariffs, and government interventions in capital and financial markets would be eliminated. These and many more in the economic and financial domains are features of globalization. In fact, the main drivers of globalization were and still are the extremely rapid advances in both transportation and communication. The economies, indeed the societies of the world, were brought very close together by the advances in communication and transport. Both Bhagwati (2004b, pp. 3, 4, 11) and Stiglitz (2003a, pp. 4, 9), who are economists, also discuss globalization in terms of the lowering or the disappearance of government controls on aspects that include international trade, flow of capital, goods, and services across borders, finance, and exchange rates. In their discussion, they concentrate on these aspects, which are considered as "economic globalization." These aspects, Stiglitz believes, are very often the subject of controversy, street demonstration, and protests in many countries. Globalization then is considered by both authors as the integration of national economies into an international economy, through the paths mentioned earlier. As we saw, there are several elements to economic globalization.

There are also "cultural globalization" and "communications globalization." All of these various facets of "globalization" have different meanings, with cultural being seen through the lenses of the arts, society, the meeting of different cultures, and vast social interaction, as a result of the advances in information technology and transportation. Communication globalization has its essence and meaning in the meteoric advances in bringing different areas of the globe together within seconds, using highly advanced communication equipment and technology, especially the Internet. There are thus several different meanings or ways the term could be defined.

For the purpose of this book, the most appropriate, short but all-encompassing definition of globalization I could see, is by Bishop et al. (2011, p. 2) who defined it as "the increasing integration and interdependence among countries resulting from the modern flow of people, trade, finance, and ideas from one nation to another." This definition actually gives the end product, but subsumes the vehicle which has made this integration and interdependence possible, which is communication and transport. For the purpose of this book, the key words are "interdependence" and "increasing." Interdependence shows that countries interact with one another, which they have been doing for centuries, and have, in many ways, come to depend on each other. The term has a connotation that what happens in one country "can" affect something in another country. It is realized that even if they are not geographically close, globalization has made it such that geographic closeness is not important when it comes to such aspects as economic, financial, and environmental interdependence. The word "increasing" indicates that with time, there is growth in the degree of closeness. Following on this thinking, in the ensuing chapters of this book, I will show that the balance of power in such interdependence is skewed in favor of those countries which have greater economic and financial resources; in other words, there is a power imbalance. Thus, we see that as in the case of the blind men, they were all, to some extent, right in their comparison of what the elephant looked like. The meaning of globalization is all of the meanings proffered by the various authors, whose thinking I discussed earlier (see Harrington 2012, pp. 3, 4, 5; Sodhi 2011, p. 562; Bhagwati 2004b, pp. 3, 4, 11). It is not static, and new aspects or ways in which the world is coming closer are shown and discovered every day.

What can we therefore put as the attributes and the key indicators of globalization? In a way, the attributes of globalization tend to be dynamic.

The attributes are thus the mobility of persons/workers, capital, information, ideas, goods, and services. Key indicators include the existence, the diversity, the volume, in terms of quantity and quality of communication, and transportation. It also includes the interaction among nations and among individuals within the nations and with other nations. An important aspect of the indicators is speed, which in some ways makes for great mobility. Although I will not attempt to do so, it could be possible to measure some or all of the indicators. This will show, among other things, the deepening of the globalization.

In a way, the attributes are the bedrock of another important concern of this book, which is development finance. Without some of the attributes of globalization, development finance would hardly have existed and certainly would not have assumed the extraordinary proportions as we know today. This is not just in terms of movement, of funds, and of capital, goods, and services acquired with the funds, but also the issue of exchange rates and more importantly of the actual operations of development finance. This latter requires the rapid movement of people, especially people with technical knowledge and expertise across Africa in particular and the globe in general, to identify, prepare, appraise, and supervise projects and programs and analyze financial statements of countries and institutions. The personnel and officials of institutions, governments, and organizations also attend meetings, workshops, and conferences in different countries, often for a few days and then return to their home base. All of these have been made possible by the rapid advances in transportation. In fact, the rapid advance in information technology has made it possible to send vast amounts of information and data across the Internet for analysis rapidly, and also for people in one continent to do instant messaging and to hold face-to-face discussions with people on another continent without moving from their offices or conference rooms. These are positive things that enhance the operations of development finance. The positive results of development finance through increased capital flows, enhanced expertise through technical assistance and scholarships for nationals of recipient countries to improve their knowledge and expertise, are other by-products of globalization.

Shall we thus say that such positive aspects, which have considerably reduced the transaction costs of doing business whether in private finance or development finance, are the consequences of globalization? Indeed without globalization, the benefits of development finance could not have been possible. Globalization has many other consequences, side effects, by-products, and implications, which some authors (see Bhagwati 2004c; Stiglitz 2003a; Sodhi 2011; Bishop et al. 2011) have discussed. These include aspects relating to, but not limited to, economic globalization, as well as to the environment and concern for the degradation of the environment; the issues of exploitation; poverty, social, and demographic inequalities; and inequalities in income distribution, all of which, they believe globalization has directly and indirectly led to. Some of the issues attributed to globalization are actually not consequences, from the point of view of cause and effect, but are more by-products of the way globalization has progressed in all its dimensions (i.e. economic, cultural interaction among individuals and groups of individual in different countries). The proliferation of organizations in the civil society, especially NGOs, is one of these by-products. Their intervention in the economies of developing countries is another by-product of globalization. The role which these organizations play in situations around the globe and more so in purely local conflicts emphasizes the importance of their activities and the perception of the population of developing countries as to the "power" they can bring to bear on local economies and societies. This was discussed by Spencer (2012, pp. 49–52) in the case of a local conflict in Mali. Tran (Tran, D.T. 2010, pp. 2, 3) discussed another of what I consider as the side effects of globalization: the impact of globalization on income distribution in developing countries.

Therefore, there are many consequences, side effects, and by-products of globalization. Such authors as Ouattara (1997a, pp. 1, 3), Bhagwati (2004c, pp. 32, 33, 228–230), and Stiglitz (2003b, pp. 7, 8, 119) have also discussed the downsides of globalization, some of which can have devastating effects on the lives of individuals, especially in developing countries. Such aspects include price movements of commodities. Movements in international commodity prices can, to some extent, cause havoc with balance of trade of developing countries. They have been the subject of articles and books for a long time; Spencer (1977, pp. 1–20) outlined some of the impact of commodity prices on the balance of trade and of payments on developing countries. Even though such movements are part and parcel of international exchange and trade, globalization has given speculators added elements, techniques, and tools in their arsenal, so that they can move their funds from agricultural produce to minerals, to foreign exchange speculation with increased rapidity. These can have adverse effects on the balance of payments of developing countries. Along this line of thinking of devastating effects, Glenny (see Grimes 2008) wrote about globalization and the criminal underworld, showing how organized criminals make use of the attributes of globalization to spread their reach beyond their own national borders. This confirms, as it were, my earlier statement that each author sees globalization through the lenses of his or her specialty or interest. This is in line with Gibsons' concept of affordances discussed earlier. It shows also that there are many downsides to globalization.

Ouattara (1997b, pp. 3, 4), Bhagwati (2004d, pp. 228–234), and Stiglitz (2007b, pp. 276–284) have each proposed measures that developing countries should take or put in place in order to remedy or mitigate the adverse effects of globalization that can reduce the number of its downsides. They have also proposed institutions, infrastructure, physical and social, as well as societal, political, and organizational changes that have to be in place or established, if they are not already in existence, for these countries to benefit fully from the positive aspects of globalization and, at the same time, minimize the negative aspects. They have discussed what the consequences would be, if these are not in place at the appropriate time, or in sufficient quantity and/or relevant quality. Although these do have a bearing on the main theme of this book, they are not directly connected to the main theme, which is perceptions of the power imbalance. One aspect that concerns this book is that of perception of power in development finance and how it has been affected by globalization and ways in which perception of power in development finance has affected globalization.

Earlier I mentioned the influence of globalization on the exercise of power in development finance. In some cases, especially for some countries in Africa that were not fully prepared for the benefits of globalization and had been weakened by the legacy of colonialism, corruption, and inappropriate economic policies in the post-independence era, globalization has facilitated the exercise of power over them. To some extent, for many countries in Africa, globalization has enabled the different sources of power to be used on their economies, strengthening the sources, as it were. I shall discuss this in Chap. 3.

Nevertheless, globalization also made it easier for the people in the different countries in Africa to become aware, through articles, books, the Internet, and the media, of the downsides of globalization. Their perceptions of the downsides of globalization that are visible in their lives, and echoed in the demonstrations and protest marches that they see in the Internet and the media, became sharpened. The job cuts they experienced, and the higher prices they had to pay for basic foodstuff began to make more sense as they perceived it rightly or wrongly as a result of some of the conditions imposed by international development finance institutions for use of their funds. Though there were fewer demonstrations in many African countries compared with those in Europe, Latin America, and Asia, the hardships experienced by many, especially youths, provided the recruiting justification for some of the internal conflicts in many parts of Africa, of which Sierra Leone and Liberia are just two. The perceptions of the young people in these two countries of the effects of globalization were, therefore, negative. Although there were other factors (e.g. poverty, corrupt practices of the leaders, and terms of trade) that entered the equation, globalization enhanced their access to information. The people saw job losses, not possible increased inflow of funds, both public and private. They saw frequent and unending electric power cuts and poor road maintenance through cuts in public expenditure, not improvement in the structure of the economy. They saw people sick and dying because of medical personnel leaving for other countries, where salaries are higher. They saw medical facilities, equipment, and supplies curtailed or left to become derelict without satisfactory repairs or maintenance, all because of cuts in the budget of the health ministry. They could not wait nor afford to wait for the promised improvements in economic well-being. Their perceptions were, as the Gibsons would say, influenced by the major focus of their "affordances." Their affordances were their well-being, their current situation, and their past experience. They believed that these perceived results of globalization were damaging and destructive to their welfare.

Perceptions like these helped to ignite the demonstrations and protest marches and, to some extent, laid the foundation for a rethinking of globalization as it was evolving. It led to international development finance institutions and international development agencies, bilateral and multilateral, putting in place such measures as debt forgiveness, such programs as the "heavily indebted poor countries" (HIPCS), budget support programs. All of these programs and measures were intended to reduce the extreme facets of the negative sides of globalization on development finance and on the economies of the recipient countries. They were also intended to enhance the factors that could bring economic growth and development. These enhancing actions were done with the hope that such growth and development would increase social well-being, enhance gender equality, and reduce poverty. This was achieved in fewer cases than expected. Some African developing countries, such as Ghana and Rwanda, attained some positive improvement in their gross domestic products (GDPs) and purchasing power parity (see World Bank data) over the years, but many of the developing countries in Africa, including those whose percentage increase in their GDP were positive between 2010 and 2013, are still in great need of development finance from the external forces.

Thus, continuing the discussion on our main theme of perceptions of the imbalance of power, globalization, and its evolution became influenced by the perceptions *and* the actions of people around the world. Although the skewness of the balance of power was not corrected, the "practice" of power in development finance benefited through globalization, from the experience of previous actions and activities of the "world citizenry." Greater attention was being paid to issues of governance, income distribution in the context of poverty reduction efforts, and inequality in the decision-making mechanisms in international institutions. Greater attention was also being given to the need to address poverty reduction in the developing countries across the globe as well as governance within these countries. Different approaches such as community-directed development programs were tried out. However, coming from the position of strength, it is difficult to see owners of the greater balance of power relinquishing such power for the good of those whose situation puts them in a position with less power. As we saw earlier, foreign aid or development finance, even when practiced in the arena of international development finance institutions, is still a tool of the foreign policy of the developed countries and to some extent that of the emerging economies/nations.

This is why some of the countries that were able to capture and use the benefits of globalization and are now "emerging powers" in their own right would like to create their own institutions as would Brazil, Russia, India, China, and South Africa (BRICS). They are mulling the idea of a BRICS development bank (Fifth BRICS Summit) that they believe would run differently from existing international development finance institutions. But would it really be operating differently from the existing international development finance institutions? Such an institution would have to follow specific financial norms and ratios. However, as Najam (2002h, pp. 155, 156) advocated, perhaps "sustainable development" and its effectiveness would become the primordial concern, superseding even financial considerations. Such an institution, born of, among other things, a rejection of all the negativity of globalization and nurtured by the perceptions of the emerging external forces of power play being exercised on them, would be mindful of how it operates; but would it? A major concern of the group of emerging nations relates to the governance structure of the existing financial institutions in which they would like to play a much more major role than what is being allowed them at present. In fact, the group is at present more of a political entity, than a united economic force; although as a group, they have considerable financial resources and could use their strength to exercise power. They represent 46% of the world's population and account for $US16 trillion in GDP; together they represent 26% of the world's land area and hold $US4.40 trillion in combined foreign currency reserves. Intra-BRICS trade was $US276 billion, in 2012. BRICS international trade rose from 29% in 2010 to 2012 to $US6.1 trillion (see BRICS 2013).

In this regard, Sidiropoulos et al. (2012a, p. 9) believe that the shape of any new alliance will affect both "global" South's view of itself and the way in which international norms and system evolve and are met. For many of these emerging powers would prefer, as Sidiropoulos et al. (2012b, p. 5) put it, to be rule makers and not rule takers. They are therefore becoming more vocal in international fora. In that regard, it is debatable whether they would not be tempted to exercise power in the old traditional ways, if the BRICS Development Bank actually takes off, working from their launching conference in Durban, South Africa, in March 2013 (see Fifth BRICS 2013). In Chaps. 3 and 4, I shall discuss in more detail the "practice" of power and show the power imbalance in development finance by the external/dominant forces, both traditional and non-traditional, on the non-dominant or less-dominant forces, especially those in Africa.

Notes and References

African Development Bank (AfDB). http://www.afdb.org/en/news-and-events/article/african-development-bank-doubles-soft-loan-funds-for-malawi-president-kaberuka-visits-malawi-1543/

African Development Bank. (2014, November). Treasury Department. ADF statement of subscription and voting powers as at 30 Sept 2014.

African Development Bank (AfDB). (2015). Facilitating regional integration in East Africa: AfDB supports Mombasa-Mariakani highway project. March 12, 2015. http://www.afdb.org/en/news-and-events/article/facilitating-regional-integration-in-east-africa-afdb-supports-mombasa-mariakani-highway-project-14047/

Alesina, A., & Dollar, D. (2000). Who gives foreign aid to whom and why. *Journal of Economic Growth, 5*(1), 33–34, 63.

allAfrica. (2008). African development bank doubles soft-loan funds for Malawi. 30 July 2008. http://allafrica.com/stories/200807300890.html

allAfrica-Lusaka. Zambia: African development bank gives country US$28 million loan. http://allafrica.com/stories/200108230084.html

Amanor-Amanor, K. S. Future agricultures South-South cooperation in context: Perspectives from Africa. China and Brazil in African agriculture project. Working paper series. Working Paper 054. http://www.future-agricultures.org/publications/research-and-analysis/working-papers/1640-south-south-cooperation-in-context-perspectives-from-africa/file

Awareness Times. (2014, August 20). Sierra Leone News: Parliament approves $23 grant. http://news.sl/drwebsite/publish/article_200526016.shtml

Axelrod, R. (1970). *Conflict of interest*. Chicago: Markham. (Cited in p. 154 by Nagel, J. H. (1975). *The descriptive analysis of power*. New Haven/London: Yale University Press).

Axelrod, R. (1973a, December). Schema theory: An information processing model of perception. *The American Political Science Review, 67*(4), 1248–1266-p.1248.

Axelrod, R. (1973b, December). Schema theory: An information processing model of perception. *The American Political Science Review, 67*(4), 1248–1266-p.1248, 1250.

Ballesteros, S. (1994a). Cognitive approaches to human perception: Introduction. In S. Ballesteros (Ed.), *Cognitive approaches to human perception* (p. 1, 3–6). Hillside/New Jersey/Hove/London: Lawrence Erlbaum Associates, Publishers.

Ballesteros, S. (1994b). Cognitive approaches to human perception: Introduction. In S. Ballesteros (Ed.), *Cognitive approaches to human perception* (p. 9). Hillside/New Jersey/Hove/London: Lawrence Erlbaum Associates, Publishers.

Ballesteros, S. (1994c). Cognitive approaches to human perception: Introduction. In S. Ballesteros (Ed.), *Cognitive approaches to human perception* (pp. 9–13). Hillside/New Jersey/Hove/London: Lawrence Erlbaum Associates Publishers.

Ballesteros, A., Nakhooda, S., Werksman, J., & Hurlburt, K. (2010a). *Power, responsibility, and accountability. Re-thinking the legitimacy of institutions for climate finance* (pp. viii, ix, 2, 4). World Resources Institute. WRI report, Washington, DC.

Ballesteros, A., Nakhooda, S., Werksman, J., & Hurlburt, K. (2010b). *Power, responsibility, and accountability. Rethinking the legitimacy of institutions for climate finance* (p. 2). World Resources Institute. WRI Final report, Washington, DC.

Ballesteros, A., Nakhooda, S., Werksman, J., & Hurlburt, K. (2010c). *Power, responsibility, and accountability. Rethinking the legitimacy of institutions for climate finance* (pp. 2, 4). World Resources Institute. WRI final report, Washington, DC.

Bejar, H., & Oakley, P. (1996). From accountability to shared responsibility. NGO evaluation in Latin America. In M. Edwards, D. Hulme, & D. Hulme (Eds.), *Beyond the magic bullet. NGO performance and accountability in the post-Cold War World* (p. 91, 95). West Hartford: Kumarian Press.

Berger, K. S. (2008a). *The developing person through the life span* (p. 166). New York: Worth Publishers.

Berger, K. S. (2008b). *The developing person through the life span* (p. 162). New York: Worth Publishers.

Berk, L. (2011). *Infants, children, and adolescents* (7th ed., p. 166). Pearson.

Bhagwati, J. (2004a). *In defense of globalization* (p. 10, 11). New York: Oxford University.

Bhagwati, J. (2004b). *In defense of globalization* (p. 3, 4, 11). New York: Oxford University.

Bhagwati, J. (2004c). *In defense of globalization* (p. 32, 33, 228–230). New York: Oxford University.

Bhagwati, J. (2004d). *In defense of globalization* (pp. 228–234). New York: Oxford University.

Bierstedt, R. (1950). An analysis of social power. *American Sociological Review, 15*(6): 7130–7138 (cited by Ledyaev, V. in p. 2 "*Power and Conflict,*" online http://www.socialsciences.manchester.ac.uk/medialibrary/politics/research/workingpapers/mancept/LEDYAEV.pdf

Bishop, T., Reinke, J., et al. (2011). Globalization: Trends and perspectives. *Journal of International Business Research,* 2. January 1, 2011. https://www.questia.com/read/1P3-2439570361/globalization-trends-and-perspectives

Brain—The brain is the center where the authors whom we discussed to a large extent agree that sensory information is processed. Some refer to that aspect as being memory, others call it cognitive activity, yet others talk of "mental content," but most use the name "brain."' These authors are: Powers in "Making Sense of Behavior" (pp. 35, 40), Robinson in "Perception" (pp. 7, 18, 193, 194, 200), Ballesteros in "Cognitive Approaches to Human Perception: Introduction," (p. 2), Ballesteros, S. & Manga, D. in "The influence of irrelevant information in visual perception" (pp. 61, 62). In Ballesteros, S. (Ed.), *Cognitive approaches to human perception.*

Braman, E. (2009). Law politics, and perception. How policy preferences influence legal reasoning. In Series: G. Ivers, & K. T. Mcguire (Eds.), *Constitutionalism and democracy* (pp. 20–24, 120–123). Charlottesville/London: University of Virginia Press.

BRICS-Fifth BRICS summit declaration and action plan posted on 27 March 2013 in Durban, Republic of South Africa. Item 9, page 3 of 11. http://www.brics5.co.za/fifth-brics-summit-declaration-and-action-plan/

BRICS. Economic data and trade statistics. http://brics6.itamaraty.gov.br/about-brics/economic-data

Brinkerhoff, D. W. (2005a). *Organisational legitimacy, capacity and capacity development*. Discussion paper 58A. June, 2005. European Centre for Development Policy Management (pp. 3–6). Publication date: August 12, 2005. http://www.rti.org/pubs/brinkerhoff_legitimacy.pdf

Brinkerhoff, D. W. (2005b). *Organisational legitimacy, capacity and capacity development*. Discussion paper 58A. June 2005. European Centre for Development Policy Management (pp. 3–6). Publication date: August 12, 2005, p. 3. http://www.rti.org/pubs/brinkerhoff_legitimacy.pdf

Brinkerhoff, D. W. (2005c). *Organisational legitimacy, capacity and capacity development*. Discussion paper 58A. June, 2005. European Centre for Development Policy Management (p. 3). Publication date: August 12, 2005. http://www.rti.org/pubs/brinkerhoff_legitimacy.pdf

Brinkerhoff, D. W. (2005d). *Organisational legitimacy, capacity and capacity development*. Discussion paper 58A. June 2005. European Centre for Development Policy Management (pp. 4, 5). Publication date: August 12, 2005. http://www.rti.org/pubs/brinkerhoff_legitimacy.pdf

Brinkerhoff, D. W. (2005e). *Organisational legitimacy, capacity and capacity development*. Discussion paper 58A. June 2005. European Centre for Development Policy Management. Publication date: August 12, 2005, pp. 6, 7.

Brinkerhoff, D. W. (2005f). *Organisational legitimacy, capacity and capacity development*. Discussion paper 58A. June 2005. European Centre for Development Policy Management. Publication date: 12 Aug 2005 (pp. 6, 7, 8).

Chimero, A. (2003). Information for perception and information processing. *Minds and Machines, 13*, 577–588. The Netherlands: Kluwer Academic Publishers (2003), p. 580.

Clark, I. (2005a). *Legitimacy in international society* (p. 3, 4, 5, 12). Oxford/London: Oxford University Press.

Clark, I. (2005b). *Legitimacy in international society* (p. 13). Oxford/London: Oxford University Press.

Clark, I. (2005c). *Legitimacy in international society* (p. 3). Oxford/London: Oxford University Press.

Clark, I. (2005d). *Legitimacy in international society* (p. 4). Oxford/London: Oxford University Press.

Clark, I. (2005e). *Legitimacy in international society* (p. 20). Oxford/London: Oxford University Press.

Clark, I. (2005f). *Legitimacy in international society* (p. 3, 4, 20, 162). Oxford/London: Oxford University Press.

Clark, I. (2005g). *Legitimacy in international society* (p. 13, (citing Bukovansky), 16, 17, 18, 27, 28). Oxford/London: Oxford University Press.

Dahl, R. A. (cited by Dowding) (1968). Power. In D. L. Sils (Ed.), *International encyclopedia of the social sciences* (Vol. 12). New York: Free Press.

Dahl, R.A. (cited by Nagel in pp. 91–96)

Domhoff, G. W. (2005). Basics of studying power. *Who Rules America?* (p. 1). http://www2.ucsc.edu/whorulesamerica/methods/studying_power.html

Dowding, K. (1996a). *Power. Concepts in social thought* (pp. 4–6, 8). Minneapolis: Open University Press/University of Minnesota Press.

Dowding, K. (1996b). *Power. Concepts in social thought* (pp. 4–6, 7). Minneapolis: Open University Press/University of Minnesota Press.

Dowding, K. (1996c). *Power. Concepts in social thought* (p. 38). Minneapolis: University of Minnesota Press.

Dowding, K. (1996d). *Power. Concepts in social thought* (p. 3). Minneapolis: University of Minnesota Press.

Dowding, K. (1996e). *Power. Concepts in social thought* (p. 3). Minneapolis: Open University Press/University of Minnesota Press.

Edwards, M., & Hulme, D. (1996). Introduction. NGO performance and accountability. In M. Edwards & D. Hulme (Eds.), *Beyond the magic bullet. NGO performance and accountability in the Post-Cold War World* (p. 8). West Hartford: Kumarian Press.

Falk, T. (2013). The Bulletin. China invests $1.1 billion in Nigerian infrastructure. July 10, 2013. http://www.zdnet.com/article/china-invests-11-billion-in-nigerian-infrastructure/

Farias, J. G., & Bustos, E. Understanding social perception and managing diversity. Organizational Behavior. University of London. http://www.angelfire.com/ak6/organizational_behav/lecture3.pdf

Faul, M. in Yahoo Finance. Nigeria gets back $227 million looted by dictator. June 19, 2014. http://finance.yahoo.com/news/nigeria-gets-back-227-million-183556491.html;_ylt=A0LEVr6Zhw9V5U4Aql4lnIlQ;_ylu=X3oDMTEzamk4b3NtBHNlYwNzcgRwb3MDMwRjb2xvA2JmMQR2dGlkA1lIUzAwMV8x

Foucault. by Faubion, J. D. (Ed.). (1984). Power. Michel Foucault. Essential works of Foucault 1954–1984. Published in the United States in 2000. In P. Rainbow, Series Editor (Vol. 3, p. 40, 41, 51, 52). New York: New Press.

Franck, T. M. (1990a). *The power of legitimacy among nations* (pp. 16–19). Oxford: Oxford University Press.

Franck, T. M. (1990b). *The power of legitimacy among nations* (pp. 51–52). Oxford: Oxford University Press.

Franck, T. M. (1990c). *The power of legitimacy among nations* (p. 47, 49, 52). Oxford: Oxford University Press.

Gordon, C. (Ed.). (1980). Power/knowledge. In: M. Foucault, *Selected interviews & other writings 1972–1977* (p. 119). New York: Pantheon Books.

Gibson, J. J. (1986a). *The ecological approach to visual perception* (p. 36, 127–134). New Jersey/London: Lawrence Erlbaum Associates.

Gibson, J. J. (1986b). *The ecological approach to visual perception* (p. 138, 139). New Jersey/London: Lawrence Erlbaum Associates.

Gibson, J. J. (1986c). *The ecological approach to visual perception* (pp. 130–136). New Jersey/London: Lawrence Erlbaum Associates.

Ghanaweb.com. Japan gives $6.8 million grant to Ghana. *Business News*, February 29, 2012. http://www.ghanaweb.com/GhanaHomePage/business/artikel.php?ID=230855

Ghana web. ghanaweb.com. Ghana to receive support from China. *Business News*. March 22, 2006. http://www.ghanaweb.com/GhanaHomePage/business/artikel.php?ID=101401

Grimes, W. (2008). Wise and fall guys, welcome to globalization. A review of the book by Glenny, M. *McMafia. A journey through the global criminal underworld*. New York: Vintage Books. *New York Times*, April 11, 2008. http://www.nytimes.com/2008/04/11/books/11book.html?pagewanted=all&_r=1&

Harrington, A. (2012). Corporate social responsibility, globalization, the multinational corporation and labor: An unlikely alliance (p. 3, 4, 5). http://www.albanylawreview.org/Articles/Vol75_1/75.1.0017_Harrington.pdf

House of Representative—US. (2002). Recovering dictators' plunder. US House of Representatives. Subcommittee on financial institutions and consumer credit, committee on financial service Washington, May 9, 2002. http://commdocs.house.gov/committees/bank/hba79943.000/hba79943_0.HTM

Hurd, I. (2007). After anarchy: Legitimacy and power in the United Nations Security Council. Princeton University Press (p. 3, 4, 5). http://press.princeton.edu/chapters/s8424.html

IFAD: These meeting are held regularly for the different regions within the development finance institutions and agencies. A sample can be found in fifth annual donor meeting on rural development for Western and Central Africa hosted by IFAD in Rome, Italy, from 9 to 11 May 2006. The synthesis can be found in: http://www.ifad.org/events/donor/report.pdf

Jacobs, A., & Wilford, R. Putting new approaches to NGO accountability into action. National University of Ireland in Galway (p. 3, 5). http://www.nuigalway.ie/dern/documents/19__alex_jacobs_and_robyn_wilford.pdf.

Karambu, I. (2015). Kenya gets Sh41 billion to finance power supply. *Daily Nation*, April 2, 2015. http://www.nation.co.ke/business/Kenya-gets-Sh41-billion-to-finance-power-supply/-/996/2673492/-/34j15dz/-/index.html

Kindornay, S., & Samy, Y. (2012a, May). *Establishing a legitimate development cooperation architecture in the Post-Busan Era* (p. v, 6). North-South Institute.

Kindornay, S., & Samy, Y. (2012b, May). *Establishing a legitimate development cooperation architecture in the Post-Busan Era* (p. 5). North-South Institute.

Kindornay, S., & Samy, Y. (2012c, May). *Establishing a legitimate development cooperation architecture in the Post-Busan Era* (p. 1, 8). North-South Institute.

Kindornay, S., & Samy, Y. (2012d, May). *Establishing a legitimate development cooperation architecture in the Post-Busan Era* (p. 2, 8, 9, 10–13). North-South Institute.

Kindornay, S., & Samy, Y. (2012e, May). *Establishing a legitimate development cooperation architecture in the Post-Busan Era* (p. v, 1, 4, 8). North-South Institute.

Kindornay, S., et al. (2012, May). For the notion of tripartite notion of legitimacy, see Kindornay, S., & Samy, Y. *Establishing a legitimate development cooperation architecture in the Post-Busan Era* (p. v, 2, 9). North-South Institute.

Lancaster, C. (2007a). *Foreign aid. Diplomacy, development, and domestic politics* (pp. 9–11). Chicago/London: University of Chicago Press.

Lancaster, C. (2007b). *Foreign aid. Diplomacy, development, and domestic politics* (p. 10). Chicago/London: University of Chicago Press.

Lancaster, C. (2007c). *Foreign aid. Diplomacy, development, and domestic politics* (p. 3). Chicago/London: University of Chicago Press.

Lancaster, C. (2007d). *Foreign aid. Diplomacy, development, and domestic politics* (p. 3, 64). Chicago/London: University of Chicago Press.

Lancaster, C. (2007e). *Foreign aid. Diplomacy, development, and domestic politics* (pp. 43–50). Chicago/London: University of Chicago Press.

Lancaster, C. (2007f). *Foreign aid. Diplomacy, development, and domestic politics* (p. 4, 6). Chicago/London: University of Chicago Press.

Lancaster, C. (2007g). *Foreign aid. Diplomacy, development, and domestic politics* (p. 6). Chicago/London: University of Chicago Press.

Lukes, S. (2005a). *Power: A radical view* (2nd ed., p. 85, 86, 92, 115,118–119). Basingstoke/Hampshire: Palgrave Macmillan/British Sociological Association.

Lukes, S. (2005b). *Power: A radical view* (2nd ed., pp. 20–28). Basingstoke/Hampshire: Palgrave Macmillan/British Sociological Association.

Lukes, S. (2005c). *Power: A radical view* (2nd ed., pp. 118–119). Basingstoke/Hampshire: Palgrave Macmillan/British Sociological Association.

Lukes, S. (2005d). *Power: A radical view* (2nd ed., p. 118). Basingstoke/Hampshire: Palgrave Macmillan/British Sociological Association.

Lukes, S. (2005e). *Power: A radical view* (2nd ed., p. 119). Basingstoke/Hampshire: Palgrave Macmillan/British Sociological Association.

Lukes, S. (2005f). *Power: A radical view* (2nd ed., p. 27, 45, 46, 47, 48, 66, 68). Basingstoke/Hampshire: Palgrave Macmillan/British Sociological Association.

Lukes, S. (2005g). *Power: A radical view* (2nd ed., pp. 26–30). Basingstoke/Hampshire: Palgrave Macmillan/British Sociological Association.

Lukes, S. (2005h). *Power: A radical view* (2nd ed., p. 20). Basingstoke/Hampshire: Palgrave Macmillan/British Sociological Association.

Lusaka Times. (2013). Government signs for a $38 million loan from the African development bank for climate change. December 18, 2013. http://www.lusakatimes.com/2013/12/18/government-signs-38-million-loan-africa-development-bank-climate-change/

Lusaka Times. ADB gives Zambia a $24 loan. http://www.lusakatimes.com/?s=african+development+bank+gives+loan+to+Zambia

Macauhub. (2009). African development bank approves loans to Mozambique and Malawi, June 26, 2009. www.macauhub.com.mo/en/2009/06/26/7309

Mack, A., & Rock, I. (1998). *Inattentional blindness*. Cambridge, MA: MIT Press.

MacLachlan, M., Carr, S. C., & McAuliffe, E. (2010). *The aid triangle, recognizing the human dynamics of dominance, justice and identity* (pp. 100–102). Halifax/Winnipeg: Fernwood Publishing.

Malikounda.com. Mali- La BAD approuve plus de 36,5 milliards de dollars US pour des projets au Mali (Translation: AfDB approves more than FCFA36,500 million for projects in Mali). September 23, 2014. http://www.malikounda.com/Economie/mali-la-bad-approuve-plus-de-36-5-milliards-de-dollars-us-pour-des-projets-au-mali.html

Martens, B. (2002). Introduction. In B. Martens, U. Mummert, P. Murrell, & P. Seabright (Eds.), *The institutional economics of foreign aid* (p. 15, 23). Cambridge: Cambridge University Press.

Martens, B. (2004). *Why do aid agencies exist?*, revised draft. November 2004. Paper presented at workshops at Pompeu Fabra University (Barcelona), the University of Indiana, Bloomington (p. 2, 6).

Miningreview.com. Chinese investment in Zambia exceeding $1 billion a year. January 11, 2011. Lusaka, Zambia. http://www.miningreview.com/chinese-investment-in-zambia-exceeding-us-1-billion-a-year/

Moore, C. Inattentional blindness: Perception or memory and what does it matter? (p. 2, 3). http://www2.psychology.uiowa.edu/labs/iapl/iAPL_people/cathleen_moore/pdfs/moore_2001_psyche.pdf

Morriss, P. (1987). *Power. A philosophical analysis* (pp. 30–34). Manchester: Manchester University Press.

Nagel, J. H. (1975a). *The descriptive analysis of power* (p. 9, 10, 11, 20). New Haven/London: Yale University Press.

Nagel, J. H. (1975b). *The descriptive analysis of power* (p. 36, 72, 73, 83–91). New Haven/London: Yale University Press.

Nagel, J. H. (1975c). *The descriptive analysis of power* (p. 24). New Haven/London: Yale University Press.

Nagel, J. H. (1975d). *The descriptive analysis of power* (p. 154). New Haven/London: Yale University Press.

Nagel, J. H. (1975e). *The descriptive analysis of power* (pp. 158–159). New Haven/London: Yale University Press.

Nagel, J. H. (1975f). *The descriptive analysis of power* (p. 158). New Haven/London: Yale University Press.

Najam, A. (2002a). Financing sustainable development: Crises of legitimacy. *Progress in Development Studies, 2*(2), 153–160. http://www.oecd.org/unitedkingdom/2083553.pdf

Najam, A. (2002b). Financing sustainable development: Crises of legitimacy. *Progress in Development Studies, 2*(2), 156.

Najam, A. (2002c). Financing sustainable development: Crises of legitimacy. *Progress in Development Studies, 2*(2), 155. http://www.oecd.org/unitedkingdom/2083553.pdf

Najam, A. (2002d). Financing sustainable development: Crises of legitimacy. *Progress in Development Studies, 2*(2), 154–155. http://www.oecd.org/unitedkingdom/2083553.pdf

Najam, A. (2002e). Financing sustainable development: Crises of legitimacy. *Progress in Development Studies, 2*(2), 156, 158, 159.http://www.oecd.org/unitedkingdom/2083553.pdf

Najam, A. (2002f). Financing sustainable development: Crises of legitimacy. *Progress in Development Studies 2*(2), 158. http://www.oecd.org/unitedkingdom/2083553.pdf

Najam, A. (2002g). Financing sustainable development: Crises of legitimacy. *Progress in Development Studies, 2*(2), 154–156.

Najam, A. (2002h). Financing sustainable development: Crises of legitimacy. *Progress in Development Studies, 2*(2), 155–156.

Ndikumana, L., & Boyce, J. K. (2011). *Africa's odious debts, how foreign loans and capital flight bled a continent* (p. 49). London/New York: Zed Books.

Ouattara, A. D. (1997a). The challenges of globalization for Africa. Address at the Southern Africa economic summit, sponsored by the World Economic Forum. Harare May 21, 1997 (p. 1, 3). http://www.imf.org/external/np/speeches/1997/052197.htm

Ouattara, A. D. (1997b). The challenges of globalization for Africa. Address at the Southern Africa Economic Summit, sponsored by the World Economic Forum. Harare May 21, 1997 (p. 3, 4). http://www.imf.org/external/np/speeches/1997/052197.htm

Pediaview.com-open source encyclopedia. Conveyed concept. https://pediaview.com/openpedia/Conveyed_concept

Powers, W. T. (1998a). *Making sense of behavior* (p. 6, 7, 9, 24). New Canaan: Benchmark Publications.

Powers, W. T. (1998b). *Making sense of behavior. The meaning of control* (pp. 8–10). New Canaan: Benchmark Publications.

Powers, W. T. (1998c). *Making sense of behavior. The meaning of control* (p. 24, 25, 29, 31–42). New Canaan: Benchmark Publications.

Powers, W. T. (1998d). *Making sense of behavior. The meaning of control* (p. 35, 40). New Canaan: Benchmark Publications.

Powers, W. T. (1998e). *Making sense of behavior. The meaning of control* (p. 12, 21, 24). New Canaan: Benchmark Publications.

Powers, W. T. (1998f). *Making sense of behavior. The meaning of control* (p. 19, 19, 22, 24). New Canaan: Benchmark Publications.

Powers, W. T. (1998g). *Making sense of behavior. The meaning of control* (p. 9, 10, 11). New Canaan: Benchmark Publications.

Powers, W. T. (2005a). *Behavior: The control of perception* (p. 8, 46–48). New Canaan: Benchmark Publications.

Powers, W. T. (2005b). *Behavior: The control of perception* (p. 3, 106, 252). New Canaan: Benchmark Publications.

Powers, W. T. (2005c). *Behavior: The control of perception* (p. 7, 10). New Canaan: Benchmark Publications.

Powers, W. T. (2005d). *Behavior: The control of perception* (pp. 148–153). New Canaan: Benchmark Publications.

Powers, W. T. (2005e). *Behavior: The control of perception* (p. 37, 38, 39). New Canaan: Benchmark Publications.

Powers, W. T. (2005f). *Behavior: The control of perception* (p. 8). New Canaan: Benchmark Publications.

Powers, W. T. (2005g). *Behavior: The control of perception* (p. 19, 35, 37, 46). New Canaan: Benchmark Publications.

ReliefWeb-reliefweb.com. (2014, December 21). World Bank approves US$170 million to improve reproductive health and education for women and girls in Africa's Sahel region. http://reliefweb.int/report/mali/world-bank-approves-170-million-improve-reproductive-health-and-education-women-and

Robinson, H. (2001a). *Perception* (Series: The problem of philosophy, p. 2, 3, 4, 8–9, 37–38). London/New York: Routledge.

Robinson, H. (2001b). *Perception* (Series: The problem of philosophy, p. 1, 4, 29, 30, 188, 191, 205). London/New York: Routledge.

Robinson, H. (2001c). *Perception* (Series: The problem of philosophy, pp. 1–2, 188). London/New York: Routledge.

Rock, I., & Mack, A. (1994a). Attention and perceptual organization. In S. Ballesteros (Ed.), *Cognitive approaches to human perception* (pp. 23–34). Hillside/Hove/London: Lawrence Erlbaum Associates Publishers.

Rock, I., & Mack, A. (1994b). Attention and perceptual organization. In S. Ballesteros (Ed.), *Cognitive approaches to human perception* (pp. 24–32). Hillside/Hove/London: Lawrence Erlbaum Associates Publishers.

Rock, I., & Mack, A. (1994c). Attention and perceptual organization. In S. Ballesteros (Ed.), *Cognitive approaches to human perception* (p. 35). Hillside/Hove/London: Lawrence Erlbaum Associates Publishers.

Sang, N. (2014). Kenya receives loan from African Development Bank for last mile electricity connectivity project. December 19, 2014. http://malawiace.com/2014/12/19/kenya-receives-loan-from-african-development-bank-forlast-mile-electricity-connectivity-project/

Schacter, D., & Badagaiyan (citing Squire 1992, Tulving and Schacter 1990). Neuroimaging of priming: New perspectives on implicit and explicit memory. *Current direction in psychological science*. American Psychological Society. http://www.wjh.harvard.edu/~rajendra/Schacter%26Badgaiyan%2701.pdf

Schacter, D., & Badagaiyan (citing Squire 1992, Tulving and Schacter 1990). Neuroimaging of priming: New perspectives on implicit and explicit memory. *Current direction in psychological science* (p. 1). American Psychological Society. http://www.wjh.harvard.edu/~rajendra/Schacter%26Badgaiyan%2701.pdf

Seabright, P. (2002). Conflicts of objectives and task allocation in aid agencies. In B. Martens, U. Mummert, P. Murrell, & P. Seabright (Eds.), *The institutional economics of foreign aid* (p. 40). Cambridge: Cambridge University Press.

Shortell, T. Weber's theory of social class. http://www.brooklynsoc.org/courses/43.1/weber.html

Sidiropoulos, E., Fues, T., & Chaturvedi, S. (2012a). Introduction. In E. Sidiropoulos, T. Fues, & S. Chaturvedi (Eds.), *Development cooperation and emerging powers: New partners or old patterns?* (p. 9). London/New York: Zed Books.

Sidiropoulos, E., Fues, T., & Chaturvedi, S. (Eds.). (2012b). *Development cooperation and emerging powers: New partners or old patterns?* (p. 5). London/New York: Zed Books.

Simon, H. A. (1969). (cited by Dowding). Notes on the observation and measurement of power. In R. Bell, D. V. Edwards, & R. H. Wagner (Eds.), *Political power: A reader*. London: Collier-Macmillan.

Sodhi, J. S. (2011). Beyond GDP: The debate on globalization and development. *Indian Journal of Industrial Relations, 46*(4), 562–570 (p. 562). https://www.questia.com/read/1G1-259078485/beyond-gdp-the-debate-on-globalization-development

Spencer, C. R. (1977). Movements in international commodity prices and the balance of trade of developing countries with particular emphasis on African countries-1972–1974. *Bank of Sierra Leone Economic Review, 2*(4), 1–20.

Spencer, C. R. (2012). *Politics, agricultural development, and conflict resolution. An in-depth analysis of the Moyen Bani Programme in Mali* (pp. 49–52). Lanham: University Press of America.

Stiglitz, J. E. (2003a). *Globalization and its discontents* (pp. 4–9). New York/London: W.W. Norton and Company.

Stiglitz, J. E. (2003b). *Globalization and its discontents* (p. 7, 8, 119). New York/London: W.W. Norton and Company.

Stiglitz, J. E. (2007a). *Making globalization work* (p. 69). New York/London: W.W. Norton and Company.

Stiglitz, J. E. (2007b). *Making globalization work* (pp. 276–284). New York/London: W.W. Norton and Company.

Sumner, A., & Mallett, R. (2013a). *The future of foreign aid. Development cooperation and the new geography of global poverty* (p. 12). Basingstoke/New York: Palgrave Macmillan.

Sumner, A., & Mallett, R. (2013b). *The future of foreign aid. Development cooperation and the new geography of global poverty* (pp. 13–16). Basingstoke/New York: Palgrave Macmillan.

Sumner, A., & Mallett, R. (2013c). *The future of foreign aid. Development cooperation and the new geography of global poverty* (pp. 14–17). Basingstoke/New York: Palgrave Macmillan.

Tandon, R. (1996). Board games, governance, and accountability in NGOs. In M. Edwards & D. Hulme (Eds.), *Beyond the magic bullet. NGO performance and accountability in the Post–Cold War world* (pp. 53–55). West Hartford: Kumarian Press.

Tran, D.T. (2010). Globalization factors in income distribution and poverty in developing countries. *Indian Journal of Economics and Business, 9*(1), 2, 3. https://www.questia.com/read/1G1-225073256/globalization-factors-in-income-distribution-and-poverty

Tran, M. The Guardian. Former Nigeria state governor James Ibori receives 13-year sentence. http://www.theguardian.com/global-development/2012/apr/17/nigeria-governor-james-ibori-sentenced

Weber, M. (1947). The theory of social and economic organization. New York: Oxford University Press. (Cited by Ledyaev, V. in p. 2, *Power and conflict.* Online http://www.socialsciences.manchester.ac.uk/medialibrary/politics/research/workingpapers/mancept/LEDYAEV.pdf

Wils, F. (1996). Scaling up, mainstreaming, and accountability. The challenge for NGOs. In M. Edwards & D. Hulme (Eds.), *Beyond the magic bullet. NGO performance and accountability in the Post-Cold War world* (p. 76). West Hartford: Kumarian Press.

Wilson, D., & Sperber, D. (2004). Relevance theory. In L.R. Horn, & G. Ward (Eds.), *The handbook of pragmatics* (pp. 607–632 [pp. 1 & 2 of 27]). Oxford: Blackwell. http://www.dan.sperber.fr/?p=93

World Bank: The annual percentage increase in GDP for 2010, 2011, 2012, and 2013 for Ghana moved from 5.5 to 12.4 and then fell to 6.4 and then came down to 5.4; for Rwanda, the figures were 4.3, 4.9, 5.8, and 1.9 and for Liberia they were 7.1, 5.9, 7.3, and 8.6, respectively. http://data.worldbank.org/indicator/NY.GDP.PCAP.KD.ZG

Xiaoguang, K., & Li, F. (2006a). NGO governance in China: Achievements and dilemmas. In L. Jordan & P. Van Tuijl (Eds.), *NGO accountability. Politics, principles & innovations* (p. 129). London: Earthscan.

Xiaoguang, K., & Li, F. (2006b). NGO governance in China: Achievements and dilemmas. In L. Jordan & P. Van Tuijl (Eds.), *NGO accountability. Politics, principles & innovations* (p. 129, 130). London: Earthscan.

Yahoo. (2013). Nigeria: $1 billion infrastructure loan from China. July 8, 2013. AP. http://news.yahoo.com/nigeria-1-billion-infrastructure-loan-china-180321812.html;_ylt=A0LEVvAonv9UJVsA03olnIlQ;_ylu=X3oDMTEzZzRibTkwBHNlYwNzcgRwb3MDMwRjb2xvA2JmMQR2dGlkA1lIUzAwMl8x

CHAPTER 3

Understanding the Exercise of Power

Sources of Power

In Chap. 2, we discussed the theoretical and conceptual aspects of power. We also discussed other concepts that will help us to have a better understanding of power. These include such concepts as perception, legitimacy, and globalization. Having had a better understanding of the concept of power from the relevant sections in Chap. 2, in this section, we shall identify and discuss the various sources of power.

To all true believers, power comes only from God. In both the Bible (The Holy Bible-Exodus 14:21–29) and the Quran (Surah 42:49–50), there are many verses that speak of and to the power of God and to the fact that God is omnipotent, and HE alone gives power to whom HE chooses, whenever HE chooses (The Holy Bible-Exodus14:21). God can and does change the nature of things as humans have come to understand them. HE also changes behavior and actions of individuals and groups of individuals. HE knows the outcome of HIS actions. Power in the Holy Scriptures is thus in conformity with power as it is understood in the non-spiritual world, changing behavior and actions and, in some cases, ensuring that behavior does not change. In the Holy Scriptures, there is a direct cause-and-effect relationship.

Power, in some sections of the Bible, is used as synonymous with "authority." With "authority," the notion of legitimacy (i.e. the notion of "lawfulness") is introduced. With notions of "lawfulness" and "legitimacy," there is the need to discuss accountability, especially in the non-spiritual

C.R. Spencer, *Western Financial Assistance to the Developing World*,
DOI 10.1057/978-1-137-58399-4_3

world. An example of power, meaning authority, in the Bible is in Matthew 8:9–13 (The Holy Bible). In that section, the Roman centurion tells JESUS, "I myself am a man under authority, with soldiers under me. I tell this one, 'Go,' and he goes; and that one, 'Come,' and he comes." They do this in spite of their own feeling of what they want to do. By indicating that he also is "under authority," he is stating that he himself has superiors who give him instructions, superiors who have power over him and power to make him do things, and superiors to whom he is accountable for his actions. He has also been vested with rights by the emperor through his superiors. In other words, he is within a pyramid structure of power.

In this example, the emperor was the highest source of the centurion's power. This centurion symbolizes six of the sources of power, which I shall discuss in this section. The centurion derived his power from the following sources:

(i) **Expert power,** which he acquired through his specialist *knowledge* of fighting in battles, the privileged *information* that he received from his superiors or from his personal assessment of the battlefields. The soldiers only received such privileged information through him. He also possessed *skills*, which he acquired through training, study, and experience over the years, which gave him the authority to lead his soldiers.

(ii) **Power of position**. As a centurion, he had obtained this position through the "power" which had been handed down to him through the administrative laws, which created his position. The ultimate source of his position was the established Roman laws. These gave him legitimacy and rights, and stipulated those to whom he was accountable.

(iii) Because he had the right to reward his soldiers and to refuse to reward them, this source is termed **Reward/Punishment power**. Through this source, the centurion could influence the behavior of his soldiers.

(iv) The fact that he could reward and punish the men under him and the law allowed him to do so, **Coercive power**, is the fourth source. This source is closely linked with the "reward power" source, because, to some extent, there is an element of coercion, which is implicit in the reward power. The outcome from the reward power source is obtained through the "anticipated reaction" of a reward or a punishment.

(v) **Personal power.** This power relates to his personality and the way his socialization process had evolved, giving him certain skills, talents, experiences, and abilities. This power source, unlike the four preceding sources, is related to his innate ability. It does not depend on what I would call exogenous factors. However, it is closely related to the first source of power, the expert power source.

(vi) I add **Connections Power** as another source of power. This is related to networking. The type, level, and power sources that these network connections bring to the table could also help to determine how much total (not absolute) power a person possesses, relative to what is required to bring about the desired change in behavior or action. In the case of the centurion, his network was very powerful, as he brought JESUS himself into his network. This enabled the sick state of his servant to change positively.

A variant of "connections power" as a source of power is linked to the rapid development of information and communication technology. As we saw in Chap. 2 under Globalization, this technology has brought people's ears and eyes within very close range of each other. This has made it possible for groups of people in different continents to see and hear what each group is doing in real time. This "capacity," as Lukes (2005a, pp. 12, 31, 34) and Morriss (1987a, pp. 14, 30, 34) would call it, has provided immense "power to" as a resource to ordinary people, not just organizations and governments that have economic/financial and other resources they can draw upon. The media—written, spoken, and now audiovisual over the Internet—has furnished ordinary people as well as organizations and governments with immeasurable power and strength. YouTube, Twitter, Instagram, Myspace, Facebook, BlackPlanet, MiGente, and online blogs are part of this people's revolution in information and communication technology. This source of power (i.e. the media/Internet) has become an agent and a tool in the hands of those who know how to use and manipulate it. It is akin to Domhoff's (2005) "collective power," which he described as "the 'capacity' of a group to realize its common goals." In the field of development finance and particularly in areas related to advocacy and environment, organized groups and ordinary people relish this source as a means to promote either specific issues with which they are deeply concerned or causes they have espoused. They can use this source as means of thwarting the power that the external forces exercise on development finance and development assistance. They also use it to break or forestall actions programmed by national governments in developing countries. This source constitutes an element in the arsenal of the recipient countries that they can use to "break the flow of power" from the external forces to their countries. The cases of the construction of the Bujagali and Gibe dams in Uganda (Nampewo 2013) and Ethiopia (see Bosshard and Pottinger), respectively, as well as the Talo dam in Mali (Fink and Meierotto 2002) are cases in point. The effectiveness of this source is still under construction; the boundaries are expanding and are being tested daily.

These sources of power, discussed by authors including Stimson, Stapleton (2007), and Mechanic (1962, pp. 349–364) are resources, which enable the possessor to influence and, in some cases, control the behavior and actions of others. There are other sources of power discussed by Poggi (2001a, pp. 18–21). These "other forms of power" that are also relevant to our study of the imbalance of power and development finance include *political power*, *economic/financial power*, *creative/intellectual power*, *ideological/normative power*, and *military power*. Poggi (2001b, pp. 27, 30, 31, 130) stated, however, that the central source of all power is political power, and the tool on which such power depends is "coercive power." In his thinking, coercion is a function of the possession by those who own political power (governments) and hence such instruments of coercive power as the police and military, on which they can call to ensure that the outcomes they desire, actually occur. In fact, coercion is, to some extent, implied and/or subsumed in the exercise of most types of power under what Nagel (1975a, pp. 16, 19) called "anticipated reaction," what Scott (1990a, pp. 4, 13, 15) discussed as the "public transcript," and what I extend in the phrase "future expectation."

How are these sources of power involved when applied to development finance to Africa? From which source or sources do the external forces derive their power when they intervene in Africa and rural Africa in particular? From the literature on power discussed earlier, there are attributes that are associated with power; these attributes inform our analysis of the imbalance of power, seen and unseen. It would be judicious to discuss briefly each relevant source and its attributes, and see how they are involved individually or collectively in the process of development finance and development assistance.

The preceding categorization puts the items discussed as sources of power. It could be argued, however, that they are in themselves different facets of the same "power," not necessarily different sources from which external forces derive their power. Power is power, irrespective of the sources from which it is derived. In development finance, and from the perspective of the developing countries, this is true. For the developing countries, especially those in Africa, governments and people only feel the effect of the power exercised on them, not the different sources. Nevertheless, for the purpose of analysis, it may be argued that different sources are used for different objectives by the external forces, and these external forces have refined the use of power to fit each particular circumstance. These circumstances may be geographic, condition-based, or time-based in a continuum of constant power play in development finance. The sources can also be used individually or in any combination that fits the circumstances. For example, the creative/intellectual power (knowledge/information) source is used in combination with expert power, as when certain conditions requiring expert or specialist knowledge are imposed on a specific project, a sector program, or a budget support program. Economic/financial power, which is considered the most important power with regard to development finance, is often combined with creative/intellectual power to design or participate in the design of intervention programs.

Expert power is often combined with position power in situations where external donors provide technical assistants to key ministries in African governments. This combination will be discussed in more detail later in this chapter. Their roles are to advise, monitor, or vet (often all three combined) all key decisions before they are approved by the political authority, which has the ultimate political power to adopt and implement decisions involving the ministry. The ultimate political power, however, is always aware that a technical assistant placed in a department or ministry wields very serious power through the "connections power" with the external donors that the technical assistant can call upon when the minister/ministry does not heed his/her advice. The anticipated reaction from such connections helps elicit acceptance of the advice given by the technical assistants. These sources are used in several different permutations, depending on the circumstances. Whatever the permutation, the underlying factor is that power can be, will be, or has been exercised. This is because, as seen earlier, the "vehicle" and the "capacity" exist. The source, from which the power has come, is often blurred in the perception of the people and government in the country recipient of the development finance. The source or sources may even be imprecise in the minds of the wielders of the power, who may have become unconsciously competent in arranging the combinations required for specific outcomes.

In the present global circumstances, where military power is not used as much as it was in the past and is often frowned upon by the international community, the main source of power of the external forces is economic/financial. Most of the other sources derive from this source. Countries like Singapore, Thailand, Malaysia, Brazil, India, and South Korea, among others, which have attained very high levels of economic and social development as evidenced by the time series of their GDP (see World Bank Data-GDP per capita) have moved from the lower strata of the pyramid structure of power described earlier. They did this in exactly the way such movement away from the structure was envisaged and mentioned in Chap. 2. They were also able to put in place the appropriate institutions, systems, and structures and ultimately take advantage of the benefits offered by globalization. They are in another type of pyramid structure, which may be based more on global geopolitical parameters.

In our discussion of economic/financial source of power, I have not taken into account the volume or level of resources required to exercise power by the external forces. In our analysis, the level and volume of resources have to be sufficient to effectively offer development financial assistance to developing countries. The particular volume or level is not relevant once that sufficiency level is attained. That sufficiency level varies by country. The level and spread of the power exercised would vary as a function of the level of resources put into the development finance "bucket." In theory, the more the resources, the greater is the power. In practice, however, the volume or level does not affect the existence of the "vehicle" and the "capacity" of that "vehicle" of the external forces to exercise power.

In general, I see a situation where the level of resources, if small, but sufficient, can give an external force "power to" on an ad hoc basis, rather than "power over," as discussed by Morriss (1987b, pp. 32–33) and Dowding (1996a, pp. 4, 5, 8). As we saw in Chap. 2, "power over" is more pervasive and longer lasting. Lancaster (2007a, pp. 193–196) illustrates the case of Denmark and its financial assistance for development to developing countries. The official development assistance figures for net disbursement at current prices for 2014 are presented hereafter in millions of $US. At $US2996 million, Denmark's official development assistance is not substantial, compared with that of France with $US10,371 million, the UK with $US 19,386 million, Japan with $US9188 million, and the

USA with $US32,729 million (see OECD). In spite of the smaller amount of development assistance Denmark gives, this small amount allows it to provide financial assistance to certain countries, thereby it the "vehicle" and the "capacity" to exercise power individually or in a group as in a joint financing or larger budget support program. Other examples of existence of vehicle and capacity to exercise power are the cases of Greece, Spain, Ireland, and Portugal. At present (2010–2015) (Mansori 2011; also Ireland after Nama 2010), given the economic and financial problems that have led to their economic and financial resources being substantially reduced, Greece, Spain, Ireland, and Portugal may not feel inclined, or even possess the financial/economic resources required to provide development finance to developing countries and so exercise power. Nonetheless, they still have the "vehicle" and the "capacity" to do so, even though this latter has been considerably reduced.

I see a link between "connections power" as a source of power and what Augsburger (1992, pp. 148, 155, 156; also Hirshleifer 2001a, pp. 18, 19) called "triangulation." This is the act of one party, party A, in a conflict with another party, party B, bringing into the conflict, a third party, party C, to strengthen its case, putting the resources of this third party on its side. Party A expects such "triangulation" to help party A to bring about an outcome of the conflict favorable to it. In other words, the "connected" or "triangulated" party would put its resources or its power to help change the mind of party B and thus produce an outcome favorable to party A. With this link, power play is seen, as Foucault (see Foucault-Faubion 2000, p. 347) and Hirshleifer (2001b, pp. 27–31) saw it, as a struggle between parties. In the fields of advocacy and environment, this analogy with struggle is very clear. Those who are "for" are struggling against those who are "against" a particular project, program, or cause.

The power exercised by some external forces derives from the colonial past of most of the developing countries, especially those in Africa. I agree with Silverman (2011) that history informs many of the concepts used in international development finance. The social, economic, and political context in which these colonies evolved before independence influenced the way the government and people look at development finance at present. During the colonial period, the countries were ruled from Europe, and "power to" and "power over" the people were vested with the colonial administration. Funds for infrastructure and other development activities were furnished by the colonial governments in Europe. Power from

Europe and "acquiescence" from the people of the colonies came with such development funding. There were instances of resistance to this power, culminating in wars against such ethnic groups, as the Ashantis of Ghana and the Zulus of South Africa (Countries Quest and also British Battles), whose acquiescence was not forthcoming in the eyes of the colonial powers. Such resistances were ultimately quelled through military power. The power of the "vehicle" (i.e. the military power and the future expectation by the population of the exercise of military power) helped the colonial governments to rule without too many instances of confrontation. The perceptions of generations of African were affected by the pervading "powers" of the colonial administrations and unequal financial and economic situation in which they found themselves even after independence.

Independent African countries inherited systems and structures that were generally photocopies of those in the developed countries, which were their colonial masters. In the words of Alemazung (2010, pp. 64, 65), this constituted their colonial legacy. Nevertheless, the structure provided resources that, had they been harnessed efficiently and effectively, could have helped the African countries move quickly from the lower strata of the pyramid structure. This would have enabled them to move away from the power grip of the external forces, which were their inheritance. These structures, ill-fitted for managing real economic and social development, even though they might have been, were made even more unmanageable by the rampant corruption, which became the order of the day in some African countries, in the post-independence period.

In their bid to shed off some of the "colonial legacy," especially aspects of the constitution and the structure they inherited, many countries in Africa, but more so Sierra Leone, modified the constitutional laws, ex post, adapting them to suit the wants and needs of the executive arm for more control. The post-independence government in Sierra Leone, for example, set the stage for corrupt practices that became very noticeable in the period between 1961 and 1967 and thereafter (see Report of the Beoku-Betts Commission of Inquiry 1967; also Caesar–Auditor-General Report 2011 and News Watch Sierra Leone 2013). The government, at that time, adopted the constitutional laws to give a lot of power and control over the legislative arm to the executive arm (Thompson 1997, pp. 26, 36, 37). There was thus little or no oversight by parliament over the actions and activities of the executive arm. These powers and control affected the everyday life of the ordinary citizen and, to a large extent, diluted the power of the legislature and, by extension, the right of the ordinary citizen and democracy.

These corrupt practices, which continue up to the present, allowed many of the leaders to deplete the resources that they inherited from the colonial setup at independence (see Ndikumana and Boyce 2011a, pp. 9, 15; also Babalola and Fatumi 2014; Faul 2014; Lacey 2003). The resources included financial, economic, physical, and what I call "software." These are systems, which were, and still are being sabotaged by some of the leaders in Africa, such that they have become dysfunctional, inefficient, and ineffective. Systems relate to judicial, transportation, communication, public/civil service, health, legal, and parliamentary systems. With the breakdown of many of these systems, the stage was set for further corrupt practices, which have provoked external forces to impose governance conditions for their development financial assistance. Unlike some of their Asian counterparts, some of the African countries were, therefore, unable to manage effectively without the continuation of development finance and assistance from external forces. Although there are several other factors including terms of trade, the weight of the "powers" of the colonial administration, and others, corruption exacerbated the situation considerably. In many cases, such endemic diseases as malaria, HIV/Aids, and the Ebola virus, as well as conflicts and poor management of the economy, compounded this poor economic and financial situation, which we shall see later on. These factors made it less possible for the countries to move away from the bottom of the pyramid structure of power.

Development finance provided over the years was intended to help get the countries out of the lower strata of the power pyramid structure. Instead, using the expert power, combined with the creative/intellectual power, the external forces used Africa to try out their theories of economic development on a real time and "live" basis. Experimenting with development theories in Africa was another manifestation of power and confirms Lewis and Kanji's (2009a, pp. 106, 173, 183, 184) statement that "ideas and ideology," especially of the neoliberal market economy and Western democracy, "often accompany development finance and assistance." Development theories and development finance provided the theorists within the external forces with economic laboratories for real time, on-the-ground experiments, with real people. Using different and often differing paradigms, policy experiments, such as Ujaama, structural adjustment programs, enhanced structural adjustment programs and the more recent budget support programs, were all tried out and are still being tried out.

All these experiments, necessary as some of them may have been, or may still be, led to the increase in the power grip of the external forces. They constitute and are elements of a major source of power by these forces. In order to understand the exercise of power seen and unseen better, it is worthwhile to appreciate the socioeconomic and financial situation of the African countries in their desire to reduce poverty and stimulate growth and development in their economies. It is thus pertinent to give a brief background of the whys and wherefores of their struggle.

The Desire for Development

In many countries in Africa, the majority of the population lives in the rural areas. They carry out mainly farming and farming-related activities. Agricultural and related activities form the backbone of the economy of these countries (see Blein and Bwalya 2013, pp. 14–15). Agriculture in these countries, however, especially smallholder agriculture, suffers from many ills. These include land tenure and land management challenges, poor access to credit, inadequate capitalization, problems caused by poor infrastructure, especially rural infrastructure. Other shortcomings include inadequate marketing and inappropriate pricing, weak extension and advisory services, policy deficiencies, corrupt practices, and unsatisfactory input supply services. The macroeconomic policies often tend to provide a disenabling environment for fostering growth and development of the agricultural sector. In many areas, these have led to low productivity and low incomes for those involved in farming and other rural area activities.

In their efforts to increase growth, improve the well-being of the rural population, and move the economy upward, African countries have strived to improve agriculture and development generally in the rural areas. The rural areas are also very often, where many of the mineral deposits are located. Mining activities in some cases tend to compete with agriculture for such resources, as land, financial, and human. Because of higher remunerations in the mining sector, people often move from agricultural and rural development activities into mining, creating even more labor shortage problems for an agriculture already bedeviled by other serious issues arising from rural exodus. In addition, mining activities in some areas, quite apart from taking up agricultural land, displace people and destroy the agricultural land; examples are open cast bauxite and rutile mining in Sierra Leone. Indeed, mining reduces the land available for farming and livestock rearing.

Some countries such as Nigeria, Angola, Gabon, and Botswana (see Index Mundi, pp. 2; and also AU/UNECA 2011, pp. 184, 185) possess substantial mineral and petroleum resources and therefore dispose of financial resources to assist with their efforts to reduce poverty. In those countries that do not have as much mineral resources or in which such resources are negligible, financial resources are very limited and the drive to reduce poverty becomes an uphill task. Financial and other assistance toward growth and development from outside their borders are then very welcome and contribute in varying degrees to the drive for improvement in the lives of citizens and to the poverty reduction efforts. In general, the poorer the country is in terms of financial and economic resources, the greater the need to have assistance from outside its borders. The less endowed the country is, especially in natural and/or mineral resources, the more limited its choice of external sources of assistance. This may be because it does not have satisfactory bargaining power or fewer assets to barter in such circumstances. Investment opportunities may also be limited due to a shortage of natural assets. In addition, the greater the urgency of the recipient country to desire external financial assistance in the short run, whether for development or operational purposes, the more likely that the options and alternative open to it may be limited. Thus, it is more likely that such a country would be subjected more to the controlling influence of external forces than one for which the urgency is not as great. Some countries have been known to have liquidity problems to pay their civil servants for some months. In such circumstances, the budgetary support provided by the external source would be very welcome. In this way, the provision of development finance, would release the government funds previously earmarked for development. These funds could then be used for operational expenditures. The cases of civil servants in the Central African Republic (IRIN 2005) reported by IRIN in November 2005, the case of civil servants in Swaziland in 2011 (Mmegi online 2011), and the more recent (2013) case of members of parliament, doctors, and teachers not being paid in Kenya (24 Tanzania-East African Reporter 2013) are examples of such a situation of urgency.

Human and financial resources are critical if African countries are to move upward in the development ladder and reduce poverty. Financial resources are very scarce in the majority of African countries. Furthermore, their need for financial resources has become greater as their need for improved economic and social development increases. In many African countries, the annual change in their real GDP continues to fluctuate in a downward trend. The World Bank data (World Bank- Global Economic Prospects) show the annual percentage change in GDP for Sub-Saharan Africa (SSA). At market prices, GDP for SSA was 5.7 in 2000–2010, it fell to 4.3 in 2011, then dropped to 4.0 in 2012. It then increased to 4.2 in 2013. It was estimated to have increased to 4.5 in 2014 and forecast to reach 4.6 in 2015 and then 4.9 in 2016.

The annual change in GDP per capita at market prices for SSA moved on average from 3.1 in 2000–2010 period to 1.7 in 2011. It dropped to 1.5 in 2012, but rose to 1.7 in 2013. It was expected to increase to 2.0 in 2014, and the estimate for 2015 is 2.1 and the forecast for 2016 is 2.4. The annual percentage change in purchasing power parity GDP fluctuated during the 2000/2010–2015 periods. It started at 5.8 in 2000/2010 period, then moved to 4.4 in 2011, and then to 4.1 in 2012, and to 4.4 in 2013. It increased to 4.7 in 2014 and is forecast to increase to 4.8 in 2015 and to 5.0 in 2016. These regional figures, however, hide the detail picture for some countries for which the annual percentage in GDP fluctuated significantly. For example, the percentage change in the GDP per capita of Guinea fluctuated from −2.9 in 2009 to 0.7 in 2010, to 1.3 in 2011; it then remained at 1.3 in 2012 and then dropped to −0.3 in 2013. The Republic of Congo, Cabo Verde, Ghana, Malawi, Mali, Niger, Burkina Faso, Zambia, and the Republic of South Africa (RSA) are also countries where the percentage change in GDP fluctuated sharply with a downward trend. The reference note will give details of these fluctuations (World Bank, GDP per capita growth).

The Reality Behind the Desire

The figures in the previous section give a foretaste of the reality behind the desire of many Africa countries in their drive to reduce poverty and foster development and growth in their economies. In contemporary Africa, development assistance and development finance have become widespread, varied, and diverse. It would appear that though the economic situation has improved in the twenty-first century, it has not improved as much as the countries would have hoped. Poverty is still very acute in many countries. According to the World Bank, despite its falling poverty rates, SSA is the only region in the world for which the number of poor individuals has risen steadily and dramatically between 1981 and 2010. It goes to state that there were more than twice as many extremely poor people living in SSA in 2010 (414 million) than there were three decades ago (205 million) (World Bank- State of the Poor). As a result, whereas the extreme poor in SSA represented only 11% of the world's total in 1981, in 2010, they accounted for more than a third of the world's extreme poor (World Bank, State of the Poor). There is more need for external assistance than before. If we take just infrastructure alone, which is the foundation for economic development, spending in 2009 was around $US45 billion per year, whereas the need is for $US93 billion per year (World Bank Press Release 2009/AFR/138; also World Bank-Transforming Africa's Infrastructure 2009).

In the 1960s and 1970s, development finance to Africa came mainly from governments in Western Europe, North America, and the Soviet Bloc countries. Other sources of development finance for the rural areas included international development finance institutions, such as the African Development Bank (AfDB), the World Bank, and the International Fund for Agricultural Development (IFAD). The Food and Agriculture Organization (FAO) also provides financial support for development in the rural areas of Africa.

It is to be noted that in recent years with relief provided under various programs by the development assistance community, especially under the Program for Heavily Indebted Poor Countries (HIPCs), the debt burden of African countries, which was 40%t of export earnings in the 1990s, has been considerably reduced. The World Bank and the IMF canceled about 90% of the external debt of Sub-Saharan countries in Africa, reducing it from $US140 billion to nearly $US15 billion. Nevertheless, in 2009, the external debt of SSA countries was still a very heavy burden at $US273.4 billion, it moved to 343.1 billion in 2012 and continued rising to $US367.5 billion in 2013 (World Bank—International Debt Statistics 2015). External debt as a percentage of gross national income (GNI) which was 27.7% in 2009, and moved to 24.3% in 2013 (World Bank—International Debt Statistics 2015). External debt as a percentage of exports moved from 82.5% in 2009 to 69.1% in 2010 and then to 78.5% in 2013 up from 72.6% in 2012, which is the latest date for which figures, are available. Debt servicing to exports moved from 4.8% in 2009 to 3.5% in 2010, and then increased to 6.3 in 2013 (World Bank—International Debt Statistics 2015).

The figures do not show the reality of the situation for some countries as regards the power of the external forces over their economies. Some countries rely on just a few external donors for a significant proportion of their external aid flows. For example, OECD (see Johnson, Martin, and

Watts—2011, p. 27) figures show that in 2009, the Malagasy Republic heavily relied on five donors for 71 % of its total overseas development aid. France supplied 24 %, the USA supplied 18 %, the European Union institutions supplied 13 %, and the World Bank and the AfDB supplied 8 % each. Equatorial Guinea is another example, with Spain supplying 60 % of its overseas development assistance (ODA). According to OECD figures, Togo, Liberia, and Côte d'Ivoire also depend on one donor for at least 50 % of their aid. With such a considerable amount of its ODA coming from a few donors, the "power over" capacity of those donors increases considerably.

With assistance from outside, comes influence or power from outside. Some may say that with the influence and power from outside, as Steven Lukes (2005b, pp. 34, 69) and Keith Dowding (1996b p. 4) would put it, come "the power to and the power over," from outside. This is similar to the "control over" which Poggi (2001a, p. 11) mentioned, citing Lewis Coser. Depending on the budgetary and financial circumstances of the countries concerned, the amount of the financial assistance from outside could be substantial and could constitute a significant proportion of the total budgetary funds available to the African governments for all purposes. For the period 2008 to 2012, ODA as a percentage of central government expenses varied widely from 695.1 in 2008 to 132.5 in 2012 for Liberia. For Sierra Leone, it was 95.2 in 2008 and moved to 57.2 in 2012. For Côte d'Ivoire, it was 16.7 in 2008 to 64.1 in 2012 (World Bank, Net ODA Received). Gross capital formation in general, for many African countries, is sourced from outside the countries. ODA as a percentage of gross capital formation ranges in 2013 from 1.4 for countries with mineral resources such as Angola, to 138.1 for non-oil exporting countries, such as Malawi. The figures for Uganda were 23.2, Burkina Faso with 28.6 and Sierra Leone with 70.9. In those cases where the ratios are moderate to high as in Malawi, Sierra Leone, Burkina Faso, and Uganda, it would be appropriate to expect that as the saying goes, "he who pays the piper calls the tune" (World Bank, "Net ODA as % of gross capital formation"). With such a large proportion of their operational and capital development resources coming from outside of the country, the "power to" and "power over" of the external forces are significant. The external forces are then in a position to "influence" important areas of the countries' policies.

Alesina and Dollar (2000, pp. 34, 38) have shown that there is, in many instances, correlation between foreign aid and openness/democracy. The more open and/or democratic the economic and political systems of the country, the more willing the donors are to provide development finance as indicated by Spencer (2012a, p. 26). Alesina and Dollar found that there is substantial evidence that aid giving is strongly influenced by political and strategic considerations. I would add economic and commercial considerations to these considerations. Martens et al. (2002a, pp. 11, 12) have shown that for many bilateral donors; domestic commercial interests have a strong influence on aid giving and aid monitoring. This is linked to Lancaster's assertion, which we discussed in Chap. 2, that domestic politics play a significant role in aid giving and project implementation. There are, however, several instances where development finance is provided for purely altruistic and/or humanitarian reasons.

The story of the Pied Piper revealed that the unpaid piper could sing a different tune. The pied piper, as Martens (2004a, pp. 11, 14) and Spencer (2012b, p. 49) indicated, may have his own separate agenda. In many situations in Africa, where financial resources are extremely scarce, external assistance may come at a price. The first question that would be asked is "who is the piper and who pays him or her?" Another question would then "to whose tune the developing countries would be dancing?" Is it that of the one who paid the piper, that is, the governments of developed countries of Northern and Western Europe and North America working under the neoliberal paradigm of free trade and market-oriented economy, or that of the piper, understood here to be the development agencies or organizations of the developed countries?

Paradigms, Delivery Systems, Development Finance, and Power

It is important also to remember that in the 1960s and 1970s, some countries in Africa, such as Guinea, Benin, Ghana, and Mozambique had adopted the centralized planning approach sponsored by the then Soviet Union, and that they received development finance mainly from countries in the Soviet Bloc. In addition, we find international NGOs who either on their own behalf and with their own agenda, or on behalf of a third party are involved in the rural areas and particularly in rural development activities. In other words, under whose power would the developing countries be operating? Some of this power, or rather the exercise of this power can be visible. Other forms of exercising or exerting power could be subtle, covert, and unseen. Lukes (2005c, p. 42) makes the difference between exerting power and exercising power. He discusses the overt and covert influences of power to control another person's action and behavior, with "exerting" requiring more effort than "exercising." In the same way, external forces could control the actions and behavior of governments and their people.

In the twenty-first century, development finance to African countries has become diversified, both in terms of source and in terms of type. Funds now come not only from governments in developed countries in Europe and North America and international finance institutions, but also from countries in the Middle East, North and South Africa, in South and Central America, in the Indian subcontinent, and in the Far East. Development financial assistance has also come from organizations. Some of these organizations have direct ownership by governments and others can be termed NGOs. Assistance from these varying sources comes in the form of human resources, capital equipment, and actual financial resource, as well as training facilities. Differing and varying degrees of influence, or of power, come with each type of assistance.

Assistance in the form of human resources, which is commonly termed "technical assistance," tends to have greater influence or power over both local human resources and policy issues than does assistance in the form of capital equipment. This latter nevertheless has its influence over the development efforts. We shall discuss this in a later chapter. The position of the technical assistant is powerful if it is located in strategic services of government of the developing countries concerned. One example was the appointment of French advisers in the key ministries of Finance, Agriculture, and Commerce during the period of the late President Houphouet-Boigny in Côte d'Ivoire. Another example was the placing of technical advisers from the Department for International Development of Britain in some ministries during the second government of the late President Tejan Kabbah in Sierra Leone (see Pflanz 2007; also Waldman et al. 2014, pp. 164, 165). This happened after his return to power following the defeat of the rebels. As we shall see later, this confirms the position of Morriss (1987c, pp. 107, 108) relating to the institutional approach to the power of a position.

The delivery of assistance over the years moved from direct specific sector project approach to broad structural adjustment programs, to sector-wide approach, and at present to direct budgetary support. In the same vein, delivery channels moved from direct funding of projects to government, incurring zero transaction costs, then funding through a third party, with some amount of transaction costs, and back to direct government funding with the budgetary support approach. Funding of projects and programs has also moved from single financier or donor per program or project to multiple financiers or donors of the same program.

The changes in the delivery arrangement of development finance have followed the prevailing paradigm for development at the time, which was that of the liberal and neoliberal thinking of free enterprise and market economy. The government, intergovernmental, and private think tanks in developed countries in Western Europe, Northern Europe, and North America championed these paradigms. In some ways, Lewis and Kanji confirmed this thinking when they indicated that flows of ideas and ideologies have often accompanied development finance from the developed countries. The adoption, by Tanzania of the "Ujamaa" policy, in the 1960s, championed by the World Bank is an example. Another example, also from the 1960s, is the adoption of the centralized planning approach, which emanated from the Soviet Union, by Guinea, Mozambique, and Benin. The Soviet bloc and China-trained technical personnel of these African countries worked with their compatriots who were trained in the USA and Western Europe to implement the different approaches to development. The product was a mixture of neoliberal market system and centralized planning.

Amanor (2013, pp. 20–30, 21) contends that the USA shaped the overarching architecture of international development through its support for agricultural research, especially, through such institutions as the Consultative Group for International Agricultural Research. In some ways, this adoption of prevailing paradigms championed from abroad, even if adapted to local conditions, is another manifestation of the power of an external force being exercised on a non-dominant internal recipient country. This may have prompted Haq (cited by Chaturvedi 2012, p. 19) to contend that the developing countries should refrain from importing concepts from abroad with different systems and cultures. He believes that developing countries should develop their own mechanisms, which could then be built around local skills and local knowledge; this would be building people around development. This is not to contend that ideas and paradigms from outside Africa are negative to African development and should be rejected.

The earlier delivery setup for development finance adopted by governments in developed countries and international development finance institutions was for the governments in the developing countries in Africa to receive the assistance directly, either in the form of human or financial resources from developed countries. The financial resources were used to acquire such capital goods as tractors, farm equipment, manufacturing machinery, or some other forms of capital equipment. With the exception of South Africa, few, if any, African countries produce capital equipment, and the majority of these capital goods were designed and imported from mainly developed countries in North America, Europe, and Asia.

Delivery Systems, Corrupt Practices, and Power

Over several years, the direct delivery system, which was discussed earlier, was used. At the end of this exercise, it was expected that there should be effective growth and visible development, and the population should see actual improvements in their lives. In many cases, these did happen; however, in innumerable instances, there were diversions of funds from the purposes for which they were programmed, to non-essential activities and in many instances, into the private bank accounts of the leaders of the countries concerned and their acolytes. The case of the late President Mobutu of Zaire was highlighted by Ndikumana and Boyce (2011b, pp. 1–4) and by World Bank report (see Voice of America 2010). The BBC also reported the case of a former state governor in Nigeria who misappropriated state funds (BBC News 2012). It was interesting to note that these African leaders and officials did not keep the funds in accounts in banks in their own countries, where they might have been loaned out to local businesses, and thereby indirectly support and foster growth and development.

They kept the funds in banks in the developed countries. This is because the holders of these accounts feared that commissions of inquiries could be held, when there is a change in government, either through democratic means or through coups d'état. These latter were rife in the 1960s and 1970s in Africa. The holders of these illegally acquired funds would then be forced to return the funds. Another reason could be that with the then frequent devaluation of the national currencies, the money would have been depleted in terms of more exchangeable currencies like dollar, francs, or pounds. For example, the exchange rate of the national currency of Sierra Leone, the Leone, which was $US1 = 0.5 Leone at its creation in 1964, is now (2015) $US1 = 4896 Leones.

The Beoku-Betts Commission (Sierra Leone Beoku-Betts Commission of Inquiry 1967) in Sierra Leone in the period 1964–1968 was one such commission. It revealed all the misappropriation of funds of some members of the government of the then prime minister, the late Sir Albert Margai. It is an exercise of power from outside for these corrupt officials to have kept the funds they misappropriated, in banks in foreign countries, mainly developed countries. In this case, the exercise of power is more the combined result of the magnetic attraction (i.e. the "active power" of the benefits of the existence of a stable and convertible foreign currency) and the cost of possible future confiscation of the funds acquired inappropriately (i.e. the dissuasive effect). This could be similar in a way to the notion of "passive power" of Morriss (1987d, pp. 99, 150). The foreign banks, as Morriss would state, have the "passive power" to receive funds from anywhere. I would agree with Lukes (2005d, p. 1) that we should think about "power" broadly rather than narrowly.

In many instances, the authorities in the developed countries, which had provided the funds in the first place, and in whose banks the illegally acquired funds were kept, were aware that the funds existed. Articles and books, which speak to the awareness by the developed countries concerned of the illegal funds entering their countries, include those by Moyo (2009) and Ndikumana et al. (Ndikumana and Boyce 2011c, p. 20). The intelligence sources and networks of the governments of the developed countries were effective in fishing out the owners of these funds, which were acquired through corrupt practices as evidenced by the return to Nigeria of funds misappropriated by the former head of state, General Abacha, and his family members (CNS News). These practices led to a change in the delivery channel for the development funds but not in the neoliberal paradigm for growth and development. They also led to a tightening of the procurement arrangements for goods and services under the development finance programs. Such tightening is another expression of power, especially in circumstances where the assistance comes in the form of a loan, which has to be repaid.

It was under these circumstances that the development agencies of the developed countries entered into the development finance equation. These agencies were created to coordinate the development financial assistance and to oversee the channeling of development financial packages to the developing countries. They were established, as Martens (2004b, p. 12) stated, to minimize, among others, the risks of failure, and to improve information concerning the assistance, for a given cost to both donors and recipients of assistance. In addition, the misappropriation of funds also led these developed countries, in several cases, to enact laws regarding illegally acquired funds. The enactment of a law to ban illegal funds from entering Canada is a case in point (see Neondo 2001). Some developed countries have also instituted proceedings to return the funds to the countries concerned. The return to Nigeria, of funds illegally acquired by the late General Abacha and by his family members, by some foreign banks is a case in point (CSN News).

External Forces, Development Finance, and Power

Finance and capital equipment are just some of the elements of the instruments used by external forces to exert or exercise power over the rural areas in developing countries. "Rural areas" here include people, their economic and social activities, and their ideas and what they think or are encouraged to think. Many types of "external forces" get involved in the rural areas and in rural development in particular. Unfortunately, not much has been written comprehensively about the power of these external forces in the rural development activities in Africa. The power relationship or, better still, the power play among the different forces and their effect on the rural areas have so far not received due attention in the development finance literature. Much less has been written on the perceptions of the people in the countries recipient of development finance.

How do they exercise or exert power in the rural space and through it on the national governments, which control these rural spaces? What could be the positive and negative aspects of these external forces and the power they have over the rural spaces? How can we better understand the perception effects they have on these economies and the concerned population? If we can better understand this effect, we can develop strategies to harness the forces they generate more positively and use them in the efforts to reduce poverty.

As we saw earlier, external forces vary in nature, source, and type. Agricultural economists and other writers on rural development, such as Moise Mensah (1994), former vice president of the International Fund for Agricultural Development, talk about external forces in economic terms. For them, external forces include such market forces as international market prices of input and output, as well as external aid transfers to agriculture. He recognizes that international cooperation is a "political act" and considers such programs as structural adjustment programs and its recent variation, budgetary support programs, as part of the external forces, which bear on rural development in Africa.

The Strategic Plan for Rural Development (the Plan), drawn up by the Indian Ministry of Rural Development (Department of Rural Development 2010, pp. 2, 3) in assessing the rural development situation in India, discussed the external factors that would influence its efforts at rural improvement. The Plan defined these as political, economic, sociocultural, technological, environmental, and legal. The opportunities, threats, enabling features, and other aspects that could militate against any positive attribute of these external factors, or what I would term external forces, were also discussed. Even though not meant in the sense as external forces, some of these external factors were brought up by Kragelund (2010a, pp. 6, 12, 24) in his paper on aid from non-traditional donors to Africa. Kragelund discusses in depth the technical cooperation for development from these sources. Kragelund analyzed the roles these interventions play in the development of the rural and urban areas in Africa. The issues are discussed in terms of potential and possible impact on the development agendas of the countries in which the non-traditional donors intervene.

In discussing causes of underdevelopment of Africa, Simensen (pp. 1, 2, 3) brought in the historical perspective going as far back as the slave trade. He proffered some interpretations and causes, which one could dispute. However, he joins Mensah and Kragelund in identifying international development aid as an external factor that has to be considered in discussing rural development in Africa. In addition, as in Mensah's paper, Simensen's paper considered external prices, especially of raw materials produced by African countries, as well as the upward fluctuating price of petroleum, as important external forces affecting rural development in Africa.

The analyses in all the papers cited earlier reflect more of an economic impact or the effect of the efforts made to improve the national and rural economies. Others discuss the efforts of the donors to attain development assistance targets established during international conferences. Such conferences are held periodically between African countries and various donors (see Kragelund 2010b, pp. 4–7, 11, 12, 13; see also France 24). Still others like Anup Shah (2014) and, to some extent, Martens (2004c, pp. 6, 7, 13) and Rena (2008) discuss what they call the underlying evidence showing the real intent of aid giving. They join Alesina and Dollar in their statement that political, economic, and strategic considerations strongly influence aid giving. The statement of the late President Kennedy of the USA confirms this, when he asserted in 1962 that foreign aid is a method for the USA to maintain a position of influence and control around the world. This is evidenced, as Lancaster stated, in Kennedy's administration of promoting development as a priority of foreign aid as a means to "the end of the Cold War containment" (see Lancaster 2007b, p. 69; see also US Congressional Budget Office 1997, p. 2). The different donors possess various tools or instruments that constitute the elements of the external forces, which affect African rural economies. These include technical assistance, training, project or program loans, policy loans and grants, sector loans and grants, and budget support grants and loans. As I explained in Chap. 2, all of these are integral parts of development finance.

We can further categorize the external forces into those that can be influenced by the African countries and those that are beyond any influence of the countries. There are also those for which the instruments can be influenced and those for which the instruments cannot be influenced. We can also classify the external factors by outcomes. Lukes (2005e, pp. 71, 72, 74, 77) and Nagel (1975b, pp. 120–121, 175) believe that outcomes are critical to evidence of power; without outcome, it would be hard to prove the existence of power. Some of these outcomes are foreseeable, whereas others are not. We discussed issues and aspects relating to these notions concerning the concepts of power and its exercise in Chap. 2. Actions or non-actions of external force can create outcomes that have impacts on the lives of people.

The instruments used by these external forces have been broken down, by some authors like Kragelund (2010c, pp. 1, 2), as coming from traditional and non-traditional donors. Burgess (2012a, pp. 225–249) followed a similar line of thinking in discussing the impact of the cooperation between Africa and China and talked of South-South cooperation. This is to distinguish it from the traditional North-South cooperation of developed countries in the Northern hemisphere to developing countries generally in the Southern hemisphere. In spite of the different categorization of the sources or the nature of the external forces used by the various authors, the important feature to retain is that they all have instruments, which they use to exercise power over another country or countries. How much power or control do these external forces exert or exercise, as Dowding would put it? In this book, power and control are used interchangeably, although they may not, in some circumstances, be the same thing.

The amount of power exerted can vary, depending on the geographic situation of the country over which the power is being exercised or exerted and the strategic importance of the country to the interest of the wielder of the external force. It can also depend on the level of development of the country and its resources, especially natural and mineral. Other factors to consider include its importance in the concerned region, and this latter is closely linked to the economic and other resources it possesses. Yet another factor is the strength of the force that is being exerted or exercised. In the context of developing countries, the amount of "force" exerted or exercised could be a function of the resistance put up by the developing countries, which in turn depends on the resources it possesses. It also depends on how critical the outcome required is to the interest of the wielder of the external force. If it is critical, the wielder will most likely increase the strength of the force.

The "criticalness" is generally strategic in nature. This latter aspect could be economic, geopolitical, or political. In a more recent development, the strategic aspect could have an underlying objective of keeping terrorists from using the country as a base for its activities or training facilities. Some of the assistance provided to some African countries by European and North American countries now include military assistance (see Tyson 2005). This assistance is intended to help combat the incursion of terror-making and terror-spreading organizations into these countries, especially those with large, thinly inhabited areas like Mali, Chad, and Niger. In fact, the recent (2012) coup d'état in Mali and the declarations by the Islamist factions in the north of the country provide a vivid example of the threat this aspect poses to peaceful economic and social development of the countries. The external forces do not always use subtle manifestation of the capacity and vehicle they possess to exercise or exert power. The threat by the USA in July 2011 to withhold military aid to Pakistan (see Dombey and Bokhari 2011) is an example, and it is reminiscent of and similar to the "gunboat diplomacy" of bygone years. The threat in 2012 by the government of the USA to withhold the assistance it gives to the military in Egypt (see Dougherty and Lawrence 2012; also Middle East Online 2011, pp. 12–31) unless it ceases to persecute and/or harass the NGO is another case in point.

Many of the emerging nations, which are now donors of development finance in what Burgess (2012a, pp. 225–249) calls the South-South technical cooperation, were or are recipients of development finance themselves (see OECD-ODA). For example, Brazil, Cuba, India, and RSA all receive development assistance. In terms of net ODA, Brazil received $US1288 million (of which 86% came from bilateral sources) in

2012; India received $US1668 million (of which 71% came from bilateral sources) in the same year; RSA received $US1067 million (of which 70% came from bilateral sources); and Cuba received $US88 million (of which 67% came from bilateral sources) in 2012. In the case of China, the amount was a negative of $US194 million in 2012, which was a drop from $US646 million in 2010; 82% of the ODA China received in 2012 came from bilateral sources. Egypt received a net ODA of $US1807 million in 2012 (of which 58% came from bilateral source, a drop from 77% in 2010). Bilateral sources include western and northern European Countries, European Union Institutions, Japan, and the USA. In other words, in the past, they too were, or are currently, still objects of the power of external forces from donor nations of the north. They must have felt or are still experiencing the power of some external forces in their economy and their rural economies. How did they react to these external forces, which wielded power over their economies then? How do they react now that they seem to be in slightly less vulnerable, or to better reflect their present status, one could say "slightly more powerful position?" Would the fact that they had experienced power being exerted/exercised over them influence the way they use their own power over the less-developed recipients of their technical cooperation? I discussed South-South cooperation, perception, and power in Chap. 2.

International Non-governmental Organizations as Power Loci

In discussing the power seen and unseen wielded by external forces in the rural areas in Africa, it is important to note that it is not the only nations that directly control the external forces and wield power. Agencies and organizations, especially NGOs, wield such powers. Ahmed and Potter (2006, pp. 14, 15) stated that NGOs, especially transnational/international non-governmental organizations (TNGOs/INGOs), have an impact on both international and domestic politics. From Ahmed and Potter's discussion of the various international relations theories and their relevance to NGOs, one could infer that these NGOs have power and can influence behavior. In fact, some of these NGOs, especially TNGOs and INGOs, have operating budgets that are much bigger than those of some of the developing countries in which they operate. Just taking the US economy alone, in 2012, 5.4% of the GDP of the USA was from the tax-exempt entities, that is, NGOs and charities. This sector contributed $US887.3 billion to the US economy (NonProfit Times 2014). The annual budget for World Vision International in 2011 at $US2.8 billion was greater than the budget of all UN agencies combined, with the exception of the World Food Programme (see Morton, pp. 325–352). Morton (pp. 325–352) stated that eight INGOs have a combined revenue of $US11.7 billion in 2011, which represented an increase of 40% over the figure for 2005. In fact, Morton (pp. 325–352) indicated that in 2011, the World Vision International global revenue was greater than the budgets of 12 out of 23 of the OECD Development Assistance Committee (DAC) donors and was more than the GNI of smaller African and European countries.

This kind of resources provide elements that could be used to exercise influence and, through influence, power. Spencer (2012c, p. 50) discussed an example of the power of an INGO to influence behaviors and actions. In this case, an INGO succeeded in halting the construction of an irrigation dam in Mali. This was done by the use of "connections power," which we discussed earlier in this chapter. The "anticipated reaction" on the part of the major external financier and the government resulted in the halting of construction of the dam. The INGO also used the media and the Internet to the fullest in its efforts to delay the construction of the dam. This action led to a protracted conflict, which lasted for more than six years.

INGOs/TNGOs, each of which is a power locus, traditionally, compete among themselves for clientele, donor fund, constituents, and media attention. All of these could be considered as elements, which could enhance their power. As Lewis and Kanji (2009b, pp. 103, 135) indicated, some INGOs/TNGOs have started to realize that their impact could increase considerably if they come together by "building alliances" through networking. As a group, they could have better outcomes from their activities and, at the same time, exercise greater power over their clientele or beneficiaries. Apart from the "connections power" that this embodies, the beneficiaries could be put in a position of having the number of alternative organizations to choose from considerably reduced. In the same vein, bilateral and multilateral donors, another set of power loci, have come together, in a bid, as they put it, to coordinate development financial assistance. This nevertheless limits the alternative options for funding open to developing countries.

All of them, governments and INGOs, through technical cooperation programs that include development finance, have come to realize that the forces they possess and use can influence and in some cases control actions far beyond their own territories, if they come together. Martens (2004d, p. 15) refers to this networking as having the common objective of maximizing aid flows. This networking nevertheless tends to limit the alternatives open to the developing countries and, in some ways, reduce the total amount of aid. These countries no longer have the possibility of going to another funding agency or donor if one agency or donor refuses their project. This situation could be assimilated to Lukes' (2005f, pp. 114, 115) concept of being "less free" and to the notion of degrees of freedom.

Although it does not concern the INGOs, one example occurred in Guinea in 1979, in West Africa, when financing for a research station as part of a joint project with two international development financiers (A and B) was being considered. One of the financiers, A, refused to finance the research station, and the government officials appealed to our AfDB team, the other financier, B, during a joint field preparation mission. The official of institution A refused to finance the research station and did not cogently explain why they had refused to finance the research station. The station was re-examined more critically. Government officials provided additional detailed analytical information, including results of work done in the station over several years. Consultations were held with the officials of institution A at their headquarters as well as with officials from such expert institutions as the FAO. On that basis, our team from institution B consulted higher authority at our headquarters in Abidjan and consequently offered to finance the research station. The official of the institution A who had refused the financing was not happy with our institution for offering to finance the research station after he had declined to consider it for financing by his own institution. He tried to get our team, which had agreed to finance the research station, to decline the financing of the station. Our team went on to include the research station in our financing package. The station turned out to be one of the best components of the project; it was well-managed and met its objectives.

It could be argued that the officials in Guinea played one external financier against the other. Although this may be true, if we eliminate the possibility of choice, it would mean that we would be limiting the possibility for the recipient countries to obtain the best possible package for its development agenda. Such a limitation of sources for financing would provide the external force with greater "capacity" to exercise power on the recipient countries. A restriction of choices of financing would make the recipient countries, as Lukes would put it, "less free to do things according to their nature and judgment." This reduction in alternative development finance sources to choose from for its development agenda thus constitutes an infringement of choices. Such a reduction, while increasing the capacity to exercise power for the external forces, reduces the number of ways the recipient countries can thwart this exercise of power. Playing one source of development finance against the other is a tool that is available to the non-dominant forces to break the flow of power, as I shall explain in Chap. 4.

Recipients, Perceptions, and Power

How do the recipients of development finance (target population as some donors used to call them), perceive the controlling influences exercised by these external forces? Do they perceive themselves as objects of power? As we saw earlier, the relationship aspect of the exercise of power has received some attention. However, the exercise of power as it relates to development finance in Africa has received even less attention. What are the perceptions or frames used by such recipients in their mental processing of the exercise of such power? Are there positive and negative repercussions on the recipients of the wielding of power? How does the end of the cold war affect their perception of the alternatives open to them in terms of "donor friends?" How could the developing countries utilize the power generated by all these external forces to move the rural development agenda forward?

In discussing power, the issue of domination crops up; however, it is important to avoid the mistake in perception that some people in rural areas in Africa sometimes make. Some of them tend to believe that the difficult situation they are experiencing in the rural areas is a result of the domination of people in the urban areas, especially the national leaders who live in these latter areas. They believe that they are powerless to change things, blaming the situation on the urban people. Although the national leaders may tend to concentrate development actions and activities in the urban area for reasons not relevant to this discourse, the rural people should not confuse this with domination. In fact, there are some people in the urban areas who are worse off than those in the rural areas. This is, in fact, a danger in thinking that Peter Morriss (1987e, pp. 41,

135) warned against. Lack of power or "powerlessness" of one group is not necessarily the result of the domination of another group. James Scott (1990b, pp. 37, 92) also hinted at this point, when he discussed the "powerlessness" of slaves, serfs, and captives to react to acts of domination. However, in the examples proffered by Scott, the "powerlessness" of one group is due to the "power" or domination of the other. In the case of the serfs, slaves, or captives, they may have "numerical strength" to change the situation of domination, but lack the ability to act in concert. However, the history of Haiti belies such generalization. Do the non-dominant recipient countries have such means or resources to reduce their "powerlessness" in development finance? We shall discuss the resources at their disposal in Chap. 4.

So far, we have been working with the hypothesis that all of these external forces possess power or at least some controlling influence over the national and rural economies of African countries. How can we be sure that what they possess is power? In fact, in Chap. 2, I discussed the conceptual issues relating to power. I have used, as did Bachrach and Baratz (cited by Lukes) (2005g, p. 21), some terms such as control and influence almost interchangeably with power, when we refer to the external forces. Are they the same and do they have any relationship to each other? Morriss (1987f, pp. 8–12) argues that power and influence are not synonymous, but believes that there are considerable overlaps with present usage. Nagel (1975c, pp. 7, 8, 9) believes that both control and influence as synonyms for power present the same problem of operationalization and measurement as the term "power" does. They cannot therefore be used to adequately define power. They can, however, be used to explain the workings and the outcome of the exercise of power.

Exercise and Exertion of Power

In some instances, we have equated the possession of resources, mainly economic/financial and political, as evidence of power; however, do these constitute power? Under circumstances where such resources can be used to obtain acquiescence from others or to ensure specific outcomes from others, through changing their behavior or their actions, they constitute potential power. This potential power can or cannot be exercised, but it is still in the possession of the external forces. This is in line with the thinking of Poggi (2001c, pp. 125, 128, 130, 136) who stated that money, that is, financial/economic resources, and power have much in common and that they can be closely linked to political power, which, he feels, represents the centrality of power. It is my contention that people with financial/economic resources exercise power. They possess, what could be termed in French in relation to a vehicle, the *pouvoir* (i.e. the ability) and, the inherent capacity, the *puissance*, as when we talk of the horsepower, and exert them in African rural development. In the case of the vehicle, it is the inherent built-in capacity (i.e. the *puissance*) that gives it the ability, which I call the *pouvoir*, to go at a set range of speed that is determined by the *puissance*. However, do these external forces really possess such power, and in sufficient magnitude, to change or influence actions and behavior? What, as Domhoff (p. 4) would say, are the "indicators of power?" Are all of the external forces endowed with powers? How much of power do they have? If they do, can it be measured?

In this regard, we should consider Morris (1987g, pp. 15–18) and Lukes' (2005h, pp. 69–70) discussions of what they call the "exercise" fallacy and the "vehicle" fallacy of power. These will be discussed as they relate to power seen and unseen in rural Africa later in this chapter. Nevertheless, we can note here that both authors conclude that power is a "capacity" that I referred to as *puissance*. This, they believe, is distinct from its "exercise" and/or its "vehicle." In the case of external forces on rural Africa, the "exercise" and the "vehicle" are both as important as the "capacity" in the perception of the national governments and their people. In some circumstances, just the existence of the "vehicle" on its own exudes power. This is because in the perception of the people concerned, the power that the "vehicle" could bring to bear or "exercise" on them in the immediate near or far-off future inspires fear of punishment. For, the possible outcome they expect from the wielding of such power could act as Damocles' sword over some aspects of the rural development activities of developing countries.

Even the non-exercise of power by these external forces could influence behavior and have outcomes, which may or may not be foreseen. Authors like Dowding (1996a, pp. 4, 5) believe that for power to have been exercised, the outcome should have been known. In our example, the outcome of behavior and action is obtained through fear of the results of the wielding of power by the more-dominant force. The non-dominant force would assess the cost of not complying with the "wishes" of the dominant force. Lukes (2005i, p. 78) discussed the notion of anticipated reaction. This notion could be linked to what I would call "future expectation," expectation of what would happen in the immediate, near, or far-off future. I presented earlier the case of what the non-dominant force should expect if their wishes are not met, as was seen in Egypt in December 2011. The BBC (see Dougherty and Lawrence 2012) reported that the US secretary of defense phoned the military ruler of Egypt requesting that the Egyptian government should "stop raids on the offices of NGOs." Some of these NGOs receive assistance from foreign bodies, including some based in the USA. If such raids were not stopped, the secretary hinted that the military rulers could lose $US1.3 billion in military assistance that the USA gives to Egypt annually.

It is this future expectation that feeds into the anticipated reaction. This could in some ways be considered akin to Nagel's (1975d, pp. 24–33) analysis of preference in causal analysis of power and his notion of anticipated reaction. This notion can also be inferred from Scotts' (1990c, pp. 4, 13, 56) discussion of what he calls "public transcript." Although not in the same context, it can be considered similar to a situation where the behavior of the dominant group or force (in this case, the donors under the "public transcript") is anticipated in the behavior of those who are objects of the wielded power (i.e. the developing countries). The latter then behaves in accordance with prescribed rules in their "public transcript." Lukes (2005j, p. 45) discusses this non-exercise of power in his discussion of the case of US Steel in Gary, as did Morriss (1987h, p. 135), with the notion of forbearing to act in the case the "powerless" people who "forbore to act" because they knew they would not get what they wanted.

Even though the context is, again, different and not all the factors are equal, an example of this non-exercise of power is the refusal to discontinue subsidies to their farmers, especially those producing cotton, by some developed countries. The existence of these subsidies and the very "ability," or power, of these external forces to give subsidies to their farmers have specific anticipated or perceived outcomes that affect the planting decisions and plans of cotton producers in Africa among other things. This "ability" and the actual provision of subsidies by some developed nations significantly influence the price, which developing countries can expect from the sale of their cotton in the international market. Chapter 2 showed us how these perceptions or perceived expected outcomes are based on experiences, whether personal or acquired through a third party by way of information and communication.

This argument could be countered by stating that apart from subsidies, other factors which include weather and existing stocks affect international prices. Although this may be true, as we have seen earlier, international prices themselves are considered, by Mensah and the Indian Ministry of Rural Affairs, as external forces. Subsidies by developed countries to their farmers encourage the farmers to produce more, even though their production costs may be much higher than in the developing countries. This exacerbates the supply situation, bringing international prices down. It could be argued that based on the perceived and anticipated outcomes, the farmers in the developing countries could factor in these subsidies into their decision-making and farm planning and so minimize the negative effects on their revenues. While this could happen, the very act of factoring the subsidies has actually affected their behavior one way or the other. Some would say that many things in one part of the country, the continent, or the world could make people change their behavior. For example, an actual or anticipated fall in the stock market of a particular stock can make holders of those stocks, that are falling or expected to fall, to move their money away from that stock. Can one then say power has been exercised? To some extent, it has. The falling or the expected fall could be considered a cost for holding that stock and the expected outcome that this would have on the holders' finances. This had given the falling stock the "capacity" and the "power" to change behavior.

Along those lines, another example is the withholding of disbursement on a loan to a government of a developing country, for whatever reason, or even the possible threat of withholding. Quite apart from the legal obligations and implications, the perception of the people regarding the expected outcome from withholding disbursement could result in behavioral change in the people. In fact, in line with the thinking of Scott (1990d, pp. 34, 35) and Lukes, the overhanging possibility of withholding disbursement would ensure compliance by the developing country, which is a recipient of a development loan or grant. Here again, it is the expected or perceived outcome that would invoke compliance or would dissuade the government from non-compliance.

In this example, the developing country considers the cost and benefit of compliance and non-compliance. The situation could even be direr, if the instrument used is a budget support grant or loan. With the "budget support approach," all possible donors would theoretically have subscribed to the program, which is being considered or which had been approved. Any other possible source of funding from, for example, the emerging powers was, as Chahoud stated (cited by Sidiropoulos et al. 2012, p. 14), perceived as a threat by the donors who have subscribed to the support program. The traditional donors would frown upon non-traditional sources intervening in the country's development agenda after a budget support program had been agreed upon. In fact, there are instances when any such move, either by a non-traditional donor or by the country receiving the budget support, would be actively discouraged. The argument often used, was that such an "outside-of-support program" initiative and funding would disrupt the finely tuned program and upset the attainment of its objectives, which would include the structural "fixing" of the country's economy. However, if the non-traditional forces wanted to participate, it would be expected of them to provide the funds and accept the program and all the terms and conditions, that had been agreed upon prior to its participation. We shall not discuss here the veracity or not of this argument, because it is not directly germane to our discussion on the exercise of power. Nevertheless, if at that particular time the need for budgetary funds is critical and no other source could become available in short notice, the emphasis here is on "short notice"; then the perception of a possible withholding of disbursement could exert compliance much faster, even if there could be circumstances that are more overwhelming not to comply. Much of the structural adjustment programs of the 1970s and 1990s, where disbursements were results based, fell under this category. What role does perception play in the exercise of power or the understanding of power and potential power?

Some authors like Martens et al. (2002b, pp. 6, 36, 41) see development finance and development aid delivery in terms of principal-agent relationship and theory. Such relationships do subsume a power play relationship and a power imbalance. Other authors, like Alemazung (2010, pp. 64, 65) and Chiriyankadath (pp. 45, 46), discuss development finance in the context of colonialism, post-colonialism, and neocolonialism. As we saw earlier, the history of the developing countries had and still has some influence on the exercise of power in development finance. It would be difficult to determine the exact magnitude of the influence. However, power play and perceptions underlie these different relationships and terminologies. We have therefore given power and the perception of power play due attention in this chapter and in Chap. 4.

As we saw, the focus is on such areas as the factors that influence the wielding of power, sources of power, and breaks in such power. The perceptions of recipients and their emotions concerning development finance constitute a major area of concern. The emphasis is to discern their "hidden transcript." As INGOs/TNGOs are very important power loci, issues related to their exercise of power are addressed. Even though I am very concerned about the heavy weight of the external public debt owed by the African countries, I have not directly discussed its power. I shall not discuss the power wielded by the external forces because of or through the huge public debt owed by the developing countries. Nevertheless, the availability of development finance, especially as loans perceived by individual countries, contributes to their being conditioned to perceive development finance from external sources as being of great necessity to move their countries away from the bottom of the pyramid. I mentioned the pyramid structure earlier, and I shall discuss it in Chap. 4. These countries are thus very predisposed for the external forces/donors to exercise power over them.

Besides, external debt is not unique to African countries. Though the nature of the external debt owed by developing countries through the vehicle of development finance is different from the debt owed through bonds, treasury bills, and notes owed by developed countries, these are still external debt. The USA has huge debts in various forms of bonds, notes, and treasury bills, owed to various entities, some of which are external. As at February 2016, China and Japan both possess 38% of the external ownership of the US debt (see Brinsley and Christie 2008 also https://www.treasury.gov/tic/mfh.tx). Many other countries and external bodies also own smaller proportions. These external elements of the US debt do have the "vehicle" and the "capacity" to "exercise" power over some aspects of US affairs. Whether they exercise it, are inclined to exercise it, or are willing to exercise it is quite a different and complex issue. The USA can never be in the same position as a developing country, and African countries in particular, where the private sectors are relatively small, compared to the public sectors. The power they can exert, given the vast private sector in the US economy, is therefore not comparable with the power of the external forces on the economies of the African countries. Another reason is that power wielded through the existence of external public debt is a vast area of study, and it cannot be thoroughly addressed within the confines of this short book. Nevertheless, I am aware that development finance, mainly as loans, is the source of the public external debt of African countries. In fact, this huge external public debt owed by African countries is a primary source of the power wielded by the external forces as a group.

The external forces most often currently wield power subtly, less overtly, or covertly, as opposed to the historical wielding of power overtly through "gunboat diplomacy" or other military interventions. I concede, though, as I mentioned earlier in the case relating to military aid in Egypt, gunboat diplomacy or variances of it has not been completely eliminated in the international development finance arena. The subtle wielding of power and the sophistication involved make it hard to discern, identify, and analyze the influence of power on the objects of such power. To carry out such an analysis is a very daunting task. This is even more difficult in the development finance field because in this field, I would like again to echo Lukes (2005d, p. 1) who stated, power could be considered at its most effective when it is least observable. In the development efforts with which external forces use advocacy and in the environmental field, the external forces use the media to their great advantage. In such circumstances, the power play could be openly observed. The media thus becomes both an instrument/agent and a tool of the external forces to attain their goals, as well as a witness to the power of the external forces.

The ways the media influence perception of people in recipient countries will be discussed further in Chap. 4. As I explained in Chaps.1 and 2, some of the vehicles of power play used in development finance include projects and programs. These are accompanied by conditions that are often used as leverage to influence and/or control the actions of the recipient countries/non-dominant forces. In the next chapter, I shall elaborate further on the forces of different types of conditions as "vehicles" of power.

Notes and References

African Union (AU) and UNECA-for countries with mineral resources see "Minerals and Africa's Development" *International study group report on Africa's mineral regimes.* Africa Union and Economic Commission for Africa. **AU/UNECA** – Addis Ababa, Ethiopia. 2011. Appendices E (p. 184, 185). http://africaminingvision.org/amv_resources/AMV/ISG%20Report_eng.pdf

Ahmed, S., & Potter, D. (2006). *NGO'S in international politics* (p. 14, 15). Bloomfield: Kumarian Press.

Alemazung, J. (2010). Post-colonial colonialism: An analysis of international factors and actors marring African socio-economic and political development. *The Journal of Pan African Studies, 3*(10), 64, 65. http://www.jpanafrican.com/docs/vol3no10/3.10Post-Colonial.pdf

Alesina, A., & Dollar, D. (2000). Who gives foreign aid to whom and why. *Journal of Economic Growth, 5*, 33–63. Kluwer Academic Publishers (p. 34, 38).

Amanor, K. S. (2013). South-South cooperation in Africa: Historical, geopolitical and political economy dimensions of international development. *IDS Bulletin, 44*(4), 20–30.

Augsburger, D. W. (1992). *Conflict mediation across cultures. Pathways and patterns* (p. 148, 155, 156). Louisville/London: Westminster John Knox Press.

Babalola, A., & Famutimi, T. (2014). UK to return Ibori's loot to Delta State. PunchAugust10,2014. http://www.punchng.com/news/uk-to-return-iboris-loot-to-delta-state/

BBC News. Former Nigerian Governor James Ibori jailed for 13 years, April 17, 2012. http://www.bbc.com/news/world-africa-17739388

Beoku-Betts. Report of the Beoku-Betts Commission of Inquiry (later the Percy Davies Commission) into the Sierra Leone Produce Marketing Board from 1 January 1961 to March 1967: The price maintenance fund.

Beoku-Betts Sierra Leone Beoku-Betts Commission of Inquiry into the Sierra Leone Produce Marketing Board. Report of the Beoku-Betts Commission of Inquiry into the Sierra Leone Produce Marketing Board: With particular reference to the sale of palm oil, rice, and coffee haulers, nut-cracking machine, and the industrialisation programme undertaken by the Board during the period from January 1961 to March 1967" Government Printer. Sierra Leone Sierra Leone. Beoku-Betts Commission of Inquiry into the Sierra Leone Produce Marketing Board.

Blein, R., & Bwalya, M. (2013). Agriculture in Africa: Transformation and outlook. *NEPAD Transforming Africa*. NEPAD. November 2013 (pp. 14–15). http://www.nepad.org/system/files/Agriculture%20in%20Africa.pdf

Bosshard, P., & Pottinger, L. *International Rivers–Protecting people-water-life*. PetitiontostopGibe3Dam. http://www.internationalrivers.org/resources/petition-to-stop-gibe-3-dam-3487

Brinsley, J., & Christie, R. (2008). China passes Japan as biggest U.S. Treasuries holder (Update 1) Far East fans of US Government Debt. November 18, 2008. http://www.bloomberg.com/apps/news?pid=newsarchive&sid=aFQwLGTYEM3Y

British Battles. The Battle of Rorke's Drift. *Britishbattles.com*. Zulu War in http://www.britishbattles.com/zulu-war/rorkes-drift.htm

Burgess, S. (2012a, July–December). Developing from the South: South-South cooperation in the global development game. *Austral: Brazilian Journal of Strategy and International Relations, 1*(2), 225–249.

Burgess, S. (2012b, July–December). Developing from the South: South-South cooperation in the global development game. *Austral: Brazilian Journal of Strategy and International Relations, 1*(2), 225–249 (especially p. 228, 234, 241).

Caesar, A. (2011). Auditor general of Sierra Leone. Sierra Leone: Auditor-general's report for 2009. June 7, 2011. http://www.thepatrioticvanguard.com/sierra-leone-auditor-general-s-report-for-2009

Chaturvedi, S. (2012). Development cooperation: Contour, evolution and scope. In S. Chaturvedi, T. Fues, et al. (Eds.), *Development cooperation and emerging powers. New partners or old patterns* (p. 19). London/New York: Zed Books.

Chiriyankadath, J. Colonialism and post-colonialism development (p. 45, 46). http://www.docstoc.com/docs/110059444/2-Colonialism-and-Post-Colonial-Development

CNS News. (2014). Nigeria gets back $227 million looted by dictator, June 19, 2014 ***CNSNews.com***. http://www.cnsnews.com/news/article/nigeria-gets-back-227-million-looted-dictator

Countries quest. History, The British-Ashanti Wars. http://www.countriesquest.com/africa/ghana/history/the_british-ashanti_wars.htm

Department of Rural Development. Ministry of Rural Development. (2010). "Strategic plan" Government of India (p. 2, 3). February 9, 2010. http://www.performance.gov.in/sites/default/files/document/strategy/RD.pdfl

Dombey, D., & Bokhari, F. (2011). US Threatens to withhold military aid to Pakistan. *Financial Times*, July 10, 2011.

Domhoff, W. (2005). Basics of studying power. *Who Rules America*, University of California in Santa Cruz, April 2005. http://www2.ucsc.edu/whorulesamerica/methods/studying_power.html

Domhoff, W. Basics of studying power. *Who Rules America* (p. 4). University of California in Santa Cruz. http://www2.ucsc.edu/whorulesamerica/methods/studying_power.html

Dougherty, J., & Lawrence, C. (2012). Egypt warned U.S. aid at risk. *CNN Security Clearance*, February 3, 2012. http://security.blogs.cnn.com/2012/02/03/egypt-warned-u-s-aid-at-risk/

Dowding, K. (1996a). *Power. Concepts in social thought* (p. 4, 5, 8). Minneapolis: Open University Press/University of Minnesota Press.

Dowding, K. (1996b). *Power. Concepts in social thought* (p. 4). Minneapolis: Open University Press/University of Minnesota Press.

Faul, M. (2014). Nigeria get back $227 million looted by dictator, June 19, 2014. http://finance.yahoo.com/news/nigeria-gets-back-227-million-183556491.html;_ylt=A0LEV7_TWT5W510AL7knnIlQ;_ylu=X3oDMTEzMnNvdWY0BGNvbG8DYmYxBHBvcwMyBHZ0aWQDRkZSQTEwXzEEc2VjA3Ny

Fink, R., & Meierotto, L. (2002). *Cultural survival* CSQ Issue 26.4 (Winter 2002). http://www.culturalsurvival.org/publications/cultural-survival-quarterly/mali/moratorium-talo-dam-construction-still-holding

Foucault, M. (2000). "Power" Volume 3. In J. D. Fabion (Ed.), P. Rainbow (Ser. Ed.) *Essential works of Foucault* (p. 347). New York: The New Press.

France 24. Africa-France summit opens in Mandela's shadow. France24.com. http://www.france24.com/en/20131206-africa-france-summit-opens-mandela-shadow-hollande-security/

Hirshleifer, J. (2001a). *The dark side of the force. Economic foundations of conflict theory* (pp. 18–19). Cambridge/New York: Cambridge University Press.

Hirshleifer, J. (2001b). *The dark side of the force. Economic foundations of conflict theory* (pp. 27–31). Cambridge/New York: Cambridge University Press.

Holy Bible. New international version. The Committee on Bible Translation June 1978, revised August 1983. Exodus 14:21.

Holy Bible. New international version. The Committee on Bible Translation June 1978, revised August 1983. Mathew 8:5–13.

Index Mundi. For oil producing countries in Africa, see **Index Mundi** "Oil Producing Countries – Africa" (p. 2). http://www.indexmundi.com/map/?t=0&v=88&r=af&l=en

Ireland after NAMA. "Ireland, Greece, Spain, Portugal: A same European 'peripheral' problem?" Posted by irelandafternama under Commentaries, Speculations in *Ireland after NAMA*. November 24, 2010. https://irelandafternama.wordpress.com/2010/11/24/ireland-greece-spain-portugal-a-same-european-%E2%80%98peripheral%E2%80%99-problem/

IRIN. (2005). See Central African Republic: Government fails to pay salaries: Civil servants continue strike. ***IRIN**, humanitarian news and analysis.* Bangui November 25, 2005. http://www.irinnews.org/report/57347/central-african-republic-government-fails-to-pay-salaries-civil-servants-continue-strike

Johnson, A., Martin, M., & Watts, R. (2011). Trends in international financial cooperation forum for LDC. Background for preparing for the 2012 Development Cooperation Forum Department of Economic and Social Affairs. Draft –April 29, 2011 (p. 27).

Kragelund, P. (2010a). The potential role of non-traditional donors' aid in Africa. Issue paper no. 11. International Centre for Trade and Sustainable Development (ICTSD) Geneva, Switzerland. http://www.ictsd.org/downloads/2011/03/the-potential-role-of-non-traditional-donorse28099-aid-in-africa.pdf. (See especially p. 6, 12, 24).

Kragelund, P. (2010b). Examples include the following cited by Kragelund, P. The potential role of non-traditional donors' aid in Africa. Issue paper no. 11. International Centre for Trade and Sustainable Development (ICTSD) Geneva, Switzerland. 2010.http://www.ictsd.org/downloads/2011/03/the-potential-role-of-non-traditional-donorse28099-aid-in-africa.pdf (See especially pp. 4–7, 11, 12, 13).

Kragelund, P. (2010c). The potential role of non-traditional donors' aid in Africa. Issue paper no. 11. International Centre for Trade and Sustainable Development (ICTSD) Geneva, Switzerland. 2010. http://www.ictsd.org/downloads/2011/03/the-potential-role-of-non-traditional-donorse28099-aid-in-africa.pdf (See especially pp. 1–2).

Lacey, M. (2003). Kenya joins nations pursuing funds stolen by ex-leaders. *New York Times,* December 21, 2003. http://www.nytimes.com/2003/12/21/international/africa/21KENY.html

Lancaster, C. (2007a). *Foreign aid. Diplomacy, development, and domestic politics* (pp. 193–196). Chicago/London: University of Chicago.

Lancaster, C. (2007b). *Foreign aid. Diplomacy, development, and domestic politics* (p. 69). Chicago/London: University of Chicago Press.

Lewis, D., & Kanji, N. (2009a). *Non-governmental organizations and development* (p. 85, 106, 173, 183, 184). London/New York: Routledge Taylor Francis Group.

Lewis, D., & Kanji, N. (2009b). *Non-governmental organizations and development* (p. 103, 155). London/New York: Routledge.

Lukes, S. (2005a). *Power: A radical view* (2nd ed., p. 12, 31, 34). Basingstoke: Palgrave Macmillan/British Sociological Association.

Lukes, S. (2005b). *Power: A radical view* (2nd ed., p. 34, 69). Basingstoke: Palgrave Macmillan.

Lukes, S. (2005c). *Power: A radical view* (2nd ed., p. 42). Basingstoke: Palgrave Macmillan.

Lukes, S. (2005d). *Power: A radical view* (2nd ed., p. 1). Basingstoke: Palgrave Macmillan/British Sociological Association.

Lukes, S. (2005e). *Power: A radical view* (2nd ed., p. 71, 72, 74, 77). Basingstoke: Palgrave Macmillan/British Sociological Association.

Lukes, S. (2005f). *Power: A radical view* (2nd ed., p. 114, 115). Basingstoke: Palgrave Macmillan/British Sociological Association.

Lukes, S. (2005g). *Power: A radical view* (2nd ed., p. 21). Basingstoke: Palgrave Macmillan/British Sociological Association.

Lukes, S. (2005h). *Power: A radical view* (2nd ed., pp. 69–70). Basingstoke: Palgrave Macmillan/British Sociological Association.

Lukes, S. (2005i). *Power: A radical view* (2nd ed., p. 78). Basingstoke: Palgrave Macmillan/British Sociological Association.

Lukes, S. (2005j). *Power: A radical view* (2nd ed., p. 45). Basingstoke: Palgrave Macmillan/British Sociological Association.

Mansori, K. (2011). Why Greece, Spain, and Ireland aren't to blame for Europe's woes in new republic. *Politics, Culture Magazine*. October 11, 2011. http://www.newrepublic.com/article/economy/95989/eurozone-crisis-debt-dont-blame-greece

Martens, B. (2004a, November). *Why do aid agencies exist?* Paper presented at workshops at Pompeu Fabra University, the University of Indiana at Bloomington (p. 11, 14).

Martens, B. (2004b, November). *Why do aid agencies exist?* Paper presented at workshops at Pompeu Fabra University, the University of Indiana at Bloomington (p. 12).

Martens, B. (2004c, November). *Why do aid agencies exist?* Paper presented at workshops at Pompeu Fabra University, the University of Indiana at Bloomington (p. 6, 7, 13).

Martens, B. (2004d, November). *Why do aid agencies exist?* Paper presented at workshops at Pompeu Fabra University, the University of Indiana at Bloomington (p. 15).

Martens, B., Mummert, U., Murrell, P., Seabright, P., et al. (2002a). *The institutional economics of foreign aid* (p. 11, 12). Cambridge: Cambridge University Press.

Martens, B., Mummert, U., Murrell, P., Seabright, P., et al. (2002b). *The institutional economics of foreign aid* (p. 6, 36, 41). Cambridge: Cambridge University Press.

Mechanic, D. (1962). Sources of power of lower participants in complex organizations. *Administrative Science Quarterly, 7*(3), 349–364. http://www.jstor.org/discover/10.2307/2390947?uid=3739704&uid=2&uid=4&uid=3739256&sid=21106472268023

Mensah, M. (1994). Policy setting and institutional framework for rural development in Africa. *Special Communication*. CTA Annual Report 1994.

Middle East Online. Egypt risks losing military aid with raids on US-funded NGOs. *Middle East Online,* December 31, 2011. http://www.middle-east-online.com/english/?id=49737

Mmegi- Online. Swaziland can't pay civil servants in ***Mmegi online***, May 12, 2011 Issue 28(69). http://www.mmegi.bw/index.php?sid=11&aid=754&dir=2011/May/Thursday12

Morriss, P. (1987a). *Power: A philosophical analysis* (p. 14, 30, 34, 38). Manchester: Manchester University Press.

Morriss, P. (1987b). *Power: A philosophical analysis* (pp. 32–33). Manchester: Manchester University Press.

Morriss, P. (1987c). *Power: A philosophical analysis* (p. 107, 108). Manchester: Manchester University Press.

Morriss, P. (1987d). *Power: A philosophical analysis* (p. 99, 150). Manchester: Manchester University Press.

Morriss, P. (1987e). *Power: A philosophical analysis* (p. 41, 135). Manchester: Manchester University Press.

Morriss, P. (1987f). *Power: A philosophical analysis* (pp. 8–12). Manchester: Manchester University Press.

Morriss, P. (1987g). *Power: A philosophical analysis* (pp. 15–18). Manchester: Manchester University Press.

Morriss, P. (1987h). *Power: A philosophical analysis* (p. 135). Manchester: Manchester University Press.

Morton, B. An overview of international NGOs in development cooperation. *Case Study, 7,* 325–352. http://www.undp.org/content/dam/china/docs/Publications/UNDP-CH11%20An%20Overview%20of%20International%20NGOs%20in%20Development%20Cooperation.pdf p. 333. Or http://www.cn.undp.org/content/dam/china/docs/Publications/UNDP-CH11%20An%

20Overview%20of%20International%20NGOs%20in%20Development%20Cooperation.pdf

Morton, B. An overview of international NGOs in development cooperation. *Case Study, 7*, 325–352. http://www.undp.org/content/dam/china/docs/Publications/UNDP-CH11%20An%20Overview%20of%20International%20NGOs%20in%20Development%20Cooperation.pdf (p. 333).

Moyo, D. (2009). Why foreign aid is hurting Africa. *Wall Street Journal*. March 21, 2009. http://www.wsj.com/articles/SB123758895999200083#articleTabs%3Darticle

Nagel, J. H. (1975a). *The descriptive analysis of power* (p. 16, 19). New Haven/London: Yale University Press.

Nagel, J. H. (1975b). *The descriptive analysis of power* (p. 29, 120–121, 175). New Haven/London: Yale University Press.

Nagel, J. H. (1975c). *The descriptive analysis of power* (p. 7, 8, 9). New Haven/London: Yale University Press.

Nagel, J. H. (1975d). *The descriptive analysis of power* (p. 16, 24–33). New Haven/London: Yale University Press.

Nampewo, A. (2013). Why damming Isimba Falls will destroy tourism on river Nile. *Daily Monitor*, September 14, 2013. http://www.monitor.co.ug/arts-culture/Travel/Why+damming+Isimba+Falls+will+destroy+tourism+on+R++Nile/-/691238/1991446/-/sc1grd/-/index.html

Nazret-Nazret.com. The first Ethiopian blog- Current Affairs, Business, Sports andStyle. http://nazret.com/blog/index.php/2011/07/29/unesco-world-heritage-committee-urges-ethiopia-to-halt-gibe-iii-dam

Ndikumana, L., & Boyce, J. K. (2011a). *Africa's odious debts. How foreign loans and capital flight bled a continent* (p. 9, 15). London/New York: Zed Books.

Ndikumana, L., & Boyce, J. K. (2011b). *Africa's odious debts. How foreign loans and capital flight bled a continent* (pp. 1–4). London/New York: Zed Books.

Ndikumana, L., & Boyce, J. K. (2011c). *Africa's odious debts. How foreign loans and capital flight bled a continent* (p. 20). London/New York: Zed Books.

Neondo, H. (2001). Canada puts corrupt African leaders on notice. *News from Africa,* March 7, 2001. http://www.newsfromafrica.org/newsfromafrica/articles/art_12376.html

Newswatch. Newswatch Sierra Leone. Sierra Leone fails the millennium challenge cooperation. *NewsWatch Sierra Leone*, November 9, 2013. http://www.news-watchsl.com/article/sierra-leone-fails-millennium-challenge-cooperation-mcc

NonProfit Times. (2014). Nonprofits worth $US887.3 billion to US economy. *NonProfit Times*, October 28, 2014. http://www.thenonprofittimes.com/news-articles/nonprofits-worth-887-3-billion-u-s-economy/

OECD. The figures are from the OECD STAT extracts. http://stats.oecd.org/Index.aspx?datasetcode=TABLE1

OECD- ODA- FOR -Brazil. http://www.oecd.org/dac/stats/documentupload/BRA.JPG China- http://www.oecd.org/dac/stats/documentupload/CHN.JPG Egypt- http://www.oecd.org/dac/stats/documentupload/EGY.JPG India- http://www.oecd.org/dac/stats/documentupload/IND.JPG Cuba- http://www.oecd.org/dac/stats/documentupload/CUB.JPG

Pambazuka. (2003). Stop the construction of Uganda's Bujagali dam. *Pambazuka News*, November 20, 2003, Issue 133. http://www.pambazuka.net/en/category.php/advocacy/18436

Pflanz, M. (2007). Blair will find dreams for Africa unfulfilled. Freetown. *The Telegraph* of London, May 28, 2007. http://www.telegraph.co.uk/news/worldnews/1552857/Blair-will-find-dreams-for-Africa-unfulfilled.html

Poggi, G. (2001a). *Forms of power* (p. 11, 18–21). Cambridge: Polity Press.

Poggi, G. (2001b). *Forms of power* (p. 27, 29, 30, 31). Cambridge/Malden: Polity Press/Blackwell Publishers.

Poggi, G. (2001c). *Forms of power* (p. 125, 128, 130, 136, 137). Cambridge: Polity Press.

Rena, R. (2008). Rich countries and their leverage on Africa. *Africa Economic Analysis*, December 4, 2008. http://www.africaeconomicanalysis.org/articles/63/1/Rich-countries-and-their-leverage-on-Africa/Page1.html

Scott, J. C. (1990a). *Domination and the arts of resistance. Hidden transcripts* (p. 4, 13, 15). New Haven/London: Yale University Press.

Scott, J. C. (1990b). *Domination and the arts of resistance. Hidden transcripts* (p. 37, 92). New Haven/London: Yale University Press.

Scott, J. C. (1990c). *Domination and the arts of resistance. Hidden transcripts* (p. 4, 13, 56). New Haven/London: Yale University Press.

Scott, J. C. (1990d). *Domination and the arts of resistance. Hidden transcripts* (p. 34, 35). New Haven/London: Yale University Press.

Shah, A. (2014). Aid as a foreign policy tool to aid the donor not the recipient. *Global Issues*, September 28, 2014. http://www.globalissues.org/article/35/foreign-aid-development-assistance#Aidasaforeignpolicytooltoaidthedonornottherecipient

Sidirpoulos, E., Fues, T., & Caturvedi, S. (2012). Introduction. In S. Chaturvedi, T. Fues, et al. (Eds.), *Development cooperation and emerging powers. New partners or old patterns* (p. 14). London/New York: Zed Books.

Silverman, J. M. From colonial administration to development finance. In *International development should........getting to demand driven development* (p.2). http://internationaldevelopmentshould.com/2011/02/15/from-colonial-administration-to-development-finance/

Simensen, J. Africa: The cause of underdevelopment and the challenges of globalization. *UTENRIKSDEPARTEMENTET* (p. 1, 2, 3).

Spencer, C. R. (2012a). *Politics, agricultural development, and conflict resolution. An in-depth analysis of the Moyen Bani programme in Mali* (p. 26). Lanham: University Press of America.

Spencer, C. R. (2012b). *Politics, agricultural development, and conflict resolution. An in-depth analysis of the Moyen Bani programme in Mali* (p. 49). Lanham: University Press of America.

Spencer, C. R. (2012c). *Politics, agricultural development, and conflict resolution. An in-depth analysis of the Moyen Bani programme in Mali* (p. 50). Lanham: University Press of America.

Stapleton, S. (2007). The five sources of a leader's power, and how (and how not) to use them. http://www.simonstapleton.com/wordpress/2007/12/17/the-five-sources-of-a-leader%E2%80%99s-power-and-how-and-how-not-to-use-them/

Stimson, T. Sources of power in CLI. http://www.consultcli.com/sources-of-power---dr-terry-stimson.html

24 Tanazania- by **East African Reporter**. (2013). Kenya's civil servants yet to receive pay as doctors, teachers threaten to strike, August 1, 2013. In 24Tanzania.https://24tanzania.com/kenyas-civil-servants-yet-to-receive-pay-as-doctors-teachers-threaten-strike/

Thompson, B. (1997). *The Constitutional history and law of Sierra Leone (1961–1995)* (p. 25, 26, 36, 37). Lanham/New York/London: University Press of America.

Tyson, A. S. (2005). US pushes anti-terrorism in Africa. *Washington Post.com*, July 26, 2005. http://www.washingtonpost.com/wp-dyn/content/article/2005/07/25/AR2005072501801.html

US Congressional Budget Office. (1997). The role of foreign aid in development (p. 2). May 1997. http://www.cbo.gov/sites/default/files/foraid.pdf

Voice of America. (2010). World Bank report claims 'quiet corruption' in Africa, March 15, 2010. http://www.voanews.com/content/world-bank-report-claims-quiet-corruption-in-africa-87800482/114188.html

Waldman, T., Barakat, S., & Varisco, A. (2014, September 28). *Understanding influence: The use of statebuilding research in British policy* (p. 164, 165). Surrey: Ashgate Publishing Co.

World Bank. Adapted from World Bank data-The GDP per capita in current $US Singapore moved from 45569.7 in 2010 to 55182.5 in 2013 in a constantly upward trend. The figures for Thailand for the same years respectively, also in a constant upward trend was 4802.7 and 5779.0, as was the case for the Republic of Korea (South) for which the upward trend for the same years was from 22151.2 in 2010 to 25977.0 in 2013. For Malaysia, the same years yielded figures which were also constantly upward from 8754.2 in 2010 to 10538.1 in 2013. Figures for India for the same years were fluctuating with slight upward trend moving from 1417.1 in 2010 to 1497.5 in 2013, having risen to 1509.2 in 2011 but fell to 1484.5 in 2012. See http://data.worldbank.org/indicator/NY.GDP.PCAP.CD/countries

World Bank. See World Bank "Global economic prospects." Sub-Saharan Africa regional forecast. Annual percentage change in GDP. http://www.worldbank.org/en/publication/global-economic-prospects/regional-outlooks/ssa; or http://www.worldbank.org/en/publication/global-economic-prospects/regional-outlooks/Global-Economic-Prospects-June-2015-Sub-Saharan-Africa-analysis

World Bank. See World Bank. GDP per capita growth (annual %). http://data.worldbank.org/indicator/NY.GDP.PCAP.KD.ZG?page=1

World Bank. The State of the poor: Where are the poor and where are the poorest?. In *Poverty reduction and economic management*. Poverty reduction and equity. http://www.worldbank.org/content/dam/Worldbank/document/State_of_the_poor_paper_April17.pdf

World Bank. See World Bank press release no: 2009/AFR/138 "New study shows that transforming African infrastructure will require an additional $31 billion a year and huge efficiency gains" MidRand, South Africa. November 12, 2009. http://web.worldbank.org/WBSITE/EXTERNAL/NEWS/0,,contentMDK:22396129~pagePK:64257043~piPK:437376~theSitePK:4607,00.html

World Bank. Transforming Africa's infrastructure. Washington, DC. November 12, 2009. http://www.worldbank.org/en/news/feature/2009/11/12/transforming-africas-infrastructure

World Bank. (2015). International Debt statistics, Sub-Saharan Africa. http://datatopics.worldbank.org/debt/ids/region/SSA

World Bank. Net ODA received (% of central government expense). http://data.worldbank.org/indicator/DT.ODA.ODAT.XP.ZS

World Bank. Net ODA received (% of gross capital formation). http://data.worldbank.org/indicator/DT.ODA.ODAT.GI.ZS

CHAPTER 4

Appreciating Perception and Power

BREAKS IN POWER SEEN AND UNSEEN

In the beginning of Chap. 3, I discussed the different sources of power and how the external forces combine these sources in the exercise and exertion of power in development finance. I explained how large the array of power is and that the strength of each source increases with each new "contract" and how the total combined force of the sources used is perceived by the developing countries. Does that mean that the non-dominant forces (i.e. the developing countries) are caught in a never-ending stranglehold?

Are these developing countries, non-dominant forces, devoid of any possibility of resisting, reducing, or thwarting the power exercised over them? Not quite, as I shall explain in this section. In development finance, donors, their governments, and their agencies, all grouped together as external forces, were and are evaluated by specific performance ratios of which the disbursement rate is one. These performance ratios include absolute disbursement amounts and disbursement amounts as a percentage of total loans. Disbursement levels/rates are compared with programmed levels/rates. These are aspects that developing countries could influence. Disbursement rates and levels are part of the upward accountability dis-

Cicero—DE LEGIBUS Volume III— "*I admit there is an element of evil inherent in the office of tribune; but without that evil we would not have the good which was the point of setting it up.*"

C.R. Spencer, *Western Financial Assistance to the Developing World*,
DOI 10.1057/978-1-137-58399-4_4

cussed in Chap. 2. The donors are accountable "upward" to a higher authority which includes their parliaments and their taxpayers. Donors and their agencies are given funds by parliaments and, in the case of some INGOs, by their board of governors or private and public donors. As we saw in Chap. 2, parliament or boards of governors require, at the end of each year, that the agencies or INGOs give account of how they spent the funds, including, in some cases, detailed audited statements of accounts. In addition, assessments of disbursement levels and rates were part of the required account statements. A report on the improvements in certain parameters, including the economic and social well-being of the population, is often also a requirement of the accountability reporting system.

The levels and rates of disbursements and improvements obtained could influence the total amount of funds that the parliaments or board of governors (the higher stratum in the pyramid structure) would allocate to governments or their agencies for the following year for development finance and development assistance. The higher the rate and/or level of disbursement in the previous year and the greater the improvement obtained, the greater the likelihood that the agency will receive higher allocations for the following year. Aid effectiveness in Europe is driven by the political need for governments in Europe to justify overseas development assistance budgets to their electorates, as Mackie (2012, p. 96) stated. This in a way is supported by statements such as that of Barder (2015) when he stated that "taxpayers (should) obtain good value for their money." The notion of higher allocation is influenced by higher disbursement level is borne out by my experience with annual budget discussion and country allocations discussion. I recall budget and country programming meetings as director of agriculture and rural development to discuss and negotiate the annual administrative budgets for departments and country loan/grant allocations for the year. The progress of the implementation of the different programs and projects and the rate, level, and total amounts of disbursements for each such program/project was a key factor in determining the allocation for the next year and years to follow. The higher level of disbursement was part of the equation to ascertain implementation progress and effective development. Thus, countries with higher level and/or higher rate of disbursement tended to receive higher country allocations. In the same vein, sectoral allocations were also influenced by the level and rate of disbursement per sector.

The level/rate of disbursement is a tool that can be used by recipient countries as a "break" on the powers of donor governments and the

INGOs. This "break," though, is still within the domain of the external forces. It is an accountability statement. At any given level in the organizational structure of the external forces, there is another level above it. The lower level is often held accountable to the higher level. In the previous example, when the disbursement level or rate is lower than the expected or programmed level or rate, the parliament of the donor country, or the board(s) of directors and/or governors in the case of international development finance institutions (IDFIs) and INGOs, is reluctant to increase the level of budgetary allocations to the government or agency. The non-increase in budgetary allocation to the donor agency could in fact make for a reduction in the resources available to the agencies of the external forces. It leads to a reduction in its operations, possibly a reduction in staff, cuts in personnel salaries, and closing down of some operations or some offices. The reduction in available resources, in some ways, reduce the spread of the power available to be exercised, not necessarily the power itself.

Knowledge of the possible reduction of available resources for the upcoming budget year influences the behavior of donors and agencies, especially toward the end of the budget year of the government or agency. The donor agency is put in a position in which it will be anxious to disburse funds with a not-too-strong consideration of the previously imposed conditions. This latter appreciation or fact has been used by some recipient countries as leverage to renegotiate, not necessarily a modification in the terms of the loan or grant but rather a review of certain conditions or more flexibility in implementation timetable or other aspects of the development finance package. In discussing some of the development assistance programs of the World Bank, Martens et al. (2002a, p. 4) observed that at times, policy targets prescribed by the interventions as conditions are not met, but the funds are disbursed nonetheless. These disbursements are made because, as Martens et al. put it, the World Bank wanted to enable the countries to service previous World Bank loans. Another reason proffered by Martens et al. is the pressure from other creditors and donors on the World Bank to help the country to continue to service its debt to them.

There is also the pressure of the political power play within the decision-making body of the institution as shown by the example given by Martens et al. (2002b, p. 12, 15). This power play among responsible institutions in the donor countries, to some extent, confirms Lancaster's (2007a, p. 6) statement that domestic politics influence development finance provided by the developed countries. Once the recipient country is aware of the preceding facts, the power wielded by the external force could be diluted by actions on the part of the recipient country to renegotiate or revisit some or all of the conditions. Another way that recipient countries/non-dominant forces effect a break in the power flow from dominant forces is by reminding the dominant forces of the high moral ground that the dominant party had set itself and which it does not seem to be respecting or adhering to. The dominant party would then be obliged to ensure adherence to the norms, guiding principles, or best practices it had set itself to respect or adhere to.

By using the preceding ways of breaking the power of the external forces, a lower stratum in the pyramid has removed some elements of the power bearing down on it by the upper stratum. Here again, however, the "dilution" is also subject to power play. The extent of the dilution is dependent upon how badly the donor agency (dominant party) wants to show its higher authority that it is achieving its goals or making an impact and/or has disbursed the funds or has attained the prescribed goals and objectives. This disbursement has to be done in a way that enhanced development in the recipient countries. The higher authority has to be made aware of the higher level of both disbursement and the development achieved. In addition, the agency has to be inclined to desire more funds for the coming year or at least desire to retain its existing level. This desire is weighed against the urgency of the need of the recipient country (non-dominant party) for the funds in the financial assistance package. When the desire by the donor for more funds for its development assistance program is greater than the urgency and the need for the development finance package of the recipient countries, the recipient countries will succeed in its renegotiation for more flexibility.

There is also in the situation where all the donors have come together in a budget support program, a recipient country can influence a donor in the external forces/donor group, with which it has close or strong ties (e.g. historical). An example is Sierra Leone getting the support of the UK, especially after the end of the civil war in Sierra Leone in 2002. Other example is France providing support for Côte d'Ivoire, again immediately after its civil war in 2011; another example of such relationship is that of the USA and the Republic of Liberia. These developing countries can use these historical ties to ask the donor countries to plead their cases within the donor group for a modification in the condition, in the time line prescribed or for extra funds. Although the fact of pleading its case is tantamount to the subtle acceptance of the power of the donors by the recipient country, it is also a break in the "power to" of the donors, because the recipient country has been able to dilute the power of the donors by modifying certain aspect(s) of the financial assistance package.

Another factor that we shall discuss later in this chapter is the existence of representatives of recipient countries in the boards of governors and directors of the IDFI, which represent the third pyramid power structure. The representatives of the recipient countries constitute an element in the arsenal of the recipients to thwart, dilute, or otherwise effect a break in the power flow from external to internal forces. Depending on the particular institution, these representatives, acting individually or as a group within the governance structure of the international development finance institution, can intervene before and/or during the process of reaching the "contract," which we discussed in Chap. 1. They can obtain, within limits, the review or modification of some of the aspects of the contract including conditionalities and implementation schedules.

Media and Perception

In development finance, outward manifestation is important, both to donor/external forces and to the recipient countries. The former group would like to be seen by their electorates that they are "doing good" to the people of the developing countries, and the latter group for its constituents to know that it is addressing the issues that are of great concern to them. The results of, or returns to development finance have to be seen or, at least, heard of. The preoccupation with perception raises issues, as we saw in Chap. 2, as to whether perception, which depends on things "seen" or "heard of," can be called real perception. As Ballesteros (1994, pp. 9–13) stated, however, in his experiments, people call on both implicit and explicit memory to provide answers to the issue of perception.

Visual presentations are useful. The media thus becomes a vector to transmit the results/returns to the public, through audio and visual presentations. These presentations, in turn, help the perceptions of people. Visual expressions of returns/results help to determine how the subject of the audio and visual expression is evaluated. The way the media reports on issues relating to development finance, especially the results of or the returns to the development finance package, is very important. It influences the way the public perceives the intervention itself or, at times, the country or countries participating in the intervention. The way this is done is critical to the perception of the recipient countries, irrespective of whether conditions were imposed, that the country found oppressive.

For example, there were instances where the visit of an appraisal mission by the AfDB to prepare a sugar project in the Kwale district in Kenya in East Africa was hailed in the media in a way that presented the AfDB as being in the district to help the ailing sugar industry in that region of Kenya. In another example, the media portrayed the appraisal mission to the Islamic Republic of Comoros, an island state in the Indian Ocean, as being there to help the small farmers in the agriculture sector of the country. These portrayals considerably helped the missions/teams to get information and data for their work from both the public and the officials of government and the private sector. In both cases, they had perceived the institution as having a positive influence on the well-being of the sugar industry, which employed hundreds of nationals in the Kwale district of Kenya. A similar perception was observed in the Comoros where the team was perceived as being there to help the small holders in the agricultural sector, which was the major sector in the economy. The team in the Comoros met with very senior politicians and top government officials. During a later period, the same positive perception was observed when I was head of a team to the Comoros to prepare a fisheries project for small-scale fishermen. The team was able to meet with very senior politicians and again with top government officials. The meetings with these top politicians and government officials were perceived by the people in the Comoros as an "endorsement" by their leaders of the work the teams were there to carry out. At all these different times, the conditions had not yet been finalized with the government team. The public and the government officials were apparently not overly concerned with the conditions relating to the agricultural sector that would have to be agreed upon with the government experts as necessary and required of the country before the team recommended the loan for approval.

Another example is again in another East African country. This time, it was a sugar project in Uganda which was visited as part of the appraisal process for an intervention in the sugar industry. Because of its allegedly poor human rights record in the early to late 1970s (see Keatley 2003; also Byrnes 1990), this country appeared to be isolated by most of the international community. It was therefore very sensitive to issues of power play from external forces. The team had discussions with senior government officials/top military officers, in the vice presidency and in the ministry of finance. One of the officials listened to the conditions, which the team listed to make the ministry aware of the conditions that we had agreed with the government experts and officials. He admonished the team not require conditions that would upset the status quo in the socioeconomic setup of the country because of the loan the institution was going to make to the country. The official was very conscious of the power imbalance between our institution and the government of the country; the development finance package should not give the team the right to think it can change the actions of the government. In other words, the loan funds should not give our institution the "capacity" to exercise "power to" over the government. In this example, the visit of the team to the ministries and vice presidency was mentioned in the local newspaper; however, it was mentioned as part of the coverage of the official delegations to the country. The report stated that a team from the AfDB was in the country to appraise the Lugazi sugar project which had been prepared prior to that by a team from the FAO of the United Nations. There was no "saving" the Lugazi sugar industry from going down in the newspaper reporting. However, because of its apparent isolation, the government, the politicians, and officials alike saw the mission as a lifesaver to the sugar industry, which, at that time, employed hundreds of nationals. In this case, the officials rightly saw that there was a power imbalance, but because of the situation of the country at that time, they had very limited room for maneuver. The country was at the lower end of the power pyramid structure.

"Economic/financial power," backed by "reward power," with a subtle hint of "coercive power," apparently got the government to accept the conditions, which were agreed with the government experts, and which were expected to improve the agricultural sector and give structure to the agricultural sector in general and the sugar industry in particular. In those circumstances, the appraisal team had also used "expert power," which is generally based on specialist knowledge and information, which we had about the economic and social situation in the country. There was also the fact that the government had an "anticipated reaction" or the "future expectation" of the reaction of the development finance institution, and what it might do. This possible "coercive power" in the perception of the government, most probably, contributed to bringing about the expected outcome. All of these sources of power, whether used consciously or unconsciously, combined to get the government to accept the conditions. The perception of both government and people was positive toward the institution, because in this instance, it was a definite case of "constellation of interests," not a case of what Domhoff (2005a, p. 1) called "enforced cooperation." In addition, in the preceding example, the ministry officials made the appraisal team privy to their "hidden transcript" which we discussed in Chap. 3.

Just as we saw in the cases of advocacy and issues concerned with the environment, the media can whip up, what Domhoff (2005b, p. 1, 2) called, "collective power." This power is considered a part of the "connections power," which is linked to Augsburger's concept of triangulation. We discussed this concept of triangulation in Chap. 3. The media can create a positive image either of the development intervention or of the institution or country involved in the intervention. There is also the possibility of the creation of a negative image. In one scenario, a hypothetical title with a possible negative image *can* be presented as follows: "China invests big money in Zambian mine where labor abuse was recorded." This positive remark is negated by the latter part of the title. The perception of the Zambians could thus likely be negative. In another scenario, even a hypothetical positive media title such as the following, "China helps Zambia, Chinese investment in Zambia over $US1 billion a year," could somehow be negated, if another article in the next column reads "Chinese mine managers shoot Zambian mine workers and are not prosecuted." This latter article, next to the positive investments of China in Zambia, could have a very harmful effect on the relationship, not necessarily of the government with China, but of the people and their Chinese neighbors, whom they will now perceive as negative, thus influencing their perception of any development financial assistance that the country receives from China.

As we saw in Chap. 2, most of the theories of perception emphasize sensory stimuli, especially visual and auditory. Thus, the media by its actions can influence perception. Nevertheless, how long will this negative perception continue, a month, several months, or a year? Would a persistent reporting of positive news about China affect the initial negative news, which had led to the initial negative perception? Unfortunately, I am not aware of any studies that have been done in this domain, which would help us answer these questions. However various the ways in which the media influences perception, may be, it does not hide the fact that whatever the circumstances, the development finance intervention involves a power play between the external forces and the recipient governments.

Source of Information and Perception

In Chap. 2, in the analysis of the perception of recipients of development finance, I explained that the current situation of the politicians in government in developing countries includes primarily the experience of enjoying the paraphernalia of power. The enjoyment of power within the context of their socioeconomic and political setup would influence their perceptions of the power exercised on the government/country through the development finance package. This will be discussed in detail later in the different models and scenarios.

Concerning the source of information received by the people in developing countries about development finance package, I asked a key question. This is related to the reliability of the sources and what information the sources conveyed. The reliability of the information conveyed about development finance packages in the recipient countries by the media is generally good. It is important to note that the "good reliability" stems from the fact that the press secretaries of the government information machinery or of the donor agency or institution make press releases to the public, including to media representatives. Most donor agencies and multilateral development finance institutions or IDFI have units or departments responsible for communications and media activities concerning the agency or institution. The press releases provide the salient points of the development finance packages. In my review of archival information among local and online national newspapers such as on Ghanaweb.com (Ghana) (Ghanaweb-2012), "Essor" and "Malikounda" (both for Mali) (Malikounda 2014), as well as online newspaper reports (Maiga 2014; also Sang 2014; Lusaka Times 2013), and such other countries as Kenya, Zambia, Malawi, and Sierra Leone (*Awareness Times* 2014), I noticed that information concerning development finance packages in the written press did not give details about the conditions accompanying the development finance package.

The disclosure policies of multilateral development finance institutions, however, require, among other things, that project appraisal reports which contain the conditions approved by the approving authorities of these institutions be released to the public and so they can be perused by anyone who so desires. In the same vein, bilateral agencies also have disclosure policies in place to release information about the activities and operations of the agencies. It is difficult to ascertain how many members of the public or press, especially in Africa, take advantage of this availability of the condition to actually request them.

Although I found that the media does not generally indicate conditions attached to approved loans and grants, I gathered from some of the comments from the general readers in the written press I reviewed (e.g. in the case of Ghana) that some were aware of conditions imposed by the Bretton Woods Institutions. A commentator was questioning why there were conditions to such assistance. Can we assume that such comments underlie some knowledge of possible power play by these institutions? In the case of a report in the media concerning a grant of 120 million GBP to Ghana for budgetary support as part of a multidonor program, one commentator's question concerned the imposition of conditions, whereas a few others were requesting tighter management by the British Government of the funds granted. A few mentioned corruption of the oversight system in Ghana as a reason for such a request (Ghanaweb 2006b).

Are we any nearer to knowing the source of information about a particular development finance or development assistance package? Yes, we saw that the written press does report on such financial assistance. The audio and visual presses also provide information concerning development finance packages. Such information is often provided by the media at the signing of the "contract" (i.e. the loan or grant agreement). Information concerning development finance packages is also provided to the public when top officials of the donor agency/government/external forces visit the country at the start of the implementation of the development project object of the financial package. At such times, information relating to the conditions is not provided to the press or the public. Therefore, using the four factors mentioned earlier in reference to Berger (2008, p. 162), the public or the people in the recipient countries do not see power play in the development package at first response to the stimuli/information. Depending on the particular "affordance" involved, the exercise of power may or may not be one of the perceived "affordances." Rock and Mack (1994, p. 31) found out that in visual arrangements, certain groupings require greater attention than do others. In the case of information concerning development finance package, it is not the specific grouping of the visual information that requires greater attention.

It is the importance of the information upon hearing or upon seeing/reading that makes the perceiver pay greater attention to the information. This could be linked to the four factors of Berger (2008, p. 162) mentioned earlier, especially that of the current situation. Of all the different concepts and notions concerning perception, which we discussed in Chap. 2, the concept of "affordance" gives the optimal explanation of perception as it relates to development finance and the issue of power play among the external and internal forces. That is not to say, as we had seen earlier, that other such concepts as "conveyed concepts" and "relevance" do not contribute to our understanding of the power imbalance in development finance, because they do. However, "affordance" contributes to our understanding best by letting us focus on the specific aspect of what we perceive, which is of greatest interest to us. This is why we feel that in perceiving information concerning development finance, the exercise of power or that of power play by external forces may not be one of the perceived "affordances" of the people in the recipient countries.

As we shall see in the models later in this chapter, other aspects of the information on the development finance package may have greater affordance. I mentioned Berger's "current situation," as being one of the factors influencing perception; in other words, how the development finance package affects their current situation would take precedence over aspects such as power play of the external forces. How can the source of the information influence perception in the context of development finance package? In a typical situation in the rural areas in Africa, information is perceived through one of the media, especially through the radio or the television. In some countries, however, the Internet is gaining popularity, especially in the urban areas where electricity and Internet connectivity could be more readily available. World Bank (Internet Users) figures for 2013 put Internet users in Africa as varying from 1.3 per 100 people in Burundi to 38.0 in Nigeria, and 48.9 in the RSA to 55.4 in Morocco. This compares with 85.8 for Canada, 89.8 for the UK, 86.3 for Japan, 81.9 for France, and 94.8 for Sweden. With regard to radio sets, the latest statistics (ITU, Radio Sets) put Africa as having 10.9 million radio sets per 1000 people. A local survey in Kenya in March 2008 (Balancing Act 2008) indicated that 10.7 million homes have television sets or radios, of which 7.5 million have radios and 3.2 million have television sets. There were more radios and television sets in the rural areas than in the urban areas, with 74% of the radio sets and 56% of the televisions sets in the rural areas (Balancing Act 2008).

In this model, in those areas where both types of media are shared in homes or in public places, the information as perceived by those listening and/or seeing will be the subject of discussions. If the information concerns a development finance package for their region, the discussion would be more intense and would concern the different implications as seen by each party. Each party will emphasize his or her own affordance, and the perceiver would go into his or her memory to help decipher the stimuli he or she has received through one of the media sources.

I recall a mission to Ghana, in 2001, in West Africa, at the start-up of an important poverty reduction program in the agricultural sector. After the technical discussions and visit to the offices of the program, a top politician/government official in the ministry of Food and Agriculture and I were interviewed for the national television station, the written press, and the radio. The television portion was aired in prime time, late afternoon/early evening, and later on during the nine o'clock news. In this and in similar interviews in the Comoros, an island state in East Africa, and in Guinea-Bissau, a small state in West Africa, the questions that we were asked focused on the amounts of the respective financial packages and the results expected. These are just a few of the many interviews and discussions with the press over several years. At no point in any of these interviews did the question turn to the issue of conditions accompanying the grant or the loan. Was the fact that no questions were asked about the conditions part of the expected public transcript or because there was no interest in the conditions or because the interviewers were not aware that conditions accompanied the development finance package and were part of the program? In such circumstances and in the examples given earlier, the discussions by the local population at their homes or in public houses would focus on aspects that the top official and I emphasized during the interviews and discussions with the press. Because of the concern for poverty reduction, the emphasis was on the objectives, the expected outcome and the returns to the participants of the programs, the benefits to the economy of the country concerned, and implementation aspects and program end date.

In discussions with some nationals, after the broadcast interviews, a few asked about the total cost of the program, and fewer still made any mention of the power the program gave to the institutions concerned to intervene in the economy of the country. Only a very discerning few, in talking about the conditionalities, referred to issues relating to the strength of external financiers in imposing conditions on African countries. These latter few, as it were, let my colleagues and me in on their "private/hidden transcripts," which were normally reserved for kith, kin, or close group members. In many similar missions to other parts of the African continent, the issue of power of the external forces was not evident except to the discerning few. However, the Bretton Woods Institutions were always associated with hard conditions, and most people in the developing world perceived the power held by these two institutions over their economies. Many leaders appreciated this power to the extent that the late Siaka Stevens, former president of Sierra Leone, in 1984 called the implementation of "harsh conditions" of the donor institutions and donor countries akin to committing political suicide (West Africa Magazine 1984, p. 2781).

More recently, in March 2012, the late president of Malawi, Bingu wa Mutharika, appreciated the power of these external forces, when they cut aid to his country in 2010. In fact, BBC reported that he actually told foreign donors "to go to hell" (BBC 2012). Unfortunately, if they did "go to hell," the economic problems of his country would not have been resolved. Their "going to hell" with his statement only reduced the funds the government could count on to fight poverty in Malawi. It also caused fuel shortages. The GDP dropped from 5627.9 million in 2011 to 3705.4 million in 2013 (World Bank GDP). The annual GDP per capita percentage growth rate of the GDP, which was 6.2 in 2007 and 5.1 in 2008, fell to 3.4 in 2010 and then fell sharply to 1.4 in 2011 and –1.0 in 2012, but rose to 2.0 in 2013 according to World Bank figures (World Bank, GDP per capita). OECD figures for Malawi put net ODA at $US1023 million in 2010; it fell to $US800 million in 2011 and rose to $US1175 million in 2012, but dropped to $US1120 million in 2013 (a 5% drop), the year after the "go to hell" statement by the then president (OECD-Net ODA). Per capita transfer of ODA dropped from $US74 in 2012 to $US69 in 2013 (a 7% drop) (World Bank- Net ODA). Much-needed funds were not being disbursed, and his government had difficulty generating the required foreign exchange for capital development from other sources. We see here the combined effect of the devastating power of the external forces and the allegedly inappropriate policies of the government on the economy. In this case, we see that power was not exercised subtly (i.e. unseen exercise of power), but was overt and a "seen" "display" of power by the external forces by cutting foreign aid. It is probable that by telling the foreign donors "to go to hell," the then president of Malawi was very much aware that the consequences of combining his "hidden/private" and "public" transcript would be a termination or a reduction of aid from these foreign sources.

I recall field missions to many African countries including Mali (Mopti agricultural project), Ghana (Food Production Poverty Reduction Project in the Ashanti Region), Guinea (Gueckedou and Kouroussa agricultural projects), Senegal (Casamance rural development project), Malagasy Republic (eight-site rural development program), Seychelles (fisheries development project), and the Comoros (fisheries development project). These missions were carried out either jointly with other external donors/lenders or individually as a single development finance institution. In many of these missions, the top politicians and very senior government officials of these recipient countries were aware of what Lukes (2005, p. 34, 71) would call the "capacity" of donors/external forces to wield power over their economies. They were also conscious of the possession by these external forces of the "vehicle" and the "capacity" to wield such power. This was manifested in the contents of the discussions these top officials and political leaders had with the members of the various missions. In one such field mission to Madagascar, in October 1976, the mission members, at the start of the mission, stayed in the country and met with top politicians and government officials. The team spent more than a month in the country. In another similar mission to the Federal Republic of Comoros in 1979, the team of which I was part met with senior government officials and top politicians in government. They were all, in sum, concerned about the conditions which the team would include to accompany the loan or grant packages and expressed such concerns.

Government ministers, highly placed civil servants, and other senior public service officials in many African countries (see Top Officials) repeated these concerns very often. In these instances, because of the African majority ownership of the AfiDB, these politicians/top government officials gave the teams insights into their "private/hidden transcripts." Such transcripts are generally reserved for "within-group" conversations/discussions, and non-members of the group rarely get such insights. Although there is no dispute as to the majority ownership of the AfDB, the question could be asked whether in the perceptions of these high government officials and top politicians, the Bank did not exercise power in its development finance transactions. These government officials and politicians perceived and tried to make the team members perceive what Berger (2008, p. 162) and the Gibson (1986, pp. 127–143) called the specific "affordance" they considered important, based on their current situation and their past experience of dealing with other multilateral and bilateral financing agencies. This affordance was the power wielded by those who provide development finance. They wanted the team members to appreciate the importance of their particular concerns and endeavor to put themselves in the shoes of the government officials or politicians, especially with regard to the attitude and perception the team members should adopt and the conditions they should require.

It could be argued, however, that these high government officials were conscious of this power wielded by external donors/forces. The politicians and government officials were aware that the African countries owned the majority of the shareholding of the AfDB; they might have been trying to influence the team members and their perceptions of the power, which they believe the institution wielded in their affairs. The outcome that these officials expected was that the team should, in the words of one top politician/official, "not try to run their countries" by imposing what the late Siaka Stevens called "politically suicidal" conditions. They were conscious of the "capacity" the institution possessed and might have been trying to work on the team members to influence them on the way they were expected to use the "vehicle" that the institution possessed. It is very plausible that they expected that any possible power play, especially with regard to conditions to be revisited, in order not to exercise such "power." Earlier, we discussed another recollection in which a very senior politician and top government official in Uganda told a field mission team not to disrupt the country for the X million dollars that the institution was going to provide for the rehabilitation of the sugar industry in the country. This is another expression of "private/hidden transcript" by the official, where the "public transcript" would have been the more appropriate expression.

It is legitimate to ask whether these politicians would have let the team into their "private/hidden transcript" if all the team members were not from Africa. On those occasions when the team members included non-Africans, they did not change the substance of their message. Can we thus conclude that they would have let the team members into their "private transcript," irrespective of the ethnicity of the composition of the team from the bank in which they felt they held majority shares? Can we otherwise conclude that what I suppose was their private transcript was in actual fact their "public" transcript? We could ask then whether these top-level politicians and government officials would have only used the "public transcript" if it were a team from one of the Bretton Woods Institutions. The answer to this question would depend on how strongly they felt about the external force and about how the "vehicle" of the institution would be used to get them to do "things" they would not want to do, for political, economic, social, or ideological reasons.

In such circumstances, as we saw previously in the case of late Siaka Stevens in 1984 (West Africa Magazine 1984, p. 2781) and late Bingu wa

Mutharika in 2012, there may not be much difference between the "private" and the "public" transcript. Under normal circumstances, however, the top-level African officials would have used their "public transcript," which is much closer to less direct talk about their feeling of the power that external forces exercised on their countries. Would a different team composition in a joint mission composed of staff from the African institution and staff from one of the Bretton Woods Institutions elicit a transcript from these officials that would have differed from the preceding? In such a scenario, I can only speculate that their statements would have been more in line with the separation of the public from the private transcripts. It is also possible that the officials would have found occasion to meet separately with the staff of each institution. In such a case, the statement of the government officials would be composed of separate transcript for each institution. It is interesting to note that as in the majority-owned African institutions, African countries also have representatives in the board of directors of the Bretton Woods Institutions. However, the African countries do not own majority shares in the Bretton Woods Institutions. Can we then surmise that the use of the private versus the public transcripts/statements is a function of the relative shareholding of the African countries in the institutions? We would be speculating on this because the answer would neither be based on scientific nor empirical evidence.

What can we say about the officials of the external forces/donors? Irrespective of ethnicity, does the fact that they work for an African institution condition them to better appreciate the situation and circumstances of the developing countries? Could the government officials and political leaders who are discussed in this book believe that the sensitization of the officials of the external African donor includes this appreciation which makes their perception more attuned to that of the population in the developing countries? In the AfDB, many of the staff members are nationals of African countries, and many actually grew up in Africa and were often recruited from their home countries. They have experience of the problems and issues of the continent, and the recruitment process at interview included questions relating to these issues. Are they then more sensitive and more sympathetic to the problems of power wielded by the institution they work for? There is no one specific true answer to this question.

Issues Relating to Perceptions and Power

In his book, "Forms of Power," Poggi (2001, p. 9, 59) wrote that the pyramid structure that can be used to illustrate the power setup in an organization does not necessarily add to the quantity of power actually available in the system. The pyramid structure can contribute to the explanation of power in the development finance field. It represents the different power loci, that intervene in the processes and the procedures relating to development finance, from the parliament of the donor country to the ultimate recipient in the Africa country. Though the quantity may still be the same, the various strata in the pyramid feel the force of the power differently. It may seem superfluous to state that the lowest stratum would feel it more than those who are above the lowest. In reality, the lower stratum is the foundation upon which the upper strata are built, because, at that level, the alternative solutions or other courses of action are limited and tend to decrease as we move from the top to the bottom of the pyramid (Figs. 4.1, 4.2, and 4.3).

In the diagram, there are three pyramid structures:

Fig. 4.1 Pyramid I—funding by international non-governmental organization (*Source*: Compiled and drawn by author)

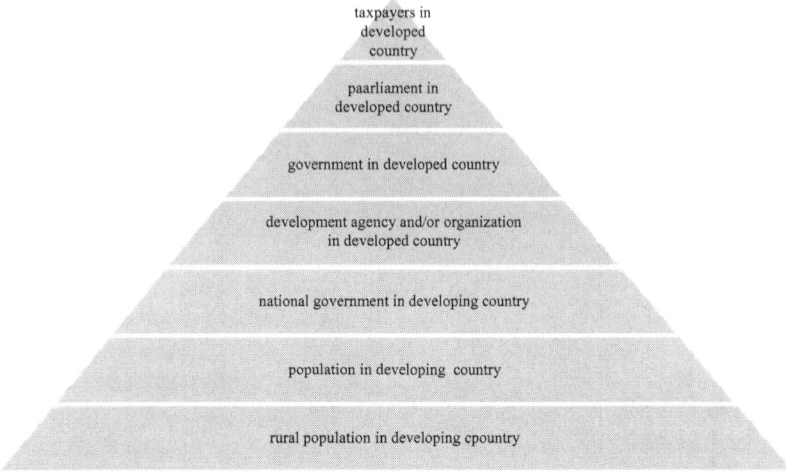

Fig. 4.2 Pyramid II—funding by bilateral donor/external force (*Source*: Compiled and drawn by author)

(i) The pyramid power structure for INGOs when they use their own funds,
(ii) the pyramid structure when funds come from budgetary allocations from parliaments of developed countries (donors), and
(iii) pyramid structure pertaining to funding from IDFIs.

Based on the arguments and the figures presented in Chap. 3, there are many countries in Africa that are very much dependent on external development financial assistance for the funding of their annual development budgets. In this discussion, we are concerned with financial assistance, which is coming from public funded sources. It may be very difficult for the lowest stratum to move out from the bottom of the pyramid. In developing countries in Africa, at any given time, the lowest stratum, in the case of development financial assistance for rural areas, contains the rural population. The rural population and the very poor people in the urban areas represent the lowest stratum under all three pyramid structures.

It may be possible for the people in the lowest stratum to move from one pyramid structure to the other (e.g. moving from under INGOs' pyr-

Fig. 4.3 Pyramid III—funding by international development finance institution (*Source*: Compiled and drawn by author)

amid to IDFIs or donors' pyramid). They cannot move out of the bottom unless they all as a group attain levels of development where they do not need assistance from outside the country or even from within the country. These two categories of the poorest segments of the population (the rural population and the urban poor), however, are the focus of more recent attention and development financial assistance. The possibility of not been subjected to power relation in the context of the power pyramid structure can exist in some circumstances, if they, as a group, pool their resources. Such pooling of their resources in some developing countries has led some rural populations to create cooperative institutions and in a further development has led to the establishment of cooperative banks, microfinancing institutions, and microfinancing networks.

The people in the lowest stratum would have a perception of power that is different from those in the other levels of the pyramid. The pressure on them is the greatest. As I explained earlier, their choices are limited. If we look at the outcomes expected of them, however, we find that there is a "constellation of interests" between what the higher echelons of the pyramid expect of them and what they would like to have as results. Both groups would like to see an increase in productivity, production, and income. Can we therefore say that power has been exercised on them? Yes, we can; for even though the outcomes expected of them may be the same or similar to what they themselves wanted to do, they have been made to do what they did because of the intervention of the strata above them. In the preceding example, it may be argued that the person on whom power has been exercised—in this case, the farmer—can modify the expected outcome by planting a different crop or not putting as much energy into his/her farming exercise as he or she should. The types of crops that can be planted on any particular piece of land, however, are circumscribed by mainly climate and soil. That argument is therefore limited in scope. The issue of not putting enough energy into the farming exercise is also circumscribed by the need of the farmer for income to feed himself and his family. One can thus make a strong argument for a meeting of minds. Even though power has been exercised, there is a meeting of minds among the farmers in the lowest stratum, the government, and the financier in all of the three pyramid structures, which is a constellation of interests, as it were.

There are circumstances, however, where some levels of the pyramid can and do influence the outcomes the wielders of power should expect from their wielding of power. They cannot, however, influence the power itself from above. This can arise in all three pyramid structures, but more especially in the IDFI structure. Developing countries, through the representatives, that they have on the boards of directors of these institutions, who represent their interests, can, to some extent, influence the outcomes of the programs concerning their countries, either at board meetings or in private sessions with the management of the institutions. Official representatives of the countries in the boards of directors of the IDFIs can influence the expected outcome from the exercise of power. In fact, by grouping together in a caucus-like setup, they can modify the "power to" aspect, but not the power structure, on an ad hoc basis. In such circumstances, the "power over" aspect which I called *puissance* and which Lukes refers to as "capacity" would remain intact. This aspect was discussed earlier as an element in the arsenal of non-dominant forces to cause a break in the power flow.

What can we then say about the perception of the farmer under these circumstances? From field supervision missions to various African countries, we found that when farmers succeeded in increasing their output, they considered the intervention by the people in the higher levels of the pyramid, the donor country, or its agency or its implementer (i.e. the INGO) in a favorable light. In this example, we can equate their favorable perception with the emotions of satisfaction in the outcome. The constellation of interests prevents them from thinking about any imbalance of power that may or may not be visible to them. We can say as with the Gibson that their affordance is focused on the returns from their effort in farming. In this context, the effectiveness of the power play in ensuring a constellation of interests and their concern with their "current situation" hide any perception the farmers would have of an external force exercising power over them to make them do something that they may not have wanted to do.

The perceptions of the government officials will take a similar path to the farmer in the preceding model/scenario and would be favorable. In a similar scenario when the constellation of interests succeeded in having a project or program that contributes to an increase in output as outcome, the official would also be seen in good light by his superior. This is expected to happen whether he or she is in the ministry of finance, which participated in the negotiations of the project or in the ministry of agriculture and rural development, which identified, designed, or implemented the project. This aspect of "being seen in good light" translates over a period of time into promotion or higher levels of increment to his salary. The manager of a successful project or program was always seen in good light by his superiors, and his or her project was always used in official speeches by ministers (*Awareness Times*, May 7 2015) to show that the ministry is doing a good job and is providing what the population needed. The view of the government official of how the project or program may affect his or her status, financial or otherwise, will affect his perception of any imbalance of power or any power play in the project process. A positive outcome of the project or program will contribute to his chances of promotion, which may increase. The fact that the government has been prevailed upon (power to) to implement or fulfill conditions that may jeopardize its continued stay in office will not have much importance in determining his or her perception. Here again, the effectiveness of the financial assistance in meeting its objective and his or her concern with his or her "current situation" would have a greater influence in determining the swing of his or her perception.

With politicians, the issue of perception of the power exercised over them to accept conditions is dependent on such factors discussed in Chap.

2 as his or her past experience, current situation, and the outcome of the intervention. In cases where the project or program succeeds in meeting its objectives, there is also a "constellation of interests" between the wielder of power and the government. Here again effectiveness is important, and it influences the perception and emotions of the politicians. However, in cases where some of the conditions accompanying the development finance package would tend to jeopardize the continued stay in office of the government and put the government in a bad light regarding its commitment to help the poor farmers, the perception of the politicians would be mixed and not as favorable as in the first case.

It is under such circumstances that the issue of the developed countries with their economic and financial resources, which give them power to dictate terms of lending and impose conditions, would become uppermost in the minds of these politicians. Here we can certainly see a visible exercise of power. In this model/scenario, the politicians have accepted these conditions because they felt they had no choice in their drive to reduce poverty. They would perceive the donors as "oppressors," since they would then consider the conditions as oppressive. In fact, some development finance interventions include conditions relating to governance as well as human right issues. Such "power over" conditions must have led Bingu wa Mutharika, the late president of Malawi, to tell the donors in March 2012 "to go to hell." This feeling of being "oppressed" is implied in the statement of the then president of Sierra Leone, the late Siaka Stevens, which was mentioned in Chap. 3. All this could nevertheless be nuanced if the team of national specialists at the disposal of the government, who had done a thorough analysis themselves and found that the conditions prescribed by the external forces as part of their intervention could be considered as sufficient and necessary for growth and development. Although in such circumstances, the perception of the politicians would be less hostile to the conditions, their preoccupation with their continued stay in office would make them fulfill the conditions, but with great anxiety as to their ultimate effect on their stay in office. An example of this was the case of Uganda mentioned earlier, where a very senior politician and top government official admonished the appraisal team not to disrupt the country because of the X million dollars.

In this context and given the situation in many African countries, where the very senior government officials tend to be partisans of the political party in government, the perceptions of the senior civil servants would also be one of anxiety. In some African countries, including Guinea

(IRIN 2011), Sierra Leone (Thompson 1997, p. 37), Kenya (The East African 2011; also Tarimo 2008), and Nigeria (Ogwu-Arizona 2009; also Ogunrotifa 2012), ethnicity and/or support for government in power has a role to play in the selection of persons for some key civil service positions. In such cases, their perceptions would be similar to those of the politicians on whom they depend for patronage. Their perceptions would be conditioned by anxiety as to whether the government and the politicians in power would lose popularity. Popularity in this sense is synonymous with electoral victory. In some francophone West African countries, it is not uncommon for a change in the minister, to lead to a change in the director of cabinet of the minister. The new minister would also often bring in his or her own chief of staff, secretaries, and even messenger. This occurs even if it is a cabinet reshuffle.

During the 1970s, development finance was geared toward the specific project approach. This is because people in developing countries generally have diagnostic frames concerning the economic problems they have in their lives or their situation. The farmers, for example, believe that they know what is wrong with their situations and tend to have prognosis and prescription for their situations.

Specific projects and programs were intended to address specific shortcomings in the rural settings, which impeded the increased productivity of the farmers and improvement in the incomes for the population in the rural areas. They addressed such issues as poor infrastructure, lack of farming equipment, shortage of transport facilities, poor and/or inadequate extension or advisory services, inappropriate pricing, ineffective marketing, and unsuitable input supply policies and procedures. The rural population experienced various stages and degrees of underdevelopment. Specific project approach, in which they saw that their concerns were being directly addressed, was a balm to the rural population. Their perceptions, which were conditioned by their "diagnostic frames," made them to see the help they were getting in terms of project, as a very good thing. Over several years of field supervision missions in different countries, the field teams from the AfDB observed that the feelings of the farmers toward the forces, which provided the financial support, were very positive and favorable. In general, the farmers often believed that such assistance came from their governments. There was not any mention made of the external forces from which the funds emanated. In those circumstances, the issue of the exercise of power was not part of the "stimuli" that they perceived. Many IDFIs and bilateral donors, however, gradually started to require that signboards be put in front of the offices of the project headquarters indicating that the funds were provided by the bilateral donors, the IDFIs, and the government. The media also helped to inform the population of the sources of the funds for the programs.

The rural population thus began to see the IDFIs as good partners to their governments and saw these bilateral donors and the IDFIs in very favorable light. However, they were not aware of the conditions, that had to be met before the bilateral donors, the IDFIs, or for that matter, the INGOs on their own, or acting as agents of both the donors and the recipients (i.e. their governments), could disburse the funds. When the project-specific approach succeeded, the population could see such physical outputs, as dams, which were providing year-round water supply for their crops directly to the farm plots, or seeds and other farm inputs becoming available which was not the case before the project was implemented. In many cases, they also perceived that they were harvesting increased products and getting higher incomes. Their perceptions were generally positive toward both the governments and the donors and their agents. The rural populations were not very much concerned about what the conditions were on the financial assistance packages.

The perceptions of these people, however, were generally different in cases where the project failed or did not achieve the specific objectives it was meant to achieve. In cases, where there were lots of delays in project implementation, disbursements, or the provision of equipment, and where facilities and farm supplies were defective, and shortcomings in project management were evident, the farmers and other beneficiaries did not see much positive change in their output and/or their incomes. In our example, not seeing any positive change in their situation seriously influenced their perception. They blamed the government and the government officials for their predicament. From West to East, through Central to Southern Africa, the people accuse their governments of mismanagement and/or corruption in the management of the affairs of state or of the public good (see News Analysis, various reports, Omolo 2010; *Nyasa Times* 2014; Tonwe, D. et al. 2012). We can therefore say that the perception of the rural population is a function of the success of the specific project or projects that were set up in their geographic locations in meeting the demands of the population and in achieving the objectives for which they were set up and implemented. Even though this may be true, it would be too simplistic a view.

Papers by Kleinman and Bradbury (2010) as well as by Hurley (2004) have shown that the perceptions of Africans about development and development activities in Africa have many factors that influence them. However, in their study, they did not ask any direct questions related to how the interviewees perceive the power of the external forces on them and their activities. From the responses provided by the interviewees, one can infer that the interviewers were, to some extent, privy to the "private/hidden transcripts" of some of these people. They showed what they really felt about such assistance, which some of them considered as displays of power from which their countries could not escape easily. Perceptions of Africans on the power of external forces are conditioned generally by past experience, the level of education, historical engagement of the external forces in the development of the country concerned, history of the people concerned, and local and world geopolitics. Other factors include what MacLachlan et al. (2010, p. 64, 65) identify as "interactional justice" and "interpersonal justice." They define the former as the feeling of being treated with respect, and the latter as that of being treated with manners, which is in fact very closely linked to the former. It means that the people in the recipient countries do not want to feel or perceive that donors or their representatives "speak down to them."

Among these factors, the level of education conditions the person's perspective on local and world geopolitics. It could be argued that the higher the level of education, the more likely that the person has been exposed to ideas from other cultures and countries. It is also more likely that the person has access to media facilities that discuss local and world issues. Again, the higher the level of education, the more balanced the views tended to be, but also the more critical of external forces and their power the person is.

In the examples given earlier, however, the governments of these developing countries were concerned with the project conditions, which had to be fulfilled. In some cases, these conditions were getting more and more stringent, and the governments were flying close to political suicide, especially for the politically ambitious. In politics in the African setting, alliances are at times volatile and fragile and are often based on ethnicity, regional affiliation, and other possible cultural affinities (see Tonwe et al. 2012, pp. 37–48; also Spencer 1977, pp. 69–86, 70, note 4). The non-achievement of the goals set for a particular project in a specific region where the majority of the population may not have voted for the government in the previous election could be a cause for serious concern for the government (see Tonwe et al. 2012, pp. 37–48; also Spencer 1977, pp. 69–86, 70, note 4).

Even in situations where the results are positive, some of the conditions could affect project output: for example, conditions that require the liberalization of the market for farm inputs (e.g. fertilizers) for which the price had been controlled and had been kept artificially low. This is the case more so as we move from the project-specific approach to policy-based approach in development finance, where conditions requiring the adoption of specific policies or the setting up of specific institutions to oversee and monitor specific policy reform are often part of the financial package. Nevertheless, even assistance under specific project approach could contain policy reform conditions. Conditions relating to price and/or import liberalization of some similar products or of the very products with which the project is concerned are cases in point. In such cases, even though the project is expected to increase production on the one hand, the very condition of allowing imports into the country of the same product or similar products with lower tariff or no duty will jeopardize the incomes, which the producers expect from the sale of their output.

In the preceding example/scenario, the perceptions thus become slightly sophisticated. Even when the results of the project in the project-specific approach are positive, this positive perception could be influenced by the low price the producers receive for their products. Thus, their perceptions become mixed. They would be favorable to the donors that provided the funds, but negative to donor countries which insist on the import liberalization. This presupposes that the information concerning the donors and their particular demands were made available to the public. This is generally not the case. This negative perception becomes greater, when they learn that these donor countries provide subsidies to their farmers that affect the prices which the farmers in the developing countries could obtain for their product in the international market or even in some parts of the domestic markets. The situation of cotton comes easily to mind.

It should be noted that in several field missions to the recipient countries and in exchanges of correspondence between the staff of the recipient countries and those of the external donors, the teams from the external financiers discuss the conditions of the grant or loan intensively and extensively. The two parties agree on the conditions before the project document is finalized, and these are the object of negotiations prior to top-level approval of the grant or loan amount. In general, conditions in the rural project-specific approach often require the setting up of institutions or adopting recommendations of studies carried out as part of the components of the project. The result of some of the studies may be expected to improve the management of the project or an aspect of the project. In some cases, say an irrigation project, the recommendations of the studies may require the government to implement changes in tariff for the sale of irrigation water to the farmers.

The fact of paying for water, which they used to get free of charge from the river with artisanal equipment, could be seen as an anathema by some farmers, even if with the implementation of the project, there were now canals capable of bringing the water directly to their farming plots. The adoption of such a recommendation by the government and its imposition on the farmers could become a serious political issue, unless the farmers have been satisfactorily informed, sensitized, as Ballesteros would put it, "sufficiently primed." In addition, they have to have willingly accepted that they have to pay for the water to their farm plots. The fact that it has been "forced" to accept the condition will affect the emotional frame with which the government will view the condition and its perception of this imposing external force will be very mixed. On the one hand, the government would welcome the funds put at its disposal to contribute to attaining its development objectives. On the other hand, it would be anxious that the rural population involved does not perceive the tariff as a form of controlling of its actions—farming actions in this case—and move its support away from the government party. This could be critical if the project or program covers a large geographic area, it is an election year, and the support of the population in that particular area or areas is crucial to its efforts to remain in office. It is assumed in the scenarios or models discussed that elections are democratic and fair. Apart from seemingly stringent conditions, there was a tendency in the early days of policy-based programs for there to be many conditions that the government of the non-dominant forces had to fulfill. These conditions were in fact meant to put the government's administrative, political, and economic arrangements in a state of readiness to implement the project and programs. The high number of conditions to be fulfilled, often before the first disbursement, frequently led to further delays in project start-up. This is one of the reasons why the new budgetary-support approach and the more recent policy-based interventions require that the state of readiness be achieved *before* the donor will engage with recipient countries. The new budgetary-support approach, in a way, enhanced the "power to" and "power over" of the external forces. Naiman and Watkins (1999, p. 12) brought up a similar situation in the health sector in Côte d'Ivoire, where a policy reform program from an external donor required the payment of user fees. This led to a reduction in visits by many of the nationals who could not afford to pay the user fees.

In this model/scenario, the perception of the government party in these circumstances and the picture it will have of the perceptions/reactions of the population would, in many instances, result in delays by government in the fulfillment of certain conditions, such as we have seen. The party in government will be reluctant to implement any specific condition that in its perception risks it losing popularity with its electorates, whether regional or national. In certain cases, the conditions would either not be complied with or fulfilled in a haphazard manner. In many instances, under the circumstances described earlier, the government would try to renegotiate the loan or grant conditions or not implement those which are considered as likely to create political or electoral problems for it. We find evidence of this in the many delays encountered in project implementation through delays in the fulfillment of the conditions. Examples in the AfDB public online archives such projects with delays in fulfillment of conditions include the Governance Reform Support Program in Chad and the Anambe Basin Rural Development Support Project in Senegal. These actions by governments and the statement by the late President Siaka Stevens, among others, of not wanting to commit "political suicide" provide concrete examples.

From the situation of delays in fulfillment, haphazard fulfillment, or the desire to renegotiate the clauses of certain conditions, one could infer that there may have been a misconception in the perceptions or in the expectations of the external forces/donor as well as in that of the governments in the recipient countries. This misconception concerns the readiness, defined here as the ability of the recipients to implement the projects or programs in accordance with the prescribed plan. Readiness is here understood to mean, having all the necessary arrangements in place for the implementation of the project. It is important to note, in this example, the pervading power of the external force to the extent that it was able to get the government of the country to accept the conditions, knowing that some aspects of its economic and social setup could be adversely affected. It also speaks to the readiness of the country at that particular time to receive development finance. Going ahead with the development finance package in spite of the apparent lack of readiness to receive assistance could be a function of the strategic importance of the recipient country to the interest of external force. Martens et al. (2002c, p. 40, 50) cite the examples of World Bank development assistance to Nicaragua in 1951–1956 and to Russia in the 1990s.

In the early days of development finance and assistance, especially for IDFIs, grant or loan conditions were almost impossible to renegotiate and tended to be rigid. In the latter part of the twentieth century, however, donors began to appreciate that the circumstances of the countries are dynamic and that there was and still is a need to revisit certain aspects of the project or program, including loan or grant conditions. This situation is even more trying for the governments in the case of budgetary support loans or grants that have become the preferred instrument these external forces use in the development finance programs. With the appreciation that situations—economic, political, and social—can change in any specific country, we do not see a weakening in the power of the external forces, but rather a rearrangement of the instruments of their power. Conditions have now become predetermined, and rather than their becoming conditions for disbursement, they became what could be called conditions prior to engagement. Countries now have to go through several predetermined processes before the external forces can consider engaging with them in the "partnership" to develop the countries. These forces use the power they possess and the "tolerable consensus" discussed in Chap. 2, to set the criteria, which have to be met before the recipient countries can become ready to receive development finance in the very broad budgetary support approach.

As I explained earlier, the source of power used is "expert power" based on knowledge and information. This is a typical example of the common phrase "knowledge is power." Not many countries in Sub-Saharan Africa have the resources, without outside assistance, to collect, collate, and analyze large amounts of economic, social, demographic, fiscal, and financial data past and present reliably and objectively and make projections far into the future in a sustained and timely manner. It could be argued that such information is now readily available all over the Internet. The information and data available on the Internet have been collected, compiled, and collated by institutions like the World Bank, the IMF, OECD/DAC, and United Nations agencies and bodies. These are generally institutions of which the governance structures are dominated by the external forces from the North. It could be further argued that economic data are neutral. Yes, they are. Their interpretation, however, is not neutral. The ways they are collected, collated, and to some extent analyzed influence the use that can be made of them. It can be conceded that several efforts have been made over the last few decades and that they are still being made to collect, collate, and standardize data on African economies, by African institutions and organizations. The Statistical Commission for Africa of the United Nations Economic Commission for Africa is one such program (see UNECA 2012).

Nevertheless, the type of data to be collected, how they are to be collected, and where they are to be collected and analyzed are strongly (not totally) influenced by paradigms, models, and concepts coming from outside the continent. These are paradigms, that Haq, cited by Chaturvedi, considers as alien and should be replaced by "mechanisms centred on local skills and knowledge." There is nothing intrinsically wrong in the fact that this influence from outside exists; however, from this influence, one could infer that the power of the external forces is present in whatever conclusions that can be drawn from the data and the process of using them. This highly influenced process produces a body of knowledge and information that are then used to define criteria, which are in turn to be used to determine the readiness of the countries to engage with the same external forces. They further influence the conditions that are set for engagement of the countries with the external forces. The power of the external forces in the rural areas thus emanate both from the knowledge/information cluster and from the economic/financial cluster in the development finance process.

I explained that at times the conditions became so disturbing for the recipient countries concerned, that there were long delays in the fulfillment of the conditions or the countries request that the conditions are revisited. The delay or revisiting of the loan or grant conditions could be considered an element in the art of resistance discussed by Scott (1990, p. 54, 57, 74, 111). Such an art is used by subordinates forces, according to Scott, to thwart the power of the superior forces from outside. It is also one of the tools that the objects of power wielded by external forces can use to influence the outcomes expected by these external forces. In budgetary support situations, especially in a situation where there are many donors in the same program, the situation could be very dire for the recipient country. The networking and coordination among donors, mentioned in Chap. 2, tend to give the external forces the power to ensure compliance with their collective will. This makes it impossible to appeal to another donor for the required funds. The coming together of external forces to support the entire development budget or a substantial portion of it of a given country makes for the availability of a large amount of funds in one single arrangement or contract package. It also reduces the country's anxiety about where it could source funds for its development and operational expenses.

It does, however, reduce the country's maneuverability in terms of not fulfilling the conditions imposed. It also reduces the possibility of the recipient country to obtain funding for the specific program from alternative sources. It thus increases the "power over" and the "power to" of these forces. In such a situation, therefore, the existence of the "vehicle" of power and the "capacity" of this vehicle combine to ensure that the "exercise" of that power will bring about the desired outcome. The future expectation of the government will be very grim without the funds, which the external forces are prepared to provide. A possible glimmer of hope for the recipient countries, in such circumstances, is found in the non-traditional sources such as the emerging nations (e.g. China, Brazil, and India). The emerging nations, such as China, Brazil, and India, do not yet participate very actively in the budget support programs.

In the case of the previous structural adjustment programs and the present budget support program, it is a requirement that the governments inform the external forces in a detailed letter of their economic and social policies and that they state their intentions as regards the implementation of these policies. This is part of the process for readiness to receive the financial assistance. After this letter is written and signed by the minister of finance or of development, and forwarded to all the external forces involved in the development finance package, these forces then have a strong commitment from the government. As I showed in Chap. 3, many of these countries do not have much in terms of financial resources. They therefore depend almost entirely on these external forces, which are now grouped together to provide them with much-needed funds to drive their development agendas and at times their operational expenses. The case of Madagascar which we mentioned earlier and in which 71 % of its external foreign aid is supplied by five countries/institutions comes to mind. In such circumstances, can we not say that these forces exercise and exert real power on the African countries that are recipients of their development financial assistance? The emotions of many put in such a position of subservience would be negative. In this scenario/model, it is important to note that the public transcript of the government and its officials will be different from their private/hidden transcript. What they say in public in front of the external donors will be quite different from their declarations when they are among themselves and away from any possibility of their being quoted.

It is to be noted that in some situations the perceptions that the recipients have of the AfDB (AfDB) seemed to have a slight positive edge over non-African institutions operating in Africa. In their pilot study relating to perceptions, Burall et al. (2007, pp. 21–24) cite a Ghanaian and a Zambian commentator. The Zambian believed that the AfDB is African and therefore has a better understanding of Africa's situation. The Ghanaian stated that the AfDB was formed specifically with Africa in mind and should have the capacity to deal with African nations. Whether this is true or is borne out by empirical data is not relevant to the perceptions of these commentators. From their statements, one could infer that the AfDB was not an external force in their perceptions. If one could stretch it a bit further, they may have believed that the AfDB was not exercising power over them.

In spite of this perception and the constellation of interests, which may arise in the case of development finance from the AfDB, the AfDB was and is still exercising power as shown in the case of the Lugazi sugar project in Uganda discussed earlier. It is possible that given the possible affinity some African governments feel for the AfDB, their "public" and "hidden" transcripts would be identical. Their perception of the non-existence of exercise of power that the African government officials and politicians might have felt or may feel is also influenced by the fact the African countries have permanent representatives in the board of directors of the institution. These representatives, as it were, monitor the actions of this "brotherly" external force. This latter fact is borne out by the marks given to the AfDB with regard to governance in the study by Burall et al. (2007 pp. 21–24). In other words, the institutional culture does not seem to create a very serious situation of dominance among the clients of the AfDB, who additionally have active permanent representatives in the administrative structure of the bank. Apart from the possibility of monitoring actions, the permanent representatives also approve policy and major procedures. These governments know that IDFIs have power and do exercise power, irrespective of their affinity. The situation with the AfDB is similar to other IDFIs where the countries have permanent representatives.

There have been instances where civil servants had supported the inclusion of policy reforms conditions by field preparation and/or appraisal missions in the days of specific project approach. They admitted that they had been trying over several years to get the government to adopt such a policy reform with no success. A case in point occurred in the artisanal fisheries project in the Comoros, where top officials in the fisheries department were in agreement with the team to include, among others, policy conditions relating to nets, boats, and licensing fees, fishing seasons, and other fisheries-related aspects. These civil servants in a way provided the team with their private transcript, because they appreciated the "power" of the external body as represented by its agents to get the government to change its behavior and agree to adopt the policy reform condition, in spite of previous strong reluctance to do so.

It is important to distinguish between the perception of the government officials and that of the politicians. An aspect to consider would be the background of these two groups: that is, not just their education, but also the fact that some are civil servants, and their remunerations are not influenced by the external force. The political affiliations of these civil servants involved, however, need to be considered. In such countries as Sierra Leone (see Thompson 1997, p. 37), Kenya (see The East African 2011), and Nigeria (see Ogwu-Arizona 2009; also Ogunrotifa 2012), an aspect that has to be considered seriously is the ethnicity of the civil servant vis-à-vis that of the majority of the members of the party in power. These are factors, which, as I explained earlier, could affect the perceptions of the civil servants concerning the development finance package and could in turn influence the perception of the rural population concerning the package.

In our discussion so far, we saw that in many cases, perceptions, especially of the rural populations, are influenced by the success or failure of the program in meeting its agreed-upon objectives, whether they are project-specific, structural adjustment, or budget support programs. In other words, the effectiveness of the intervention is a key factor in determining whether the perceptions are positive. However, the positive nature of perceptions does not preclude that the "hidden transcript" could be negative, especially with regard to the exercise or the exertion of power. I recall instances as in the case of the Food Production Poverty Reduction Project in the Ashanti Region of Ghana. After an official ceremony to recognize the positive outcome of a program, politicians and government officials unofficial remarks concerning the conditions. The gist of these remarks was that we must not lose sight that they have been "bullied" into accepting some conditions, with which they still were not happy. These conditions concerned were actually standard, general conditions inserted into all development finance packages and agreed upon as such by their representative in the governing council of the Bank. This was done even prior to the beginning of procedures for what we called the "contract," in Chap. 1. In fact, the general conditions had been agreed to prior to the Bank starting its operations in 1964 by the governing council composed of high-level government officials of the various member countries. The government officials were not aware of this, even though it was explained to them, and they felt nevertheless, that power has been exerted on them. We thus became privy to what Scott (1990, p. 9, 14, 15, 120) called the "hidden/private transcript" of these top-level officials.

It is important therefore to understand the indicators that influence this perception with regard to effectiveness. This preoccupation with effectiveness in development finance could be seen as a result of growing interest by bilateral agencies, which have translated the notion of result-based management and its associated tool of having a balanced scorecard to monitor management actions and activities. This notion is also applied to multilateral organizations. In a bid to assess the effectiveness of development finance, several surveys have been carried out, and networks have been established (see Massa 2011, pp. 2–4). Most of these have developed indicators to evaluate the effectiveness of assistance from multilateral organizations. Some surveys also attempt to evaluate the perception of recipients of development assistance using specific indicators relating to effectiveness. Some of these indicators include the rapidity of disbursement, flexibility of funding and procurement sources, concessionality of the loan, the number of conditions attached to the assistance package, and the transparency of funding decisions. These indicators are endogenous to the external forces providing the financial assistance. Among the factors, which can influence the indicators, we find the organizational structure and internal and external communication lines of the donor and/or its agent, the harmony in principal-agent relationship between donor and its agent, and the incentive structure for personnel of the donor/agent and also of the recipient country. These factors should be dynamic and reviewed periodically in light of, and adapted to, changing circumstances. When they are efficient and effective, they influence positively on the indicators, especially on those that relate to the effectiveness of the donors/agents.

How does this donor effectiveness translate into perceptions of the recipient countries and their peoples? As we saw earlier, effectiveness on the donors' side would mean rapid and timely disbursement, flexible funding, well-understood procurement rules, concessional loans, and reduction in conditions. However, the preceding factors do not have much influence on such aspects as the organization, structure, and communication lines of the implementing institutions of the recipient countries. If they are deficient, these aspects could lead to a reduction in any effectiveness gains on the project from the perception of the loan recipients and/or farmers, fisherfolk, or other rural entrepreneurs. Thus, the perception of the farmers, which we saw in the example/model earlier, is influenced by the effectiveness of the program or project in achieving its goals. This effectiveness is dependent on several factors exogenous to the farmers. If there is lack of synchronization in efficiency/effectiveness between the donor/agent organization and the recipient organization, the project or program will fail to deliver what it was supposed to deliver. If that happened, there would be a situation where the "public transcript" of the farmers is similar to the "hidden transcript." Both transcripts will be unfavorable to both the donor and their own government.

Differences in Perception: North-South, South-South, North-South-South, and South-South-South

In our earlier discussion, we saw that development finance from external forces is classified into North-South, South-South, North-South-South, and South-South-South. The traditional form of technical and economic cooperation was for countries in the North (i.e. the developed countries) extending assistance to developing countries in the South. In their papers, Kilimani (2011, pp. 16–20), Kragelund (2010, pp. 2–4), and Mei (2010, pp. 53–56) discussed these other cooperation sources mentioned earlier. What are the perceptions of the African countries and the population regarding bilateral South-South and trilateral North-South-South and South-South-South cooperation? What factors influence their perceptions? Is there any difference in perception between the traditional and the new cooperation arrangements?

So far, we have been discussing perception, models/scenarios as regards the power wielded through the North-South cooperation, whereby countries in the North provide development finance to countries in the South. Other forms of cooperation depicted a different type of power structure and power play. These other forms include South-South, South-South-South, and North-South-South. In the first category, as Kilimani (2011, pp. 16–20), Simensen (2008), and Kragelund (2010, pp. 2–4) indicated, all the countries involved in the cooperation are classified as developing countries, as are all the countries in the second category. In the third category, at least one of the countries is classified as a developed country, and the other two are developing countries. This last category is also called trilateral or triangular cooperation.

These more advanced developing countries/emerging economies have resources they can make and have made available to less-advanced developing countries, which may be in a position of need. Examples of the first category is the deal offer of R100 million solidarity grant South Africa made to Cuba, and the R250 million line of credit it extended to Cuba (see Money Web 2014). In 2014, South Africa wrote off R1.1 billion of debt which Cuba owed to it (see Politics Web 2010). Other examples abound. Cuba established schools of medicine in the Gambia and Equatorial Guinea and sent Cuban professors to teach in medical schools in Eritrea, Uganda, Ghana, and South Africa (see *Asia One Education* 2008). In the second category, we can cite the Group of 77 meeting in Havana, Cuba, in 2000, during which the better-endowed African states agreed to finance 3000 Cuban doctors to work on the African continent (see South-South Cases-Task Team, p. 4). The financing of medical staff from Cuba by South Africa to work in Mali and the support of Germany for health staff from Cuba to work in Niger (see South South-Task Team, p. 4) are other examples. In the third category, the financial, technical, and logistic resources of the developed country are utilized. In this category, we find the assistance from a developed country in the North providing financial and/or technical support to the country in the South which furnishes assistance to another country in the South. An example of this triangular transaction is the German support to Niger mentioned above; also, the October 2013 announcement that the United States Agency for International Development (USAID), the American aid agency, will partner with three Indian organizations to provide low-cost agricultural innovations and technologies to African countries is another example (Parti 2013).

As I indicated in Chap. 3, many of these southern donor countries were or are themselves the recipient of development finance and assistance of some form. This is the case with India, Brazil, South Africa, Cuba, and Egypt. Financial assistance from these donors or countries from the South has become very important in the development finance field. In fact, according to the latest figures it published, the United Nations Development Programme (UNDP) (UNDP-ODA) estimated that global assistance from non-DAC countries was around $US15.3 billion in 2008.

As I explained in Chap. 3, in the case of the traditional North-South cooperation, the set of conditions, which accompany the development finance package, is the most important element of the power play. In fact, the conditions are the major tools that external forces utilize to exercise power in development finance. It is worthwhile in the analysis of power in the context of the non-traditional, South-South cooperation, to see if conditionalities are also used regularly. If they are, what form do they take? If they are not, what tools, if any, are used in their place in the financial arrangements? In fact, it would be instructive to see whether there is power play in the South-South cooperation. Do the sources of power, which we discussed earlier, play any part in this non-traditional cooperation arrangement?

Much of the debate about South-South cooperation tends to focus on the issue of data and information about the different aspects of the cooperation. These include volume, type, and terms. There are very few discussions of the issue of the imbalance of power and of power play and the factors, which influence such power play. In the debate, there is not much discussion concerning conditions. On the issue of conditions, the donors in the South-South cooperation indicate that they do not include such conditions as the ones imposed by the traditional North-South donors. I explained that some of these conditions which accompany North-South development packages cover governance issues, economic and financial management of the recipient countries' economies, and issues relating to policies aimed at poverty reduction in general. China, India, Cuba, and South Africa, the four South-South donors, indicate that they do not include such conditions (see Lancaster 2007b, p. 1; also Hong 2012, p. 137, 157, 161; also Sidiropoulos 2012, p. 232). China undertakes its development finance cooperation with the guiding principles of mutuality (i.e. self-respect) and non-interference in the affairs of the recipient countries.

China's development financial assistance was originally provided in the general struggle, during the days of the "cold war," as a way to combat imperialism (see Hong 2012, p. 154) and provide an alternative to the "conditioned" assistance from Europe and the USA. In more recent declarations, the vice commerce minister insisted that Chinese assistance is still based on "mutual help between developing countries" as an alternative to donors who impose conditions, especially political conditions on recipients of assistance (see Hong 2012, p. 154). China's own national interest has recently surfaced as an important consideration. Even though declarations of Chinese officials at home and abroad talk of mutual benefits and non-interference, China is aggressively insisting that recipient countries recognize only one China as a condition of its assistance, thereby dropping Taiwan, if they had previously recognized Taiwan as being the nation of China. In its assistance to neighboring countries in Asia, the expulsion of Uyghurs from their countries is another seemingly non-negotiable condition (see Matta 2015) for China. The issue of China's growing need for energy and natural resources and its rise as the major donor in the South-South cooperation has become a major subject of discussion.

China's funding of and investment in natural resources projects raise questions as to the real motivation behind China's aggressive development finance and assistance efforts. It is allegedly secretive in its operations and is often accused of not sharing or not publicizing information about its development finance and assistance activities compared with traditional Northern donors, especially the countries in OECD/DAC. This is another cause of disagreement in most discussions. Given the great demand by China for natural resources for its development, it could be argued that China's development assistance to some natural resource-rich countries is in reality barter trade (i.e. exchanging money for oil, minerals, or other natural resources). In that regard, as was mentioned in Chap. 1, all development assistance contains some element of barter trade. As we indicated earlier, China is the largest donor in the South-South category, competing as it were, with countries in the OECD/DAC. The way it goes about dispensing development finance and assistance is thus bound to attract discussion.

OECD donors generally allow the recipient countries to implement their own projects, and donors only provide funds, technical expertise, and "advice." For some projects in Africa, especially those which involve construction, including in agriculture, China allegedly provides a large amount of manpower for many of its projects. The debate about Chinese investment in, and development finance, to Africa, focuses on the safety standards and the alleged labor abuses in some of the mines it is operating, especially those in Zambia. The Human Rights Watch Campaign group has written a report on these issues (Human Rights Watch 2011; also Magistad 2011), and it is mentioned that the then (2011) elected president of the country, Mr. Michael Sata, had been critical of the conditions in Chinese-run mines. We shall discuss later how these relate to power and how they could affect the perceptions of the population.

As we saw earlier, Cuba, South Africa, and India like China do not require recipient countries of their assistance to fulfill conditions relating to governance, or economic and financial issues. Media reports show that India and South Africa are setting up development agencies to manage their development finance programs (see IRIN-South Africa 2011; also Patel 2011). The setting up of agencies would help bring coherence and better coordination to their development finance and development assistance programs. In the case of China, the management of its interventions is done from the various embassies abroad (see Hong 2012, p. 149, 150). How does this seeming closeness of decision-making to the recipient affect the perception of the recipients? Is the decision-making power actually within the embassies or in Beijing? We will discuss the former question later; however, we cannot answer the latter, given the dearth of information about China's development finance and assistance program.

The RSA is the strongest economic bloc in the African continent. It receives development finance from developed countries in the North and medical technical assistants from Cuba, among others (see Media Club South Africa 2012). In declarations (see IRIN-South Africa 2011), South African officials have recently indicated that RSA, being the strongest economic bloc in the continent, needs to provide assistance to other countries in the continent. Creating the South African Development Partnership Agency (SADPA) mentioned earlier is therefore an expression of RSA's foreign policy agenda. The director-general of international relations and cooperation stated that the creation of the agency "was not only a reflection of altruistic motives, *but* also of how to advance RSA's *own interest.*" This agency represents the vehicle through which RSA can influence other countries, in its desire to "advance its own interest." It is the gateway to its exercise of power.

With the formation of a South-South forum (Mail and Guardian-Staff Reporter 2010) (i.e. the BRICS), RSA could, if it so desires, enhance the power available to it through possible "connections power" with the other BRICS members. This would be much the same way that traditional Northern donors exercise power, using the "budget support" approach. It is revealing to note that in the establishment of the SADPA, RSA called upon the creative/intellectual and the "expert powers" of, as the director-general put it, "Western development agencies on the best approach to managing aid programs." This represents another manifestation of the subtle power of the external forces over affairs of non-dominant forces.

In terms of motivation, the assistance provided by Cuba was described in a 1991 speech in Havana, by former RSA president, the late Nelson Mandela (Malapanis and Kane 1995) as "selfless." Hammett wrote (Hammett—University of Edinburgh) that many developing countries perceive Cuban assistance as devoid of any imperialistic ambitions. In a review of Gleijeses book, "Visions of Freedom," Elizabeth Schmidt (2014) confirms Gleijeses comments on the degree of idealism that underlie Cuban assistance to Africa. Thus, it is logical to state that Cuba does not exercise "power over" or "power to" on the recipients of its development assistance, even though it has the capacity to do so. This idealism, he found, was unusual in the foreign affairs of all categories of states. It is important to note that given the ever-present sanctions against Cuba by the USA, Cuban assistance to other developing countries helps it to reduce the isolation that these sanctions are causing. It is worthwhile to note that with the recent restoration of diplomatic ties between Cuba and the USA (Baker 2014), the argument concerning isolation is dissipating. I can state that Cuba, through its ideological belief in non-interference in the affairs of other countries, does not impose conditionalities on its assistance package.

India has traditionally focused its assistance on countries in Asia with Africa receiving below 10% of total assistance. In recent years, there has been a dramatic rise in assistance to Africa. Prime Minister Singh stated that India would offer $US5 billion over the next three years under lines of credit "to help achieve the development goals of Africa." It will grant an additional $US700 million to establish new institutions and training programs (Newsome 2015). Although an important portion of its assistance goes through export credit, the traditional approach is the project approach. It does not engage in policy dialogue with recipient countries, and its disbursement of its assistance is not in any way linked to decisions of the IMF or the World Bank.

Thus far, I have used development finance very broadly, but not too broadly to include direct trade interventions, assistance to the military, or humanitarian interventions after catastrophes. Military and humanitarian assistance, however, contribute to the total cumulative amounts, and as I explained earlier, this increases the "capacity" of the "vehicle" to exercise both "power to" and "power over." As I indicated in Chap. 2, I refer to development finance as assistance, which enhances the well-being of the peoples in the recipient countries. These include grants, loans, concessional loans, studies, and technical assistance operations. In addition to direct finance to countries, many of the donors from the South channel a good portion of their financial assistance through such multilateral development finance institutions as the World Bank, the Asian Development Bank, the Inter-American Development Bank (IDB), and the AfDB. As I explained in the pyramid structure, IDFIs are also involved in development finance and assistance to Africa. These include such institutions as the World Bank, the UNDP, and the AfDB. Others include the Arab Bank for Economic Development in Africa (BADEA), we never say the IFAD, and the International Fund of the Organization of Petroleum Exporting Countries (OPEC Fund). We should add development finance institutions set up by some countries in the Middle East to this list including the Kuwait Fund, the Saudi Fund, the Islamic Development Bank (IsDB), and Arab Development Agencies. The essence of this list is to show that through their development finance and assistance to Africa, these development finance institutions have the "vehicles" and the "capacity" to exercise power.

The World Bank, the UNDP, and IFAD are all part of United Nations system, and the funds are generally sourced from the North. Notwithstanding that, such other countries as China and South Korea provide the United Nations system with substantial funds. The funds for the others, apart from the AfDB, come mainly from countries in the Middle East and North Africa. We could therefore classify them as coming from the South. The AfDB, like the other regional bank in the Asian Development Bank (AsDB), and the IDB have membership that includes developed countries. Their sources of funds come from a mixed bag of developing and developed countries. The AfDB and its soft window, the AfDF, which provides concessional loans and grants to African countries, receive funds from developed countries. The funds for the AfDB are also sourced at low interest rates from the international capital markets. The source of funds for the AfDF is mainly from countries in the North, called "state participants." Do the institutions, which source their funds from countries in the South, operate differently with regard to conditions from those whose funds come from the North?

From the preceding discussion concerning RSA, Cuba, India, and China, which are donors that do not impose conditions for their assistance, we would expect that institutions sourcing funds from the South not to impose conditions. In fact, theoretically, most of them do not. Neither BADEA nor the IsDB has economic policy conditionalities, nor do they engage in macroeconomic policy dialogues with countries; IsDB discusses sectoral policy issues, when cofinancing with other donors/lenders. On the other hand, the AfDB discusses macroeconomic and sectoral policies with recipient countries. It also engages in macroeconomic policy dialogue with recipient countries and imposes economic and governance conditions. As we saw in Chap. 3, the recent trend toward budget support interventions makes conditionalities the subject of discussion among the parties involved in providing the total funding well before the fund approval stage is arrived at. Under these circumstances, the conditionalities constitute tools with which power can be exercised. However, is it only through the imposition of conditions that power can be exercised in development finance and development assistance?

Even without imposing conditions, power can still be exercised through the existence of both the "capacity" and the "vehicle." These notions combined with the concept of "anticipated reaction" or "future expectation" tend to ensure that power can be and is exercised, overtly or covertly even in the case of non-traditional donors/external forces. An example is China. As we saw earlier, China does not impose economic or political/governance conditions on its financial assistance; nevertheless, it wields enormous power. PRI.org reported on 28 September 2011 (Magistad 2011) that allegedly the Chinese government threatened to pull out its investment in Zambia if the late Mr. Michael Sata were elected president. The Chinese investment and development finance in and to Africa are very substantial. The exact amount is the subject of constant debate and conjecture, as China itself does not share the exact figures with the international community.

The case of the INGO discussed earlier, which halted the construction of the irrigation dam in Mali, is an example that shows that conditionalities in development finance package are not the only tool used by external forces to control behavior and actions in developing countries. The example also countries have the capacity to control behavior and so exercise power.

In Zambia, for example, China invests more than $US1 billion a year (Mining Review 2011). This is a substantial amount, considering that in 2010, the World Bank (World Bank-GNI) puts the gross national income for 2013 (GNI Atlas method in current US$) of Zambia at $US26.3 billion; Chinese annual investment represents around 4% of the GNI or 4% the GDP ($US26.8 billion in current dollars) of Zambia in 2013 (World Bank GDP). With one country responsible for 4% of the GNI and GDP, China wields significant powers without imposing conditions. This is an example of economic/financial power. Despite issues relating to alleged labor abuse, poor safety standards in the mine it runs, and general negative perception of the Zambian people and the critical view of the president of Zambia, nothing much seem to have changed in terms of the "vehicle" or the "capacity" and the "willingness" to exercise power unseen.

The Chinese managers in the Collum mines in Zambia who allegedly shot and wounded thirteen mine workers, who were protesting against poor safety standards and low pay, apparently went on trial and the Zambian prosecutors decided not to prosecute the case, apparently because of a lack of witnesses (Lusaka Times 2011). The injured Zambian mine workers were compensated by the Collum management (Lusaka Times 2010). Did the economic/financial power possessed by the Chinese through their cumulative investment and development finance have anything to do with the unwillingness to prosecute entered by the Prosecutor's Office? Was there any hint of "anticipated reaction" that played a part in this? Unfortunately, not being privy to any unpublished information, we cannot precisely answer these questions and can only speculate.

In this example, we see the manifestation of what was discussed in Chap. 1 about the cumulative strength of total development finance. In this case, this is combined with the total magnitude of the investment amount. It could be argued, as would Nagel (1975, p. 16) that rightly or wrongly, the alleged "anticipated reaction" by the Zambian prosecutor and other top government officials of the Chinese government possibly withholding further finance and investment could have activated the exercise of the "unseen power." This withholding of further finance could not even have taken place. In the perception of those in authority in Zambia, however, the mere possibility that this could happen could have been sufficient and necessary to modify the behavior of the Zambian prosecutor. "Reward power and punishment power" combined with "economic/financial power" could have been used covertly "behind the scenes." These are suppositions based on our earlier models, because no detailed explanation was made public. Similar cases of possible Chinese "abuse of workers" exist in Nigeria (*Daily Trust* 2007). Can we say, however, that the use of such power did not succeed in preventing the expulsion of 600 Chinese nationals and the closure of three firms in the Democratic Republic of Congo (DRC) since 2007 for violating labor and environmental laws? (Clark et al. Bloomberg 2008). Although the exercise of such power did not directly concern development finance as such, the power exercised was sourced from the "economic/financial power" that China possesses through its huge development finance and investment in these countries. Luke's saying that effective power is that which is "least observable" receives resonance in these cases.

What then can we say about the perception of recipients of financial assistance from non-traditional donors, of power exercised over them? What factors influence their perception under these circumstances? Can we say that, among the factors, the concepts of "interactional and interpersonal justice" which we discussed earlier have some influence? These two factors play some role as they affect the psychology of the recipients. Though MacLachlan et al. discussed these two concepts in the context of organizations, they were discussing these in the field of development finance. The notion of "being treated with respect" is a factor, which the population in the developing countries attribute more to non-traditional sources of development finance. We saw that conditionalities provide the tool for power and the effectiveness of the interventions of the external forces in meeting its objective, greatly influence the perception of power by the recipients under the traditional North-South arrangements. Is the perception of the recipient countries, however, concerned directly with the exercise of power or with the countries themselves or with other actions/activities of the donors not directly relating to development finance?

When there are no conditions accompanying the interventions, can we say that these external forces have exercised power? They have not tried to change behavior, actions, or policies, nor have they specified the outcome of their exercise of power. Thus, apart from China, which imposes the "one China" policy as a condition, no action is required of the recipient country, apart from those that relate directly to the implementation of the project, such as establishing project-managing body or providing counterpart funds. With the "one China" policy, China's condition, and the fact that such countries in Africa as DRC, Sierra Leone, Liberia, Senegal, and Malawi have acquiesced, by switching from Taiwan to China, show that China effectively influenced the behavior of these countries. We believe that the source of power, which was decisive in swinging the issue in favor of China, was economic/financial.

As at 2011, however, some African countries either did not initially recognize China or still recognize or re-recognize Taiwan. Those in Africa include Burkina Faso, Sao Tome, and Swaziland. These are relatively poor countries. Development finance and investment from China would improve the economies of these countries, had they recognized China? Why did they not change from Taiwan to China? Was there any factor that affected their perception of China and that worked in favor of Taiwan? It is probable that the "financial/economic pull" from China may not have matched the push caused by the negative perception of some aspects related to Chinese interventions. There is also the relative pull of Taiwan or the issue of loyalty, which they may have felt for Taiwan, being themselves small countries. There is the possibility, mentioned in Chap. 3, that these countries are relatively small and that apart from Sao Tome, which has oil and other mineral resources, they do not have any major mineral resources or at least, not in significant quantities. By major mineral resources, I mean minerals such as metals and/or oil, which are necessary to facilitate industrial growth. Therefore, they may not have been of major interest to China.

Nevertheless, in November 2013, The Gambia, in a move which allegedly took the government of Taiwan by surprise and which was supposedly a shock to the government in Taiwan, cut diplomatic ties with Taiwan (BBC 2013). In spite of this, the office of the president of The Gambia expressed the hope that The Gambia will remain friends with the people of Taiwan. It is interesting to note that as far back as 2008, it was made known that The Gambia was marketing its production of zircon and rutile to China through the joint Australian/Chinese Company, even though there were no diplomatic relations (see Mukumbira 2008). This ties in with the president's statement a day after cutting diplomatic ties with Taiwan, that "the national strategic interest of Gambia" was a major factor in cutting ties with Taiwan. Sao Tome and Principe, one of the other three remaining countries with diplomatic ties to Taiwan, announced, also in November 2013, that China planned to open a trade mission to promote projects there (Reuters 2013). In both cases, the "reward" source of power is combined with the "economic/financial" source. Although it was not made public that The Gambia intended to open relations with China, in a twist of the "anticipated reaction" discussed earlier, the countries are anticipating that they would be "rewarded" with some of the economic and financial resources that China, in the case of the Gambia, would provide for cutting diplomatic ties with Taiwan. In the case of Sao Tome and Principe, we can proffer that a "trade mission" would be a precursor of diplomatic ties. This is another example of unseen power being exercised.

The perception of recipient countries in the case of non-traditional donors is influenced by the experience, which the people and the government have of the non-traditional donor. The presence and activities of the Indian businesses in West and East Africa, for example, influence the perception that the population of West and East Africa has of India and Indians. Their everyday interactions with the population, through their trading activities, are at times seen as one of dominance of a foreign trader/business people over small national retail buyers. This translated into dominance of the East African economies by Indian and Asian businesses. This was a factor in the expulsion from Uganda in 1972 of Asians who did not take Ugandan nationality (BBC 1972). Though India does not impose conditionalities on its development finance and assistance interventions, the experience of the nationals with their businesses could translate into a negative perception, as if it is an extension of the trader/buyer experience. This can be interpreted as "past experience," which Berger noted as one of the factors influencing perception. In the same vein, because of its earlier interventions in many African countries, where it built sports stadiums, China was perceived as a positive influence in these countries. Sports in many of these countries represent a common denominator for people of all economic and social levels in the countries. The provider of stadiums would receive both high marks and a positive perception in the minds of the people.

The motivation behind the provision of development finance plays a part in the perception of the recipient countries. For example, as discussed earlier, Cuba assists developing countries, with what the late President Mandela called "selflessness." Its interventions are thus perceived favorably. China generally benefitted from this type of perception, until some of the issues became known through the media to the population in other countries, and questions about its true motivation started to be raised. The problems it had in the DRC, Nigeria, and Zambia exacerbated the issue of how the population in the recipient countries perceives its development finance. This may have prompted the ministers attending the Fourth Confederation of Indian Industry (CII) EXIM Bank Conclave on India-Africa Project Partnership 2008 in New Delhi (*The Hindu* 2008) to declare that Africa needs "shareholders," not "stakeholders." This could be interpreted to mean "involved" partners in the development process not "self-interested" investors. For, involved partners/shareholder would exercise less "power over" on recipient countries.

It is therefore reasonable to infer that in recent years, development partners from the South are more and more tending to behave in ways similar to those in the North, with national interest as a primordial theme. In the same way, perceptions of the recipient countries are gradually changing. These countries are getting to see that power is power, and most external forces intervening with development finance in Africa are using their power sourced from the categories we discussed earlier. In fact, given the vast natural resources, especially the mineral resources of Africa, it could be possible for external forces from either the North or the South to collaborate and divide Africa into "zones of intervention," as was done in the past during the period of the "Scramble for Africa" in the 1880s. This may be the reason why Chaturvedi et al. (Sidiropoulos 2012, p. 5) believe that there seems to be a growing divergence of interest between the emerging regional and global powers on the one hand and the rest of the developing world on the other. This could be interpreted to mean not just covert exercises of power, but open and visible exertions of power. We are seeing the beginning of this with the collaboration for budgetary support operation.

In fact, the UNDP used to chair regular weekly meetings of donors and potential donors in some of these countries in Africa; I attended two such meetings in Burundi (1994) and Senegal (2005). Discussions centered on the provision of information on interventions of the various donors in the countries. Ways to coordinate these interventions and monitor progress in the interventions were discussed, in a bid to "avoid duplications." Avoidance of duplication was and is very important in the drive to sustainability, project effectiveness, and reduction of transaction costs to both the donors and recipients. However, avoidance of duplication should be monitored from the central development/planning offices of the recipient countries concerned, through the regular supply of up-to-date information to the central planning office of the government of the recipient countries and weekly meetings with donors and potential donors, chaired by the permanent secretary of the planning ministry. These weekly donors' club meetings were another tool that strengthened the power of the external forces and tended to limit the maneuverability of the recipient developing countries with regard to options in sources of development finance. Apparently, the national officials of the countries did not attend, or were not invited to attend, some of these weekly meetings. This does not mean that multidonor budget support interventions are not useful, urgent, and necessary, and weekly coordination meetings among external donors are not worthwhile and productive. However, from the standpoint of exercising power by external forces, such collaboration provides excellent platforms for such an exercise of power.

What then can we say about perception of the population in countries recipient of development finance and the exercise of power by external forces from both North and South? Both traditional and non-traditional lenders/donors *can* and *do* exercise power. For some, mostly the non-traditional, both the "vehicle" and the "capacity" exist but the "exercise" may not occur and developing country recipients can use the "normative/ideological" argument to remind these non-traditional external forces of the norm, on which the latter built their development finance and assistance programs of not imposing conditions. This can be so, because it can especially be shown that such exercise of whatever power through the "capacity" that they possess would be tantamount to what they felt when they were recipients of development finance and other assistance from the external forces from the North. As I explained earlier, the perception of power play is very often not visible to many of the people in the countries recipient of development finance. Their perceptions of the power imbalance and of power play are influenced or in some ways clouded by their past experience, current situation, historical ties, and inputs from the media. These factors intervene such as to either hide any power play or accentuate the negative feelings or perception of the country/external forces involved in the power play. All of these combine in the cognitive process of the population individually as well as in groups, either homogenous or heterogeneous. The stimuli thus received induce them to view individual development activities or actions of any particular external force favorably or unfavorably.

With this background information and from an objective standpoint, has the existence of the "vehicle," the "capacity" of the vehicle, and the "exercise" of power or non-exercise of power by the "vehicle" been productive in the way Foucault meant? What advantages and disadvantages have been derived from the different sources of power we identified in Chap. 3? Are there intrinsic elements in power play that can be said to be of great value such as to "positivise" the negative perception people in the recipient countries may have of the power play? In Chap. 5, I shall discuss such factors and elements. I shall look at these positive and negative results/products of power play and determine whether the benefit or the inconvenience is for the population, directly or indirectly, or for the economies of the countries concerned.

Notes and References

African Development Bank. Chad: Governance Reform Support Programme (PARG)—Reform support aspect Completion report. http://www.afdb.org/fileadmin/uploads/afdb/Documents/Evaluation-Reports-_Shared-With-OPEV_/Chad._Governance_Reform_Support_Programme__PARG___EN_.pdf

African Development Bank. Senegal: Anambe Rural Development Support Project (PADERB) Completion report. http://www.afdb.org/fileadmin/uploads/afdb/Documents/Evaluation-Reports-_Shared-With-opev_/senegal-anambe%20basin%20rural%20development%20support%20project%20%28paderba%29-pcr-30-06-2011.pdf

ASIA ONE-See. (2008). Study medicine for free. *AsiaOne Education.* September 17, 2008. http://news.asiaone.com/News/Education/Story/A1Story20080916-88124.html

Awareness Times. (2014, August 20). "Sierra Leone news: Parliament approves $23 million grant" from International Development Association of the World Bank. *Awareness Times.* http://news.sl/drwebsite/publish/article_200526016.shtml

Awareness Times. (2015, May 7). Sierra Leone news: YACAN celebrates tenth anniversary. http://news.sl/drwebsite/publish/article_200527572.shtml

Baker, P. (2014). U.S. to restore full relations with Cuba, erasing a last trace of Cold War hostility. December 17, 2014. http://www.nytimes.com/2014/12/18/world/americas/us-cuba-relations.html?_r=0

Balancing Act-See Telecoms, Internet and Broadcast in Africa. (2008, April 4). Broadcast- *Balancing Act.* (26). *10.7 Million Homes Own TV or Radio.* http://www.balancingact-africa.com/news/broadcast/issue-no26/broadcast/kenya-107-million-ho/bc

Ballesteros, S. (1994). Cognitive approaches to human perception: Introduction. In S. Ballesteros (Ed.), *Cognitive approaches to human perception* (pp. 9–13). Hillsdale/Hove/London: Lawrence Erlbaum Associates.

Barder, O. (2015, January 12). In the foreword to essay by Lankester, T. "In Defence of British Overseas Aid". *Center for Global Development.* http://www.cgdev.org/publication/ft/defence-britains-overseas-aid

BBC. (1972). 1972: Asians given 90 days to leave Uganda. *BBC.com*, August 7, 1972. http://news.bbc.co.uk/onthisday/hi/dates/stories/August/7/newsid_2492000/2492333.stm

BBC. (2011, November 3). http://www.bbc.com/news/world-africa-15569310

BBC. (2012, March 5). Malawi's President Mutharika tells donors "go to hell." www.bbc.com/news/world-africa-17256718

BBC. (2013, November 15). Gambia severs diplomatic ties with Taiwan. *BBC.com.* http://www.bbc.com/news/world-africa-24951115

Berger, K. S. (2008). *The developing person through the life span* (p. 162). New York: Worth Publishers.

Burall, S., Mease, K., Mall, P., et al. (2007). *Assessing key stakeholder perceptions of the effectiveness of multilateral organisations.* Final report. Overseas Development Institute. June 2007, (pp. 21–24). http://www.odi.org/sites/odi.org.uk/files/odi-assets/publications-opinion-files/239.pdf

Clark, S., Smith, M., & Wild, F. (2008). China lets child workers die digging in Congo mines for copper. *Bloomberg.* July 22, 2008. http://www.bloomberg.com/apps/news?pid=newsarchive&sid=aW8xVLQ4Xhr8

Daily Trust. (2007, July 4). Nigeria: Chinese and the abuse of Nigerians. *Daily Trust.* http://allafrica.com/stories/200707050526.html

Domhoff, W. (2005a). Basics of Studying Power. *Who Rules America* (p. 1). Santa Cruz: University of California, April 2005. http://www2.ucsc.edu/whorulesamerica/methods/studying_power.html

Domhoff, W. (2005b). Basics of Studying Power. *Who Rules America* (p. 1, 2). Santa Cruz: University of California. April 2005. http://www2.ucsc.edu/whorulesamerica/methods/studying_power.html

Ghana Web. (2006a, March 22). Ghana to receive support from China. *Business News.* GhanaWeb.com. http://www.ghanaweb.com/GhanaHomePage/business/artikel.php?ID=101401

Ghana Web. (2006b, March 22). UK grants Ghana GBP 120m budgetary support. *Business News in Ghanaweb.com.* http://www.ghanaweb.com/GhanaHomePage/business/artikel.php?ID=101402. (Source: GNA, with comments starting 3–22, 2006–19:08).

Ghana Web. (2012, February 29). Japan gives $6.8 million grant to Ghana. http://www.ghanaweb.com/GhanaHomePage/business/artikel.php?ID=230855

Gibson, J. J. (1986). *The ecological approach to visual perception* (p. 36, 127–143). London: Lawrence Erlbaum Associates.

Hammett, D. P. *From Havana with love: A case study of South-South development cooperation operating between Cuba and South Africa in the health care sector.* Edinburgh: Centre for African Studies, University of Edinburgh. https://www.era.lib.ed.ac.uk/bitstream/id/1185/DanHCuba.pdf/;jsessionid=6B73C73C82391E7627F01F490BA80BF6

Hong, Z. (2012a). China's evolving aid landscape: Crossing the river by feeling the stones. In S. Chaturvedi, T. Fues, & E. Sidiropoulos (Eds.), *Development cooperation and emerging powers. New partners or old patterns* (p. 137, 157, 161). London/New York: Zed Books.

Hong, Z. (2012b). China's evolving aid landscape: Crossing the river by feeling the stones. In S. Chaturvedi, T. Fues, & E. Sidiropoulos (Eds.), *Development cooperation and emerging powers, new partners or old patterns* (p. 154). London/New York: Zed Books.

Hong, Z. (2012c). China's evolving aid landscape: Crossing the river by feeling the stones. In S. Chaturvedi, T. Fues, & E. Sidiropoulos (Eds.), *Development cooperation and emerging powers, new partners or old patterns* (p. 149, 150). London/New York: Zed Books.

Human Rights Watch. (2011). Zambia: Workers detail abuse in Chinese—owned mines. *Human Rights Watch*. November 3, 2011. http://www.hrw.org/news/2011/11/03/zambia-workers-detail-abuse-chinese-owned-mines

Hurley, C. (2004). Perceptions of development in Ghana. *African Diaspora* ISPs Collections. SIT Graduate Institute/SIT Study abroad. Digital Collections @ SIT. April 1, 2004. http://digitalcollections.sit.edu/cgi/viewcontent.cgi?article=1059&context=african_diaspora_isp

IRIN. (2011). Guinea: Avoiding ethnically-driven elections. *IRIN Humanitarian News and Analysis*. Conakry, December 6, 2011. http://www.irinnews.org/report/94405/guinea-avoiding-ethnically-driven-elections

Irin-South Africa. (2011). Aid agency to be launched. *IRIN News*. Johannesburg, January 17, 2011. http://www.irinnews.org/report/91651/south-africa-aid-agency-to-be-launched

ITU-International Telecommunications Union-Encyclopedia of the Nations. Radio sets (per 1000 people)-infrastructure-development outcomes-African development indicators. http://www.nationsencyclopedia.com/WorldStats/ADI-radio-sets2.html

Keatley, P. (2003). Idi Amin. http://www.theguardian.com/news/2003/aug/18/guardianobituaries; and also Byrnes, R. (1990). *Military Rule Under Amin*. Uganda: Country Study Washington. http://countrystudies.us/uganda/10.htm

Kilimani, N. (2011). *Study on the impact of Official Development Assistance (ODA) flows to Africa: The case of China*. Report for the Economic Development and NEPAD Division (EDND) of the United Economic Commission for Africa (UNECA) (pp. 16–20), November 14, 2011.

Kilimani, N. *Study on the Impact of Official Development Assistance (ODA) flows to Africa: The case of China*. Report for the Economic Development and NEPAD Division (EDND) of the United Economic Commission for Africa (UNECA) (pp. 16–20).

Kleinman, M. & Bradbury, M. (2010). Local perception of US "hearts and minds" activities in Kenya. *Humanitarian Exchange Magazine*. Issue 47, June 2010. http://www.odihpn.org/humanitarian-exchange-magazine/issue-47/local-perceptions-of-us-hearts-and-minds-activities-in-kenya

Kragelund, P. (2010). *The potential role of non-traditional donors' in aid in Africa*. ICTSD Programme on Competitiveness and Sustainable Development (pp. 2–4), Issue Paper No. 11, Geneva, Switzerland, February 2010.

Lancaster, C. (2007a). *Foreign aid. Diplomacy, development, domestic politics* (p. 6). Chicago/London: University of Chicago Press.

Lancaster, C. (2007b). Chinese aid system. *Center for Global Development* (p. 1). http://www.cgdev.org/files/13953_file_Chinese_aid.pdf

Lukes, S. (2005). *Power. A radical view* (2nd ed., p. 34, 71). Basingstoke/Hampshire: Palgrave Macmillan/British Sociological Association.

Lusaka Times. (2010, November 18). Collum management, shooting victims agree not to prosecute the Chinese officers. *Lusaka Times*. http://www.lusakatimes.com/2010/11/18/collum-management-shooting-victims-agree/

Lusaka Times. (2011, April 1). State enters nolle prosequi involving Chinese collum mine shooting. *Lusaka Times*. http://www.lusakatimes.com/2011/04/01/state-enters-nolle-prosequi-case-involving-chinese-collum-shooters/

Lusaka Times. (2013, December 18). Government signs for a $38 million loan from African Development Bank for climate change. http://www.lusakatimes.com/2013/12/18/government-signs-38-million-loan-africa-development-bank-climate-change

Mackie, J. (2012). Aid effectiveness and emerging donors: Lessons from the E.U experience. In S. Chaturvedi, T. Fues, & E. Sidiropoulos (Eds.), *Development cooperation and emerging powers, new partners or old patterns* (p. 96). London/New York: Zed Books.

MacLachlan, M., Carr, S. C., & McAuliffe, E. (2010). *The aid triangle, recognizing the human dynamics of dominance, justice and identity* (pp. 64–65). Halifax/Winnipe/London/New York: Fernwood Publishing/Zed Books.

Magistad, M. K. (2011). http://www.pri.org/stories/2011-09-28/chinas-investment-zambia. September 28, 2011.

Maiga, F. (2014). Sahel: la Banque Mondiale debloque 85 milliards de FCFA pour la sante reproductive. *ESSOR* .ml decembre 26, 2014. http://www.essor.ml/sahel-la-banque-mondiale-debloque-85-milliards-de-fcfa-pour-la-sante-reproductive.html

Mail & Guardian – Staff Reporter. (2010, December 24). South Africa invited to join Bric group. *Mail & Guardian*. http://mg.co.za/article/2010-12-24-south-africa-invited-to-join-bric-group

Malapanis, A. & Kane, R. (1995). Mandela: "Cuba shared the trenches with us" S. African President Praises "Unparalleled Internationalism". *The Militant, 59*(39), October 23, 1995. http://www.themilitant.com/1995/5939/5939_1.html

Malikounda. (2014). Mali-La BAD approuve plus de 36, 5 milliards de dollars US pour des projets au Mali. *malikounda.com*, Septembre 23, 2014. http://www.malikounda.com/Economie/mali-la-bad-approuve-plus-de-36-5-milliards-de-dollars-us-pour-des-projets-au-mali.html

Martens, B., Mummert, U., et al. (2002a). *The institutional economics of foreign aid* (p. 4). Cambridge: Cambridge University Press.

Martens, B., Mummert, U., et al. (2002b). *The institutional economics of foreign aid* (p. 12, 15). Cambridge: Cambridge University Press.

Martens, B., ith Mummert, U., et al. (2002c). *The institutional economics of foreign aid* (p. 40, 50). Cambridge: Cambridge University Press.

Massa, I. (2011). *Impact of multilateral development finance institutions on economic growth* (pp. 2–4). London: Overseas Development Institute, August 2011. http://www.odi.org/sites/odi.org.uk/files/odi-assets/publications-opinion-files/7312.pdf

Matta, B. (2015, February 18). China to neighbours: Send us your Uighurs. *Aljazeera News*. http://www.aljazeera.com/indepth/features/2015/02/china-neighbours-send-uighurs-150217103722697.html

Media Club. (2012, January 13). South Africa, Cuba to train more doctors. *Media Club South Africa*. http://www.mediaclubsouthafrica.com/youth-and-education/2730-cuba

Mei, H. (2010). *South countries combining their strengths—the perspective of Sino-South African cooperation in development assistance to Africa. in "A brave new world of 'emerging', 'non-DAC' donors and their differences from traditional donors"* (pp. 53–56). Norrag: Network for international policies and cooperation in education and training, NN44, September 2010. http://www.norrag.org/en/publications/norrag-news/online-version/a-brave-new-world-of-emerging-non-dac-donors-and-their-differences-from-traditional-donors/detail/south-countries-combining-their-strengths-the-perspective-of-sino-south-african-cooperation-in-dev.html

Mining Review. (2011). Chinese investment in Zambia exceeding US$1 billion a year. *Mining Review Com*. Lusaka, Zambia. January 11, 2011. http://www.miningreview.com/chinese-investment-in-zambia-exceeding-us-1-billion-a-year/

Money Web. (2014). South Africa signs a R350m deal with Cuba. *MoneyWeb*, September 26, 2014. http://www.moneyweb.co.za/uncategorized/south-africa-signs-a-r350m-economic-assistance-to/

Mukumbira. (2008). For information about sales of zircon China see: Mukumbira, R "Gambia's President forcing Australia's Carnegie Minerals out of country". *Mine Web*, January 17, 2008. http://www.mineweb.com/archive/gambias-president-forcing-australias-carnegie-minerals-out-of-country/

Nagel, J. H. (1975). *The descriptive analysis of power* (p. 16). New Haven/London: Yale University Press.

Naiman, R., & Watkins, N. (1999, April). *A survey of the impacts of IMF structural adjustment in Africa: Growth, social spending, and debt relief* (p. 12). Washington, DC: Center for Economic and Policy Research CEPR, April 1999. http://www.cepr.net/documents/publications/debt_1999_04.htm

Newsome, M. (2015). Act of faith. *India Africa Connect*. May 21, 2015. http://www.indiaafricaconnect.in/index.php?param=news/2688

Nyasa Times. (2014). Malawi economic woes created by greedy politicians. *Nyasa Times*, January 22, 2014. Reporter. http://www.nyasatimes.com/2014/01/

22/malawi-economic-woes-created-by-greedy-politicians-atupele/comment-page-3

OECD. Net ODA receipts per country in millions of US$. http://www.oecd.org/dac/stats/documentupload/TAB25e.xls

OECD- Recipient Countries Perspectives in Evaluating Performance of Multilateral Financial Institutions. A case study of the Commonwealth Secretariat's efforts. OECD. http://www.oecd.org/site/oecdgfd/37998702.pdf. (p. 26).

Ogunrotifa, B. (2012). Federal Civil Service Reform in Nigeria: The case of democratic centralism. *A Journal of Radix International Educational and Research Consortium* (Vol. 1), October 10, 2012. http://www.academia.edu/2046090/FEDERAL_CIVIL_SERVICE_REFORM_IN_NIGERIA_THE_CASE_OF_DEMOCRATIC_CENTRALISM

Ogwu-Arizona, C. (2009). Northernization. *Nigerians in Nigeria*. June 17, 2009. http://www.nigeriansinamerica.com/northernization/

Omolo, L. O. (2010). Various reports-for a sample of these see the following: Kenya, Tanzania, and Uganda: Governments are blamed for mismanagement of Lake Victoria. *News Analysis by Leo Odera Omolo in Kisumu City*. April 21, 2010. http://blog.jaluo.com/?p=5140

Parti, M. (2013). United States and India help improve farming in Africa. *USAID*-Wednesday. October 30, 2013. http://www.usaid.gov/india/news-information/press-releases/united-states-and-india-help-improve-farming-africa

Patel, Nishika. (2011, July 26). India to create central foreign aid agency. *The Guardian.com*. http://www.theguardian.com/global-development/2011/jul/26/india-foreign-aid-agency

Poggi, G. (2001). *Forms of power* (p. 9, 59). Cambridge: Polity Press.

Politics Web. (2010, December 08). SA cancels R1.1bn of Cuban debt—Jacob Zuma. *Politics Web*. http://havanajournal.com/business/entry/south-africa-forgives-140million-of-cuban-debt-offers-more-credit/

Reuters. (2013, November 14). China to open mission with tiny Sao Tome, despite its Taiwan links. *Reuters*. http://www.reuters.com/article/2013/11/14/us-china-saotome-idUSBRE9AD0CJ20131114

Rock, I., & Mack, A. (1994). Attention and perceptual organization. In S. Ballesteros (Ed.), *Cognitive approaches to human perception* (p. 31). Hillside/Hove: Lawrence Erlbaum Associates Publishers.

Sang, N. (2014). Kenya receives loan from African Development Bank for last mile electricity connectivity project. December 19, 2014. http://malawiace.com/2014/12/19/kenya-receives-loan-from-african-development-bank-for-last-mile-electricity-connectivity-project/

Schmidt, E. (2014). Review of visions of freedom. *H-Diplo Roundtable Reviews, XV*(41). http://www.academia.edu/7721243/Review_of_Piero_Gleijeses_Visions_of_Freedom

Scott, J. (1990a). *Domination and the arts of resistance. Hidden transcripts* (p. 54, 57, 74, 111). New Haven/London: Yale University Press.

Scott, J. (1990b). *Domination and the arts of resistance. Hidden transcripts* (p. 9, 14, 15, 120). New Haven/London: Yale University Press.

Sidiropoulos, E. (2012). South Africa: Development, international cooperation and soft power. In S. Chaturvedi, T. Fues, & E. Sidiropoulos (Eds.), *Development cooperation and emerging powers, new partners or old patterns* (p. 232). London/New York: Zed Books.

Sidiropoulos, E., Fues, T., & Chaturvedi, S. (2012). Introduction. In S. Chaturvedi, T. Fues, & E. Sidiropoulos (Eds.), *Development cooperation and emerging powers, new partners or old patterns* (p. 5). London/New York: Zed Books.

Simensen, J. (2008). Africa: The causes of under-development and the challenges of globalization. *Utenriksdepartementet.* See also. November 14, 2011. http://www.nairaland.com/2008935/africa-causes-under-development-challenges#28226589

South South-Task Team on South-South Cooperation. Cuba Africa—"Promoting integrated health services" Case and evidence (p. 4). http://southsouthcases.info/casosafrica/caso_15.php

Spencer, C. R. (1977). *Politics, public administration, and agricultural development: A case study of the Sierra Leone Industrial Plantation Development Program, 1964–1967*(pp. 69–86, 70). Macomb: Western Illinois University, 12(1), October 1977, note 4.

Tarimo, A. (2008). *Politicization of ethnic identities and the common good in Kenya*. Aquiline Tarimo, S. J.—Santa Clara University. April 2008. http://www.scu.edu/ethics/practicing/focusareas/global_ethics/kenya.htm

The East African. (2011). See shock of Kenya ruled by ethnicity. *The East African*. April 8, 2011. http://www.theeastafrican.co.ke/news/-/2558/1140072/-/o3wqvtz/-/index.html

The Hindu—Special correspondent. (2008, March 23). Be a shareholder in Africa's development. *The Hindu*. http://www.thehindu.com/todays-paper/tp-national/article1225149.ece

Thompson, B. (1997). *The constitutional history and law of Sierra Leone (1961–1995)* (p. 37). New York/London: University Press of America Inc.

Tonwe, D., Ojo, G. U., & Aghedo, I. (2012). Spoils politics and environmental struggle in the Niger Delta region of Nigeria. http://www.academia.edu/1886300/Spoils_politics_and_environmental_struggle_in_the_Niger_Delta_region_of_Nigeria. also in Inkanyiso. *Journal of Humanities and Social Sciences, 4*(1), 37–48. http://www.ajol.info/index.php/ijhss/article/view/80068/70331

Top Officials of Recipient Countries-These included Principal Secretary of the Ministry of Finance of The Gambia, Director General of the National Food Corporation (NAFCO) of Tanzania, Director General of the Tea Authority in

Ethiopia, the Director General of the Seychelles Fisheries Authority, the Minister of Agriculture of Ghana, and senior officials of Vice Presidency and Ministry of Finance of Uganda.

UNDP. Official Development Assistance, No. 5, UNDP. http://www.undp.org/content/dam/undp/library/Poverty%20Reduction/Inclusive%20development/Towards%20Human%20Resilience/Towards_SustainingMDGProgress_Ch5.pdf

UNECA-United Nations Economic Commission for Africa. (2012). For proof of the existence of the Commission, see United Nations Economic Commission for Africa. *Third Meeting of the Statistical Commission for Africa.* January 21–23, 2012. http://www.uneca.org/statcom-africaiii

West Africa Magazine, 1984. 2781

World Bank. GNI Atlas Method in current US$. World Bank. http://data.worldbank.org/indicator/NY.GNP.ATLS.CD.GDP in current US$.

World Bank. http://data.worldbank.org/indicator/ny.gdp.mktp.cd

World Bank. Internet users per 100 people in http://data.worldbank.org/indicator/it.net.user.p2/countries

World Bank. "Net ODA received per capita" in current US $. http://data.worldbank.org/indicator/DT.ODA.ODAT.PC.ZS?page=2

World Bank. GDP (current US$). http://data.worldbank.org/indicator/ny.gdp.mktp.cd

World Bank. GDP per capita growth (annual %). http://data.worldbank.org/indicator/ny.gdp.pcap.kd.zg

CHAPTER 5

Perceptions, Outcomes, and Power: Positives and Negatives

Pertinent Questions

So far, using concepts and notions discussed in Chap. 2 to assist in a better understanding of the subject, I have explained the exercise of power and discussed issues relating to the appreciation of perception and power. The perception of power imbalance and of the power play of the external forces held by the people in the countries recipient of development finance would appear, in general, to be negative. In other words, the recipient countries do not consider favorably the power exercised on them. We have explored the different ways power can be, and has been, and is being exercised on developing countries, especially in development finance. We discussed "passive" and "active" exercise of power. I explained that a major manifestation of "active" exercise is represented by the conditions which accompany the development finance packages. It is important to note that it is not only the developing countries that are subjected to conditions that accompany financial assistance packages. The recent (2015) refusal of the Eurozone leaders, especially Germany, to accept any changes by the new Greek government to the bailout plan between Greece, the Eurozone leaders, and the IMF agreed on with the previous Greek government is a clear manifestation of "power to" on the part of the Eurozone leaders (Ehrenberg 2015). The bailout plan itself and its conditions are similar to those imposed on developing countries by the external forces discussed in previous chapters.

C.R. Spencer, *Western Financial Assistance to the Developing World*,
DOI 10.1057/978-1-137-58399-4_5

In this chapter, I shall look objectively and in depth at some of the conditions imposed on developing countries that are the indicators of the exercise of power, and try to assess their intrinsic value. I shall discuss ways in which the exercise of power has been "productive" and positive as well as ways in which such exercise could be considered as not being beneficial or negative. I touched on this in Chap. 3. Can we say some outcomes of power or power play are beneficial to the individual or groups of individuals in the recipient countries, whereas others are not? Are there other outcomes which are beneficial to the economy as a whole while not being beneficial or positive to the individuals or groups of individuals?

Based on this beneficial element, has the exercise of power been positive? If there are positive/beneficial outcomes or results, situations are certain to exist where the outcomes of the exercise of power were not beneficial to anyone. The basic question, then, is: "was there anything productive about the exercise of power?" In this statement, I equate "productive" with "positive," which may not necessarily be the case. I use the word "productive" in line with Foucault's statement about power being "productive." We discussed this in Chap. 2. Some things could be productive and negative at the same time. In cases where I feel that what has been produced is negative, I shall discuss why this is so.

Does perception have anything to do with whether the exercise of power was positive or negative, or is there some objective scale or criteria that can be used to determine the "positiveness" or "negativeness" of the exercise of power? Can we find intrinsic value in the power play, which is not subsumed in the way the recipients perceive the power play or the wielder of the power? If perception has some influence on the issue of the positive or productive nature of the exercise of power, the question could be asked as to whose perception we are talking about. Whose perception considers the outcome positive? Is it the perception of the people in the recipient countries or of the people who constitute the external forces? The Gibson's (1986, pp. 127–143; also Berger 2008, pp. 162–163) theory of "affordance" will come into play in the case where perception has some influence irrespective of whose perception is involved. What the recipients of development finance would perceive as "positive" may not necessarily be the same as what the external forces would consider or determine as positive. In this book we are concerned with the perception of the recipient countries. Can the perception of the donors/external forces influence the perception of the people in the recipient countries as far as the positive element in the exercise of power much like I discussed under Legitimacy in Chap. 2? Is it possible to examine the different sources of power and identify which ones can result in positive or negative outcome of power?

It is important to be certain that the results or outcomes are attributable to power and the exercise of power. I will endeavor to distinguish between these preceding outcomes and those that are the results of the programs or projects around which the power play revolved (i.e. the results of the activities of development finance). It is a daunting task to try to distinguish between outcomes that are purely and directly attributable to the exercise of power and those which come about because of the elements that development finance directly brings to the mix. Rather than working from the different sources of power, I will identify aspects of the exercise of power and discuss their "positiveness" and locate whether the sources of power played any part in bringing about this positive result of the particular aspect. I shall also identify which source of power was responsible or contributed to the positive aspect of the result and the way the result is perceived.

Conditions as Manifestation of Power

I had explained that by complying with the conditions, the recipient countries are allowing the external forces to dictate their actions whether willingly or unwillingly. It is appropriate, then, to center the analysis of perception, outcome, and power on the conditions. I shall therefore discuss typical categories of conditions in this regard. I shall then ascertain whether the result of the power play involved was productive or positive and whether the result was solely attributable to the exercise of power or other factors. The first category includes those conditions that are directly concerned with the management of the programs. These often relate to the appointment of personnel, the provision by government in the national budget of the necessary funds to implement and operate the program or project. The compliance with these, alone, may not constitute a manifestation of the exercise of power by the external forces, because the appointment of personnel, whether in the project approach, the program approach, the sector-wide program approach, or the budget support approach, is a necessary item in any agenda that the government may have for the management of its economy. As regards the budget support approach, the personnel are generally already part of the civil service, and the project under this approach becomes integrated into the normal work of the relevant department of the civil service. In the case of non-budgetary support projects, the conditions that require the appointment of personnel constitute a "constellation of interest," as discussed in Chaps. 3 and 4. As I discussed in Chaps. 2 and 3, however, the existence of constellation of interest does not nullify the presence of the exercise of power.

Is there anything productive and positive that has resulted from this exercise of power, even though it might be considered "benign?" Benign, in this sense, means, without negative, short-term or long-term effect. In this particular case, power was exercised even though there was a constellation of interest. In cases of such conditions, the potential appointees have to be approved by the external donors. The vetting by the external force provides a productive and a positive element that in some cases ensures that the appointees meet the standard required for the satisfactory management of the various parts of the programs. The fact of vetting the appointed candidate is an indication of "power to" which we discussed in Chap. 2. This issue of vetting may seem trivial compared to some of the other aspects, which we shall discuss later. The oversight or the "power to" that the external forces possess, however, helps to ensure that political considerations or political expediency does not get the government to put a mediocre candidate appointed, which could be detrimental to parts of the program or the whole program. In this example, the coercive power and the power to reward and punish were in evidence.

The other part of this type of conditions, which I mentioned earlier, is that which safeguards the activities of the program by getting the government to provide funds for those activities that the money from external forces does not cover. The outcome of this exercise of power in this instance is positive. However, there are instances where despite the willingness to provide the required funds for the operations on a regular basis, the financial situation of the country makes it impossible to have the funds available in sufficient quantity and in a timely manner, for some particular operation or activity or at some point in time during the life of the program. Although power was exercised and is perceived as positive by the recipient countries and the external forces alike, a "break in power," therefore, is experienced because of the inability to provide the required funds. Does this negate the positive outcome of the power? Not at all; for the result of the exercise of power would only be suspended but not completely eliminated. The government would still be legally bound by the "contract" of the development finance package to provide the funds either from its own resources or from another internal/institutional or external donor.

Another category of conditions requires the carrying out of studies concerning certain key aspects either of the concerned sector or the entire economy. The external forces or donors provide the necessary funds within the program budget for the implementation of the condition, which is the study. An example of such a study in the agricultural sector is the study on water pricing for irrigation water provided by the irrigation project to the farmers. Another example is the study on the liberalization of market of a product that the program or project will be producing or a similar or even a competing product. The pertinent question in this case would be whether the condition imposing "the carrying out" of the study and the compliance with it reflect an exercise of power or not. This question is important, especially as the study then becomes an activity of the project or program to be carried out in line with the "contract" agreed upon prior to the provision of the finance. Although it could be argued that the condition (i.e. the study) did produce an outcome and the outcome was positive, the outcome itself was an activity of the project or program. Therefore, the condition and the compliance with it, which are an indication of the exercise of power, have in a rather indirect way been positive. The positive nature of the outcome of this power play is closely linked with the findings of the study, the recommendations of the study, and the implementation of these recommendations. In these cases, the recommendations of the studies on pricing of irrigation water and liberalization of the import of the product could include some recommendations, which may be disadvantageous to the farmers as individuals and as a group even though beneficial and positive to the economy.

In some programs, there is a category of conditions that requires the government to establish an institution or dissolve an existing institution. In the agricultural sector, these are often public or semi-public institutions, or they could be parastatal. There are also instances when the government is required to privatize an existing institution. In all of these cases, when the governments of the countries recipient of development finance packages comply with the conditions, as I explained in Chaps. 3 and 4, power was exercised on them. The outcome of the power play was the dissolution of an institution, the establishment of an institution, or the privatization of a parastatal. The establishment, dissolution, or privatization had been determined by the external forces and agreed upon by the recipient countries as something that would be beneficial to their economies. If we assume that this is based on solid evidence and rigorous and thorough analysis, then these actions would have a positive effect on the economy. In the cases of dissolution of an institution or an organization, such an action would be injurious to those who would lose their jobs. In many instances, as was the case in Uganda, Zimbabwe, Côte d'Ivoire, and other countries, jobs were lost, and some farmers did not have positive gains in their income (see Naiman and Watkins 1999, pp. 8–13). In the case of the establishment and/or privatization of an institution, there would be gains as jobs would be retained (i.e. not lost) and new jobs created. In the event of a privatization of an existing institution, because the private sector in many instances provides higher remunerations, those who gain jobs in the newly privatized institutions would have higher salaries.

In addition, the loss to the economy that the institution was creating by not being efficient and cost-effective and losing funds would be stopped. In these cases, the outcomes are attributable to the exercise of power and are not the result of the provision of the development finance, which was only indirectly relevant. Examples of dissolution in the agricultural sector are the dissolution of the produce marketing boards in Ghana and in Sierra Leone in the late 1970s and 1980s, respectively, at the instigation of, among others, the Bretton Woods Institutions, as part of the structural adjustment initiatives. These outcomes of power play were of mixed perceptions. There were aspects which were perceived as beneficial to the economy, as in the case of the parastatals, which were hemorrhaging the economy due mainly to poor management and corrupt practices (see Spencer 1977, p. 84). As was mentioned earlier, these outcomes of the exercise of power were positive to the economy of Sierra Leone at the time and also to those who got jobs because of the establishment of the institution, but unfavorable or negative to those who lost their jobs. If, however, the basis or the assumptions of the analysis for the conditions were neither solid nor rigorous nor thorough as they should have been, or were flawed in any way, the result would be wrong, and the outcomes would have been perceived as positive, even though they should have been perceived as negative.

(Re)structuring the Economy

Another category of conditions worth discussing in the context of the exercise of power concerns the economy in general and such specific sectors as agriculture in particular. These conditions accompanied the structural adjustment programs and are often some of the prior conditions that constitute some of the more recent budget support programs. They are imposed in the effort to restructure the economies of the recipient countries. Under this category, I shall discuss those that require

(i) reducing the expenditure of government,
(ii) liberalizing imports, by removing import tariffs and government subsidies,
(iii) making some key appointments,
(iv) improving the general governance in the management of the economies.

I shall examine each category in terms of their relevance to the exercise of power.

The general notion underlying this category of conditions in (i) above is that the government is spending money that it does not have, or it can ill afford, or is spending on certain items, activities, functions, or posts that are not cost-effective and should be terminated. In other words, these expenditures are supposedly neither cost-effective nor do they have positive returns in terms of cost-benefit analysis. The condition requiring a reduction in expenditure of the recipient country's budget is generally the result of analysis done by the external forces using their own country strategy documents of the recipient country. These documents have different names, depending on the external force. The external forces also use the financial and operational strategy documents, and the strategy documents of the recipient countries. These include the national strategy paper, the national poverty reduction strategy paper, the national development plan, and the national accounts. Based on the analysis, and using the expert power of the external forces, a reduction in expenditure is prescribed. In the 1980s, in the days of "structural adjustment" programs when such decisions concerning expenditure reduction were the trend, expenditure was cut often drastically, and these led to losses of jobs, reduction in social sector programs, reduction in the maintenance of infrastructure, and shortage of funds for operating public administration activities, among other such reductions. These resulted in very serious hardships among the population. Thus, the population perceived the exercise of power as negative. The statement by the then president of Sierra Leone mentioned in Chap. 3 was a result of this perception of the power exerted by external forces to reduce public spending.

More recently, the budget support programs and the policy-based operations that are financed by external forces are more cognizant of the social impact of such exercises of power, which required a reduction in government expenditure that often included a downsizing of public-funded personnel. This accounts for the heavy reference to the national economic policy papers and plans prepared by the governments (see AfDB 2009), often with strong support and assistance (e.g. intellectual, technical, and financial) from the external forces. There are also periodic consultations between the external donors and the officials of the recipient countries. The resultant budget support programs factor in this concern for the circumstances, conditions, needs, and aspirations of the people of the recipient countries. Under such circumstances, it is logical to assume that there is a "constellation of interest" in the need to adopt appropriate reforms in the effort to streamline public expenditure. Therefore, the outcome of the exercise of power in this type of situation is perceived as positive and beneficial to the economy of the recipient country. Nevertheless, it must be remembered that as we saw in Chaps. 3 and 4, the external forces still possess the reward and punishment powers, the "vehicle" and the "capacity," as well as the economic/financial power to ensure compliance. In these particular circumstances, the benefits of the exercise of power are attributable directly to the power play, not to development finance activities as such. In our analysis, we have tried to dissipate any fuzziness that might tend to cloud the "attributability" to power play directly.

In discussing some of the conditions which sometimes accompany development finance packages in the agriculture sector, we examined conditions that required the liberalization of import market and the reduction and/or elimination of import tariffs. Some of these conditions concern more than one sector and relate to the economy as a whole. These are instances when the conditions required the elimination of subsidies and allegedly hidden subsidies on some agricultural produce or industrial products by the governments of the recipient countries. The cases of subsidies on fertilizer and import duties on textile products are examples. In some cases, such actions also negatively affect the fledgling industrial complex/manufacturing industries in the recipient countries. Imposing conditions under such a situation and the compliance with them are the obvious display of the exercise of power, and any outcome from such exercise can be attributable only to such. Is there any positive element in this outcome? If there is, who perceives it as positive?

In the general effort of the World Trade Organization (WTO) to increase world trade and to reduce and/or eliminate barriers to trade in the developed and developing countries, the existence of such tariff and subsidies are seen by WTO as impediments to increased world trade. Therefore, the conditions to liberalize trade are intended to foster trade. Although WTO rules allow developing countries time for adjustment to the provisions of WTO concerning non-discriminatory trade by countries, however, the developing countries and their industries do not play on a level playing field. In many developed countries, their industries are well-established and had benefited in the past and in some cases are still benefiting from government assistance. Some countries in Africa, therefore, especially the Cotton-Four (Fibre2Fashion 2009; also Mutume 2003, p. 18), perceive any exercise of power that requires them to continue to play in the uneven playing field as regards the elimination of trade barriers as unfair, unfavorable, and negative. They perceive this in the context in which some developed countries (e.g. the USA) continue to provide subsidies and other economic incentives to their own farm producers, especially cotton producers (Fibre2Fashion 2009). Between 1995 and 2012, cotton subsidies in the USA totaled $US32.9 billion (EWG-Farm Subsidies). Some articles put the annual figure of farm subsidies at $US24 billion. These subsidies had been ruled by WTO as illegal (WTO 2004). In addition, the subsidies provided by some of the developed countries that are producers of cotton tend to keep world market prices artificially low, by allowing relatively higher-cost producers in such countries as the USA to produce cotton and sell in the international markets. They thus increase the supply and bring the prices down. These artificially low prices are much to the detriment of the producers in developing countries in general and particularly to Africa countries for whom the exercise of power was and still is unfavorable.

In the third category listed earlier, one set of outcomes of the exercise of power is expected to be the appointment of officials in some key areas of the economy. These appointments are generally perceived by the external forces as critical to the efficient and effective management of the economy. The government, whether deliberately or because of the inadequacy of budgetary provisions, often does not make these key appointments, especially in the area of financial management of the economy. Some of the positions left vacant—at times for lengthy periods of time—are those of accountant-general and auditor-general. In some cases, the annual accounts for some ministries have not been prepared for a considerable time. In other cases, even when the accounts are up-to-date, there is a backlog in the auditing of these accounts (Modern Ghana-GNA 2009; also SADCOPAC-Auditor-General-Republic of Uganda 2008; also Awareness Times 2015). In fact, in countries where the management of the economies leaves much to be desired, governments may not be happy to finalize the accounts of some ministries or of the whole government (see Auditor-General Sierra Leone 2010). The appointment of an accountant-general and an auditor-general would thus be a low priority for governments in such situations. In fact, appointing a person in an acting capacity in the two positions mentioned would tend to buy the government time and also put in place personnel who may or may not be very qualified for the positions and who would be willing to do the bidding of the government in order to ensure that their appointments become permanent. In such circumstances, the exercise of power by the external forces in insisting that these key positions, among others, are filled is a positive, and the provision of a clause to vet the candidate appointed and in some cases providing the necessary funds for his or her remuneration are also positive. In this case, the "positiveness" is in the perception of the external forces and the objective nationals of the recipient countries. It is also good for the country as a whole. The government would also perceive such an exercise of power as positive, if shortage of funds was the stumbling block in appointing personnel permanently to these positions. However, if mismanagement, whether inadvertent or deliberate, was part of the problem for not making permanent appointments, the perception of the outcome of this exercise will be negative for the government or the politicians in power.

Governance: A Major Concern

The final category of conditions mentioned earlier concerns the broad classification of "governance." "Governance" in effect is a concept that transcends sectors and concerns all sectors of the economy of the countries. Under this broad classification, we find the following specific types which include conditions that require

(i) reforming certain institutions,
(ii) activating certain key national committees,
(iii) preparing some key final accounts,
(iv) enacting some crucial laws, and

(v) preparing and adopting or ratifying some important economic, financial, or social policy documents.

Under (i), the first type, which I examined briefly with regard to the agricultural sector, I will discuss the case of national tender boards. Depending on the country, these boards have the final approval authority for all things to be acquired with public funds. In other countries, these boards have the final recommending authority before the ministerial head of department/ministry approves. Once the tender board has recommended purchase, the approval by the minister is often a formality. Given the vast amount of items acquired or activities funded and carried out by governments, the amounts are substantial, and the power of the relevant tender board is immense. There have been instances where the board could be influenced by political considerations, political expediency, or outright corrupt practices. In such cases, a reform of the board is in the best interest of the nation, but not necessarily in that of those who have a propensity toward corrupt practices (see Caesar-Auditor-General Sierra Leone 2010). The affordance of these two parties (i.e. the external forces and the not honest government officials) will differ considerably with regard to their perception of the exercise of power, which this condition embodies.

Another institution that the conditions tend to target under the general classification of "governance" is the parliament. Parliaments act as oversight bodies in many countries in Africa and are part of the governance superstructure. However, because of reasons which include budgetary constraints and heavy workloads, it winds up having backlogs (see Muriuki 2006) in the processing of its debates, reports, and other documents that are part of its workload. The budgetary constraints often do not permit the managers of parliament to make such key appointments as clerk of the house, editor of debates, and even satisfactory numbers of lower-level personnel. This situation has a deleterious effect on the normal running of the affairs of government and of the economy. Conscious of this, some donors under policy-based operations impose conditions in their development finance package to countries for these positions to be filled with competent candidates. A condition under this circumstance and the compliance by the recipient countries, although a manifestation of the exercise of power, will have a positive outcome on the management of the economy.

Those conditions, especially in policy-based operations, whereby the external donors require parliament to enact laws are very closely linked with financial management of the economy. Some of the laws that are relevant in these cases include laws relating to the management of commerce and financial accounting. Others relate to the efforts of the government to reduce poverty in the country. All of these conditions are allegedly imposed with the best interest of the people of the recipient countries in mind. Another set of conditions that also concern parliament is the preparation, adoption, or ratification of important policies in areas or domains similar to the ones mentioned earlier. These conditions lead to outcomes that are perceived by the external forces as critical to the efficient and effective management of the economies of the countries concerned. Do the recipient countries themselves perceive them as crucial? Are the outcomes negative or positive?

In Chaps. 3 and 4, I had discussed issues relating to the effectiveness of development activities financed under the development finance packages and how these affect the perception of the different segments of the population. In those chapters, I remarked that the conditions are generally not publicized, and the issue of power play by the external forces is therefore not always visible. However, these conditions exist and make an impact on the economy of the countries concerned. Some of the laws, which require enacting or revisiting, include laws that reinforce the protection of private investment and private property, as well as laws that spell out procedures for dealing with aspects of financial management of the economy. The enactment of these laws by parliament means that the government accepts that there were gaps or loopholes in the existing body of laws of the country. Another possible argument was that the economies of these countries were dynamic and were evolving; new situations and circumstances require adapting the old laws or enacting new laws to address the dynamics of the evolving situation. As a result, the power exercised in ensuring these laws are enacted by parliament should be considered as positive.

Under normal circumstances, and in a democracy, all bills to enact laws are debated upon before they become laws. It is therefore logical to expect that the external forces anticipate that while exercising "power to" and "power over," there will be discussion in parliament on the advantages/benefits and disadvantages of the law, which is required to be passed. The external forces also envisage that the government has the necessary majority or political clout to get the laws through parliament successfully. This may not be the case, and the final version of the law may not meet their expectation. This is unlikely to happen in many developing countries, especially as both government and opposition are aware that the provision of a lot of money under the development finance package hinges on the enactment. The financial assistance provided by the external forces is crucial to the developing countries to advance their development agenda. Neither the party in government nor the party or parties in opposition would want to take the blame for "losing" such critical funding. Here again, the anticipated reaction of parties in the recipient countries appreciates the power of the "vehicle" and its "capacity" to punish for non-compliance and to reward for compliance. It is not always that such a support for the law is a foregone conclusion. It is not also always that the party in government consults or table motions concerning external financial assistance in parliament, as the recent (8 September 2015) IMF support to Ghana showed. In that case, the minority in parliament accused the government of failing to seek parliamentary approval for a three-year extended credit facility from the IMF (Vinorkor 2015). What can we say about the outcome of this power play? Is it positive or negative? It is reasonable to believe that if the laws to be enacted are to protect investment and private property, these would be beneficial to the country and to individuals who invest or have private property within the country.

Another set of conditions under the "governance" umbrella targets corrupt practices and wastage. These often concern either the setting up of effective and efficient procurement committees or tightening the procedures by which the existing committees do business. These conditions are expected to produce outcomes that are considered or perceived by the external forces to be beneficial to the country. People in the recipient country who work toward eliminating corruption and cutting wasteful costs that would ultimately be disadvantageous to them would also perceive them as positive. For these people, the outcome of this exercise of power would be perceived as positive. However, for those whom missing accounts and/or receipts would benefit (Caesar-Auditor-General, Sierra Leone 2010; also ugandaradionetwork.com 2013), the power play is negative to their interest, much in the same way we discussed in Chap. 4, as it is for the government officials whose fortunes were aligned to the party in power and whose integrity is questionable.

Still in the context of "governance" and enactment of laws, two critical positions that are often the object of conditions are editor of debates and clerk of the parliament. Any backlog in the agenda of parliament or in the preparation of the agenda, or in the preparation of debates will be reflected in delays in enacting and/or finalizing the enactment of laws. These could jeopardize the smooth flow of the affairs of government, hence the need to ensure that competent and efficient persons are in these positions. The exercise of power under these circumstances will be perceived by both the recipient and the external forces as beneficial and positive. In cases where the resources are provided by the external forces for the remuneration of the concerned staff, as we saw earlier, the recipient's budgeted funds would then be used for other purposes. The provision of funds for the salary and other expenses by the external forces will be perceived by the recipient as doubly beneficial.

Herbert (2012, p. 69), however, stated that such provision of funds by external forces is not positive. He stated that it tends to relinquish the government from accountability to taxpayers and electorate for the use of its own funds. This may be so; however, whatever the source of funds, the government has to account for its use, hence the preparation of final accounts and the auditing of these accounts as discussed earlier. In fact, in an overt display of the reward and punishment power, the Millennium Challenge Corporation established by the US Congress gives grants to governments in recipient countries which meet standards of good governance and also have plans with measurable indicators for facilitating long-term economic growth (see Amanor 2013, p. 28). In this way, governments are rewarded for good governance. Those who do not meet the required standard, although they are not punished as such, are put in a position whereby they will not benefit from the grant and would want to work toward benefiting. This latter aspect is another unseen exercise of power or pressure on the recipient countries to do what the external forces consider as beneficial for their economy. To be able to justify the requirement of meeting standards of good governance, the governments have to prepare final accounts and get them audited. These are elements in the process and procedures of good governance. It was seen previously that improved governance is a positive and favorable element for economic and social development and growth. It would be perceived as such by both the external forces, and objective nationals and governments of recipient countries. However, the conditions attached to this grant are still to be considered as an exercise of power.

Under the assumption that those positive aspects of the exercise of power discussed earlier help to improve governance and efficiency in the concerned recipient countries, the general perception of the recipients and of the external forces alike would be favorable. Thus, it is to be expected that the countries would be in an improved position with regard to governance and progress in the journey toward general socioeconomic development and economic growth. In fact, Amanor believes that after the traditional donors have ensured that governance and the general economic situation have improved, through their exercise of power, non-traditional donors benefit from the situation when they intervene in the same countries. Even though they do not impose conditions on the provision of their funds, these non-traditional external forces, in effect, would have positive returns to their development finance efforts because of the previous groundwork accomplished by the traditional external donors through their conditions and the compliance with them, a type of "sunk cost" as it were. Can we then say that both types of external forces would consider the exercise of power as positive? If so, it is consistent to believe that the exercise of power as manifested by the imposition of conditions expected to improve governance, economic indicators, and economic management was and is positive and beneficial to the recipient countries.

Even though this may be so, it is important not to lose sight of some of the sociological and emotional aspects of the exercise of power, especially for the people in the recipient countries. These include the issue of dominance and possible perpetual dependence and their effect on perception. As shown in Chap. 3, people in many recipient countries are already dependent on external forces for resources to operate their economies. Their perceptions of the exercise of power on them as I explained in Chaps. 3 and 4 are often very strongly influenced by the tangible benefits they gain as a result of the actions and activities of the development finance package. Nevertheless, dominance and dependence have a negative connotation. In fact, according to the public transcript of the non-traditional, South-South donor countries, they understand the feeling of being dominated of the poorer recipient countries. This is why they are not overly or primarily concerned with macroeconomic issues and the exercise of power to ensure that their intervention succeeds. From the discussion in Chap. 4, they state that the countries in which they intervene have their own plans and strategies, and they need finance to help move their development agenda forward. This is why the interventions of these non-traditional external forces mainly involve providing development finance. Because they have traveled the road themselves or are still traveling it as recipients of development finance, they do not consider the exercise of power by traditional North-South donors as being positive. Is it then possible to state that despite their disinclination to assess the instances of the exercise of power which predated their own interventions in a country, their later interventions piggybacked on these and had the "sunk cost" benefits that I mentioned earlier? Logically, if the exercise produced beneficial outcomes for the economies concerned, yes we can. As we saw earlier, however, not all of these instances produced positive or beneficial outcomes. In some cases, the outcomes left some individuals and/or groups of individuals worse off than before the exercise of power. At other times, the negative elements and the positive elements crossed out each other, and the individuals or groups of individuals were left in an unchanged position.

What can we conclude from this short exploration into the perception of people in the countries recipient of development finance packages as regards the balance of power? Do development finance packages that are accompanied tacitly or openly by the exercise of power on them through the imposition of conditions make the recipients perceive the exercise of power positively? Are there instances when the exercise becomes exertion and they would rather not receive the packages and say to the external forces, as did the late Malawian president, "go to hell?" (BBC.com 2012). As we saw in Chap. 3, their choices are constrained. This brings us to our concluding chapter, where we shall succinctly summarize the outcomes of the exercise of power and the perceptions of these outcomes and the lessons we can learn.

Notes and References

AfDB. (2009). *An example of such programmes is the "Chad: Governance Programme"* approved by the African Development Fund on October 12, 2005 and which was completed in 2009. See: http://www.afdb.org/en/news-and-events/article/chad-governance-programme-3593/ for approval announcement by the AfDB, and for the completion report, see: http://www.afdb.org/fileadmin/uploads/afdb/Documents/Evaluation-Reports-_Shared-With-OPEV_/Chad._Governance_Reform_Support_Programme__PARG___EN_.pdf

Amanor, S. (2013, July). South-South Cooperation in Africa: Historical, geopolitical and political economy dimensions of internal development. *IDS Bulletin, 44*(4) (Published by John Wiley and Sons Ltd., p. 28).

Awareness Times. (2015). For Sierra Leone, confirmation by the president of Sierra Leone and head of state that backlog existed in audit. Tonkolili Correspondent- "Sierra Leone News: 'I was the first to call for an Audit' - EBK tells Mile 91". *Awareness Times*, February 23. http://news.sl/drwebsite/publish/article_200527219.shtml

BBC.com. (2012). Malawi's President Mutharika tells donors 'go to hell'. *BBC News*, March 5. http://www.bbc.com/news/world-africa-17256718

Berger, K. S. (2008). *The developing person through the life span* (pp. 162–163). New York: Worth.

Caesar-Auditor-General Sierra Leone. (2010). *For an example of ministries not being happy to submit accounts for auditing, see: Audit Service Sierra Leone.* "Auditor General's Report on the Accounts of Sierra Leone for the year ended December 31, 2009" issued December 2010. http://www.auditservice.gov.sl/report/assl-auditor-general-annual-report-2009.pdf

Ehrenberg, B. (2015). Merkel refuses to budge on Greek debt repayments: 'Europe's credibility depends on us sticking to the rules'. *City A.M.*, February13. http://www.cityam.com/209395/merkel-refuses-budge-greek-debt-repayments

EWG Farm Subsidies. Cotton subsidies in the United States totaled $32.9 billion from 1995–2012. http://farm.ewg.org/progdetail.php?fips=00000&progcode=cotton

Fibre2Fashion. (2009). Cotton-4 African countries in US to discuss subsidies. *fibre2fashion.com*, July 28 (United States of America). See http://www.fibre-2fashion.com/news/cotton-news/newsdetails.aspx?news_id=75441

Gibson. (1986). For an explanation of the concept of "affordance". See Gibson, J. J. (1986). *The ecological approach to visual perception* (pp. 127–143). Hillsdale and London: Lawrence Erlbaum Associates.

Giles, W. (2004). WTO rules against EU sugar, U.S. cotton support, backing Brazil. *Bloomberg*, September 8. http://www.bloomberg.com/apps/news?pid=newsarchive&sid=as4.wnubGOWw

Herbert, R. (2012). Sixty years of development aid: Shifting goals and perverse incentives. In S. Chaturvedi, T. Fues, & E. Sidiropoulos (Eds.), *Development cooperation and emerging powers. New partners or old patterns* (p. 69). London and New York: Zed Book.

MMC in Millennium Challenge Corporation. https://www.mcc.gov/pages/about

Modern Ghana-GNA. (2009). Auditor-general's department has a backlog of 27 reports for Parliament. *Modern Ghana*. Accra, September 18. http://www.modernghana.com/news/239529/1/auditor-generals-department-has-a-backlog-of-27-re.html

Muriuki, M. (2006). Kenya: Backlog of bills awaits MPs as parliament opens. *allafrica.com*, March 20, Nairobi. http://allafrica.com/stories/200603201018.html or http://allafrica.com/stories/200603201018.html

Mutume, G. (2003, May). Mounting opposition to northern farm subsidies. *Africa Recovery, 17*(1), 18. http://www.un.org/en/africarenewal/vol17no1/171agri4.htm

Naiman, R., & Watkins, N. (1999, April). A survey of the impacts of IMF structural adjustment in Africa: Growth, social spending, and debt relief. Center for

Economic Development and Policy Research (CEPR) (pp. 8–13). http://www.cepr.net/documents/publications/debt_1999_04.htm

SADCOPAC-Auditor-General. (2008). Implementation and follow-up of audit recommendations in Uganda: Mechanisms, challenges and strategies. *SADCOPAC Conference*. http://sadcopac.pac-networks.org/file/detail/Uganda+Case+Study.doc. Republic of Uganda-public financial management performance report, Final report (pp. 18, 19, 21), June 2009.

Spencer, C. R. (1977, October). Politics, public administration and agricultural development. *Journal of Developing Areas, 12*(1), 84.

ugandaradionetwork.com. (2013). More rot in government as auditor general releases a new report. Kampala, Uganda, June 28. http://uganadaradionetwork.com/a/story.php?s=53916

Vinorkor, M.-A. (2015). The government failed to seek parliamentary approval for IMF support. *Graphic Online*, September 8. http://graphic.com.gh/news/general-news/49130-govt-failed-to-seek-parliamentary-approval-for-imf-support-minority.html

World Trade Organization (WTO). Understanding the WTO. What we stand for. https://www.wto.org/english/thewto_e/whatis_e/what_stand_for_e.htm

WTO. (2014). WTO rules U.S. cotton subsidies & EU sugar subsidies are illegal. *Organic Consumers Association*, September 8 (Bloomberg). https://www.organicconsumers.org/old_articles/corp/sugar091004.php

CHAPTER 6

Conclusions

The last five chapters have explored the issues of perception and power as they relate to development finance. We looked at various concepts that are relevant to understanding the perceptions about the exercise of power on the people in countries recipient of development finance. We have seen that possession of power by someone over another can make the object of power do things that the possessor of power wants him or her to do, even against his or her will. The possessors of power in the context of development finance are the donors who provide finance to developing countries in general and to African countries in particular.

Through the discussion of perception, we were able to appreciate that perception is very individual, and it is very unlikely that two individuals can be said to have identical perceptions of the same object. Even the same individual can view the same object at two different times and will recall different things of the object. This is in line with the Gibson's (1986, pp. 127–143; see also Berger 2008, pp. 162–163) theory of affordance as well as theories by such authors as Rock et al. (1994, pp. 23, 34, 35) relating to inattentional blindness. The fact that no two individuals can always have the exact same perception of the same object makes it difficult to analyze perceptions of groups of individuals in the recipient countries. How can we be certain that all the members of the group reacted to the same stimuli? As we saw in Chap. 4, in the context of development finance, the basic contents of the messages about development finance packages received from one of the media were the same, irrespective of the nature

C.R. Spencer, *Western Financial Assistance to the Developing World*,
DOI 10.1057/978-1-137-58399-4_6

of the media. As I explained, however, perceptions are varied and are influenced by factors that I explained in Chap. 2 and summarize here.

In this regard, we saw that the perceptions of people are influenced by several factors, including current situation, past experience, and the type and nature of the various visual and auditory stimuli. These stimuli include media information. We saw that the media often convey information about development finance packages without mentioning the conditions that accompany the packages. We also saw that the information about development finance packages received by many nationals of recipient countries is most often what I called "secondhand." They receive the information from people who got it from one of the media sources. Thus we saw that the concepts of conveyed concept and obsolescence of the information influence the information they received. As I will explain shortly, these concepts and notions would contribute to them focusing on immediate issues relating to their major concerns, especially benefits they would derive from the development finance activities rather than on any exercise of power that may have occurred.

Based on the models/scenarios and the examples in the preceding chapters, this focus does not differ much as we saw in Chap. 4, even when we deal with officials of the recipient countries who were and are privy to the information first hand and are aware of the conditions that accompanied the development finance packages. From this, can we conclude that knowledge of the conditions and of the exercise of power would not create opportunities for different perceptions of power play on the people who are objects of such power play? Not at all! We saw that their perceptions are different in the various specific examples of us being privy to the private transcript of some of the people concerned at various levels of the society. People in the recipient countries do not perceive favorably any exercise of power on them. From the analysis, we saw that they are concerned with their present difficult situations and are focused on the outcome and the benefits to them of the development finance package and of the accompanying power play. As we discussed in Chaps. 3 and 4, they perceive that they do not have many alternatives and even fewer choices. However, they do not like the power play, which accompanied the development finance packages.

We saw that the economic situation of many African countries is very critical, and poverty is a serious pervading feature. We understood that many of these countries feel that they do not have the financial resources to pull themselves out of the situation without outside assistance. They are therefore in need of external financial funds, even though many of these countries, especially many of those in Africa, have extensive and rich natural resources. These natural resources can only bring wealth and prosperity to the people of those countries which possess them, if they are fully brought into production. Until efficient and effective management of their economies is instituted and corrupt practices are eliminated, however, African countries will continue to need the financial resources that the external forces can muster and provide.

In order to provide these financial resources, the external forces have their own agenda. This is so whether we categorize them as traditional, North-South donors or South-South, non-traditional donors. The common denominator for all of these donors is that they are mostly external to the African continent. As I have explained, their development finance often comes at a price. They have their own motives, which could be political, strategic, economic, or commercial. There are, however, other motivations for development finance, including historical ties, as well as philanthropic and altruistic concerns. As shown in Chap. 3, whatever the motivation, providing development finance to the African countries gives these external forces the occasion and the opportunity to exercise power. As Lukes (2005a, pp. 31, 34) and Dowding (1996, pp. 3, 4) would put it, the provision gives them the "capacity" and the "vehicle" to exercise "power over" and "power to" on the recipient countries.

How they choose to use this, as shown in the preceding chapters, is a function of their motivation. For external forces, we saw that providing development finance is, in many cases, an instrument of their foreign policies intended to enhance their own national interests and influence among other nations. Many developing countries that are recipients of development finance are also often very much more concerned with the amount of the total development finance package and the smooth flow of these funds into their countries than they are with any power play that might exist. As we saw in Chaps. 3 and 4, they are thus, as Herbert (2012, p. 79) stated, compelled to accept any initiatives and any modifications in strategy that the external forces recommend. As a result, as shown in Chap. 1, most books on development finance, especially concerning Africa, tend to discuss issues of motivation of aid, its purpose, its volume, the effectiveness of the interventions, or the amount and flow of funds. Lancaster (2007, pp. 3–7, 43), Sumner and Mallett (2013, pp. 31, 32), and Fues et al. (2012, pp. 250–251) are some of the authors in this category. When the issue of perception is raised, it is often about the perception of the external forces about development, and development prospects in Africa. Authors like Aryeetey (p. 17) come to mind. Few authors such as Burall et al. (2007, pp. 8–12) and MacLachlan et al. (2010) look at perception from the perspective of the population in the recipient countries and the different segments that make up the population.

Using models/scenarios based on real-life examples drawn from experience in development finance, on both sides of the development finance divide, the perception of various segments of the population showed that their perception could be positive or negative depending on the outcome of activities of the development finance package. When the development finance activities led to an improvement in their current situation, they perceived the donor and any power play as favorable. Their major concern was not the exercise of power that the external donor displayed; rather it was their own specific interest and the benefit for them. In fact, from an examination of newspapers in some African countries, we can conclude that the conditions that accompany the development assistance package are rarely made known to the general public. As I explained in Chaps. 1 and 5, these conditions are the major manifestation of the exercise of power by the donor/external forces. Thus, the average citizen does not actually know the conditions that their governments have to comply with or fulfill before they could enjoy the benefits of the finance package. They are thus not aware of any exercise of power on them or their governments. We saw that in the few cases where they had some knowledge of conditions, they were not at ease with the power displayed and the exercise of power on them. In some instances, we were able to enter into their confidence and obtain what Scott (1990, pp. 6, 9, 15) call their private and hidden transcripts as opposed to their public transcript. These private and hidden transcripts told us what they really felt about the power exercised on them, and this was unfavorable.

Even though in many cases they were not aware of the conditions, we saw that in line with what we discussed in Chap. 2 on power, power was effectively used to obtain compliance. Such compliance was obtained by the external forces calling upon one or more of the several sources of power that they possess and which I discussed in Chap. 3. These sources provided them with the "vehicle" and the "capacity," and they had the willingness to exercise power. In fact, we were able to appreciate the distinction between "power to" and "power over." We saw that "power over" is more encompassing than "power to." The former is longer-lasting whereas the latter tends to be "ad hoc" (i.e. used for specific one-off exercise).

We saw that in many cases, as was in the case of Zambia (see Mining Review 2011; also Lusaka Times 2010, pp. 2010), "power over" builds up cumulatively with each new development finance package introduced. In fact, we saw that when we add purely investment packages to the total development finance packages, the external forces wield enormous power much beyond the context of just development finance. External forces which have got to such a position can wield power in diverse ways, often in unseen ways. This is as Lukes (2005, p. 1) puts it, power is at its most effective when least observable. The examples and models/scenarios we discussed in Chaps. 3 and 4 showed that the different segments of the population perceived any outcome of the exercise of power through the lenses of the effect it would have on their current and future situation. This is very much the case for government officials and politicians. In general, we found that any external force that imposes conditions which affect the continued stay in office of the party or government in power was perceived negatively by the government or the party in power. In some cases whenever possible, the government/party in power will try to find ways to defer the compliance with the conditions or dilute them, making them more politically "palatable."

We saw that with the trend toward program interventions and policy-based operations, conditions are getting more and more into the policy domain of government. This is policy domain that governments in many developing countries consider as their own "private" domain. Governments, especially in developing countries, tend to assume that with such entry into their "private" domain, they have lost sovereignty. Even though this may be true, in the present geopolitical situation in the world, sovereignty is relative. No nation can claim to have perfect sovereignty. As we saw, not even the USA, with more than 60% of its treasury bills and bonds in foreign hands, can claim perfect sovereignty. Nevertheless, some nations have more sovereignty than others. As we saw in Chap. 4, in the different organizational pyramid diagrams, developing countries have less sovereignty, especially those receiving external development finance and more so those in Africa.

We saw also that unlike traditional donors, non-traditional donors do not impose conditions on the disbursement of their development finance. Under the circumstances, and on the premise that African countries are not comfortable with conditions being imposed on them, non-traditional donors should normally be their donors of choice. Except for China, the total resources of the non-traditional donors, though substantial, are not as large as those of the traditional North-South donors (UN Organization—also UNDP). While this may be so, we saw that some donors, like China, India, and the Republic of South Africa, have established external development finance agencies that are moving to manage and coordinate their development finance agendas. These agencies are the potential vehicles by which these non-traditional donors could exercise power. In some cases, these agencies are the forerunners of the push by these non-traditional donor countries for their influence in the international geopolitical stage. For them, development finance has also become an instrument of foreign policy and a tool to project their individual national interest or personality. Be that as it may, it is important to note that the existence of non-traditional donors provides welcome players in the world of development finance. They provide alternatives to the seemingly rigid establishments of traditional donors. This is all the more welcome in the context of multidonor development finance packages, where, as we saw, traditional donors tend to frown upon developing countries getting financial resources from donors, not within the multidonor budget support package. As a group, non-traditional donors seem to be a threat to the supremacy of the traditional external donors in the world of development finance. In many ways, non-traditional donors of development finance provide a dilution in the power of external traditional forces.

Given the situation of inefficient and ineffective policies and procedures, and a more or less degree of corrupt practices in some developing countries, it is debatable whether the power wielded by external forces on the developing countries, especially in Africa and in the context of development finance, is such a bad thing. We saw in Chap. 5 that there are instances when the conditions imposed by external forces do have outcomes which we rated as beneficial to the economies of the recipient countries and by extension to the people. These are times when the conditions contribute to the improvement of governance and the reduction of the potential for corrupt practices within the countries concerned. We also saw that, again in Chap. 5, that some of the conditions provide improved settings to facilitate growth in the economies of the recipient countries. These include instances where certain enactment of laws or the carrying out of studies or instituting modifications to certain policies is part of the requirements of the conditions. The elimination of organizations or institutions that are inefficient, are ineffective, and make substantial losses to the economy required by some conditions of the development finance package represents instances of positiveness of the exercise of power.

It could be argued that the government did not need a condition imposed on it for it to enact these laws or dissolve these institutions. In some cases, the benefits would not be obtained without these conditions. There are, however, many countries that had not done so, because they felt that they were neither necessary, nor relevant, nor important. The fact that the need and relevance were brought to their attention by the external donor is a reflection of the expert power of these external donors, which, with or without the input of the recipient countries, had identified these shortcomings.

We saw also that globalization is an important factor which helped to change aspects of the way traditional donors were doing business in developing countries. Globalization is linked to what I call "connections power." It is a double-edged sword. As we saw in Chap. 3, the "connections power" can contribute to thwarting the desire for development and actions of developing countries. The construction of dams for power generation or irrigation, some of which external forces, especially the international non-governmental forces, considered as having negative impact on the physical or social environment, can run afoul of the connection power as we saw in Mali with the Talo dam (see Spencer 2012, pp. 49–53) and we are seeing in Ethiopia with the Gibe III dam (International Rivers-UNESCO 2011).

What then can we conclude about perception of recipient countries of the external forces that seem to dominate development finance in Africa? Power breeds a feeling of being dominated, a feeling of dependence, and a feeling of frustration. It is important therefore for developing countries to understand the issues of perception and sources of power in-depth, and how these sources operate in the context of development finance. It is crucial for government officials and "contract" negotiators in developing countries to be familiar with the concepts, notions, and ideas contained in this book. This knowledge will help them to realize that they are not without power of their own as I explained in Chap. 4. There are breaks in power which can assist them to negotiate better packages for the different sectors of their economies. These development finance packages will contribute considerably in their drive to reduce poverty and inequality in their economies. This book will facilitate putting together development finance packages that they will perceive as facilitating growth and development while also being the least repugnant to them in terms of exercise of power.

Are there other lessons that we can learn from this analysis of perception and power in the field of development finance? As is being done with the various political subregional groupings (e.g. Mano River Union, ECOWAS, COMESA, and SADC in Africa and ASEAN in Asia), countries can draw strength from greater coordination of their efforts and development activities. This coordination is being done at present, but there is room for greater consultation and coordination. Such coordination will go a long way toward greater cohesion. In Western Africa, a case can be made for the combination of efforts to exploit in common and control the fisheries resources in the Exclusive Economic Zone (EEZ). The joint exploitation of resources will contribute to a reduction in poaching and also contribute toward reducing the exercise of power in the fisheries domain, especially as the European Union often negotiates fishing rights in West Africa on behalf of its members. The cooperative exploitation of offshore petroleum resources in subregional groupings will help to improve the strategic importance of the countries and thus contribute toward the reduction of the power of the external forces in this domain as well. These will contribute toward diluting the strength of the power that will be exercised on them individually and collectively. Another important lesson is that countries should strive to take advantage of the positive aspects of globalization, which will help them improve their economies and help them move away from the very bottom of the pyramid structure.

Moving away from the bottom of the pyramid will mean that the amount of power exercised on them will be less, but more so, they will have more elements to break the flow of power on them. They will be in a better position to negotiate a better "contract" in the development finance package. In addition, the conditions, which, as we saw, are manifestations of power, will not be as stringent as when they are desperate for development funds. In short, higher socioeconomic development would make for less power being exercised on them.

In our analyses, we discussed the different sources of power that are used in the context of development finance. But are these the only sources involved in the exercise of power generally and the exercise of power in the context of development finance? I also explained that these powers are used individually and in combination to obtain the desired outcomes. It is logical to expect that some sources come into play more often than others. Why is this so? Is there any intrinsic element in each source that makes that specific source more appropriate in a variety of circumstances? Are there ways in which the different sources of power can be measured individually in the context of development finance? These are some of the questions on which more light could be thrown by further research and enquiries; but are these questions very significant to the debate? Are there other areas that should be researched? In fact, I explained that in the perception of the people in the recipient countries, power is power. They do not perceive the different sources that we discussed. They perceive "power" as being exercised on them.

With regard to the conditions that accompany the financial assistance, I used them as the major manifestation of the exercise of power in the context of development finance. I also discussed some of the other ways in which power is exercised in development finance. Are there other avenues through which the external/dominant forces exercise power in development finance?

The perceptions of the different segments of the population in recipient countries are influenced by factors which we discussed in Chap. 4. Are there other factors that contribute to the specific type of perception of the exercise of power? These are topics that more research could help further strengthen the analyses of perception of the exercise of power in development finance. Have the interventions of the non-traditional donors that intervene in developing countries benefited from the outcomes of the exercise of power by the traditional donors? It would be interesting to explore these and other questions. Would it be worthwhile, then, for non-traditional donors to strengthen the economies of the recipient countries further by imposing conditions of their own? That would mean that the recipient countries have a greater number of external forces exercising power over them. Further research would help elucidate these questions. It is interesting to note that corrupt practices tend to contribute to the increase in the exercise of power on developing countries. They also prolong the period over which the power is exercised.

This book is a contribution to the debate on development finance, the debate on the exercise of power, the debate on perception, and the debate on all these combined as well as the perception of exercise of power in the context of development finance. The teaching staff of universities, graduate students, and senior undergraduate will find it very worthwhile and instructive. Senior government and public officials and the informed and/or educated public in the developed and developing countries will benefit from a knowledge of, and familiarity with, the concepts, notions, and analyses in this book.

Notes and References

Aryeetey, E. Taking Africa seriously: A case for enhanced resource flow to facilitate development and reduce poverty (p. 17). http://www.uib.cat/depart/deaweb/smed/pdf/aryeetey.pdf

Berger, K. S. (2008). *The developing person through the life span* (pp. 162–163). New York: Worth.

Burall, S. Mease, K., Mall, P., & Datta, A., et al. (2007, June). *Assessing key Stakeholder perceptions of the effectiveness of multilateral organisations.* Final report. Overseas Development Institute (pp. 8–12). http://www.odi.org/sites/odi.org.uk/files/odi-assets/publications-opinion-files/239.pdf

Dowding, K. (Ed.). (1996). *Power* (p. 3, 4). Minneapolis: University of Minnesota Press.

Fues, T., Chaturvedi, S., & Sidiropoulos, E. (2012). Conclusion: Towards a global consensus on development cooperation. In S. Chaturvedi, T. Fues, & E. Sidiropoulos (Eds.), *Development cooperation and emerging powers. New partners or old patterns?* (p. 250, 251). London and New York: Zed Books.

Gibson. For an explanation of the concept of "affordance" see Gibson, J. J. (1986). *The ecological approach to visual perception* (pp. 127–143). Hillsdale and London: Lawrence Erlbaum Associated.

Herbert, R. (2012). Sixty years of development aid: Shifting goals and perverse incentives. In S. Chaturvedi, T. Fues, & E. Sidiropoulos (Eds.), *Development cooperation and emerging powers. New partners or old patterns?* (p. 79). London and New York: Zed Books.

International Rivers-UNESCO. (2011). UNESCO World Heritage Committee: 'Halt all construction on the Gibe III dam'. *International Rivers*, July 21. http://www.internationalrivers.org/resources/unesco-world-heritage-committee-halt-all-construction-on-the-gibe-iii-dam-3390

Lancaster, C. (2007). *Foreign aid. Diplomacy, development, domestic politics* (pp. 3–7, 43). Chicago: University of Chicago Press.

Lukes, S. (2005a). *Power. A radical view* (2nd ed., p. 31, 34). Basingstoke and New York: Palgrave Macmillan.

Lukes, S. (2005b). *Power. A radical view* (2nd ed., p. 1). Basingstoke and New York: Palgrave Macmillan.

Lusaka Times. (2010). Management, shooting victims agree not to prosecute the Chinese officers. *Lusaka Times*, November 18. http://www.lusakatimes.com/2010/11/18/collum-management-shooting-victims-agree/

MacLachlan, M., Carr, S., & McAuliffe, E. (2010). *The aid triangle. Recognizing the human dynamics of dominance, justice and identity.* Halifax and Winnipeg/London and New York: Fernwood/Zed Books.

Mining Review. (2011). For an example of cumulative increase in power through development finance and investment, see "Chinese investment in Zambia exceeding US$1 billion a year". *Mining Review.com*, Lusaka, Zambia,

January11.http://www.miningreview.com/chinese-investment-in-zambia-exceeding-us-1-billion-a-year/

OECD-Figures for assistance DAC countries are estimated by OECD for also for 2008asUS$56.5billion. Seehttps://data.oecd.org/oda/country-programmable-aid-cpa.htm

Rock, I., & Mack, A. (1994). Attention and perceptual organization. In S. Ballesteros (Ed.), *Cognitive approaches to human perception* (p. 23, 34, 35). Hillsdale, Hove and London: Lawrence Erlbaum Associates.

Scott, J. (1990). *Domination and the arts of resistance. Hidden transcripts* (p. 6, 9, 15). New Haven and London: Yale University Press.

Spencer, C. R. (2012). *Politics, agricultural development, and conflict resolution. An in-depth analysis of the Moyen Bani programme in Mali* (pp. 49–53). Lanham: University Press of America.

Sumner, A., & Mallett, R. (2013). *The future of foreign aid. Development cooperation and the new geography of global poverty* (pp. 31–32). New York: Palgrave Macmillan.

U.N. Organization-The United Nations Organization estimates total non-DAC (excluding China) global assistance in 2008 at US$15.3 billion. Figures for assistance DAC countries are estimated by OECD for also for 2008 as US$56.5 billion.

UNDP. For figures concerning non-DAC countries, see Official Development Assistance, 5, UNDP. http://www.undp.org/content/dam/undp/library/Poverty%20Reduction/Inclusive%20development/Towards%20Human%20Resilience/Towards_SustainingMDGProgress_Ch5.pdf

Bibliography

African Development Bank. (2014, November). Treasury Department. ADF statement of subscription and voting powers as at 30 Sept 2014.

African Development Bank. Chad: Governance Reform Support Programme (PARG) – reform support aspect. Completion Report. http://www.afdb.org/fileadmin/uploads/afdb/Documents/Evaluation-Reports-_Shared-With-OPEV_/Chad._Governance_Reform_Support_Programme__PARG___EN_.pdf

Ahmed, S., & Potter, D. (2006). *NGO'S in international politics*. Bloomfield: Kumarian Press.

Allafrica.com. African Development Bank doubles soft-loan funds for Malawi. 30 July 2008. http://allafrica.com/stories/200807300890.html. Also in http://www.afdb.org/en/news-and-events/article/african-development-bank-doubles-soft-loan-funds-for-malawi-president-kaberuka-visits-malawi-1543/

Alemazung, J. (2010). Post-colonial colonialism: An analysis of international factors and actors marring African socio-economic and political development. *The Journal of Pan African Studies, 3*(10), 64, 65. http://www.jpanafrican.com/docs/vol3no10/3.10Post-Colonial.pdf

Alesina, A., & Dollar, D. (2000). Who gives foreign aid to whom and why. *Journal of Economic Growth, 5*, 33–63. Kluwer Academic Publishers.

Amanor, K. S. (2013). South-South cooperation in Africa: Historical, geopolitical and political economy dimensions of international development. *IDS Bulletin, 44*(4), 20–40. Published by John Wiley and Sons, Oxford.

Anane, M. C., & Abiwu, C. Y. (2011). Independent study report of the ADDAX bioenergy sugarcane to ethanol project in the Makeni region in Sierra Leone.

C.R. Spencer, *Western Financial Assistance to the Developing World*,
DOI 10.1057/978-1-137-58399-4

http://www.brotfueralle.ch/fileadmin/deutsch/01_Service/Medien_Texte/Mediencommuniques/Independent%20Study%20Report%20Addax%20Final.pdf

Aryeetey, E. *Taking Africa seriously: A case for enhanced resource flow to facilitate development and reduce poverty* (p. 17). http://www.uib.cat/depart/deaweb/smed/pdf/aryeetey.pdf

Augsburger, D. W. (1992). *Conflict mediation across cultures. Pathways and patterns.* Louisville/London: Westminster John Knox Press.

Awareness Times. (2014, August 20). Sierra Leone News: Parliament approves $23 grant. http://news.sl/drwebsite/publish/article_200526016.shtml

Axelrod, R. (1973). Schema theory: An information processing model of perception and cognition. *The American Political Science Review, 67*(4). American Political Association. http://www.jstor.org/stable/1956546

Ballesteros, S. (Ed.). *Cognitive approaches to human perception.* New Jersey/Hove/London: Lawrence Erlbaum Associates/Publishers Hillsdale.

Ballesteros, A., Nakhooda, S., Werksman, J., & Hurlburt, K. (2010). Power, responsibility, and accountability. Rethinking the legitimacy of institutions for climate finance. World Resources Institute. WRI Final report. Washington, DC.

Barder, O. in the foreword to essay by T. Lankester (2015). In defence of British overseas aid. 1/12/2015. Center for Global Development. http://www.cgdev.org/publication/ft/defence-britains-overseas-aid

Baxter, J. Oakland Institute. Understanding land investment deals in Africa. Country report: Mali. http://www.oaklandinstitute.org/understanding-land-investment-deals-africa-mali

BBC News. (2012). Former Nigerian Governor James Ibori jailed for 13 years. 17 April 2012. http://www.bbc.com/news/world-africa-17739388

Bebington, A. J., Hickey, S., & Mitlin, D. C. (Eds.). (2008). *Can NGOs make a difference. The challenge of development alternatives.* London/New York: Zed Books.

Berger, K. S. (2008). *The developing person through the life span.* New York: Worth Publishers.

Berk, L. (2012). *Infants and children. Prenatal through middle childhood.* Boston/Columbus/New York: Allyn and Bacon.

Bierstedt, R. (1950). An analysis of social power. *American Sociological Review, 15*(6), 7130–38.

Bhagwati, J. (2004). *In defense of globalization.* New York: Oxford University Press.

Blein, R., Bwalya, M., et al. (2013). Agriculture in Africa – transformation and outlook. *NEPAD Transforming Africa* (pp. 14–15). NEPAD. http://www.nepad.org/system/files/Agriculture%20in%20Africa.pdf

Braman, E. (2009). Law politics, and perception. How policy preferences influence legal reasoning. In Series: G. Ivers, & K. T. Mcguire (Eds.), *Constitutionalism and democracy*. Charlottesville/London: University of Virginia Press.

Brinkerhoff, D. W. (2005). *Organisational legitimacy, capacity and capacity development*. Discussion Paper 58A. European Centre for Development Policy Management. Publication date: 12 Aug 2005.

Brinsley, J., & Christie, R. (2008). China passes Japan as biggest U.S. Treasuries holder (Update1). Far East fans of us Government debt. 18 Nov 2008. http://www.bloomberg.com/apps/news?pid=newsarchive&sid=aFQwLGTYEM3Y

Bukovansky, M. (2002). *Legitimacy and power politics. The American and French revolutions in international political culture*. Princeton/Oxford: Princeton University Press.

Burall, S., Mease, K., Mall, P., et al. (2007). *Assessing key stakeholder perceptions of the effectiveness of multilateral organisations*. Final report. Overseas Development Institute (pp. 21–24). http://www.odi.org/sites/odi.org.uk/files/odi-assets/publications-opinion-files/239.pdf

Burgess, S. (2012). Developing from the South: South-South cooperation in the global development game. *Austral: Brazilian Journal of Strategy and International Relations, 1*(2). e-ISSN 22386912. ISSN22386262. July–Dec 2012.

Business News. (2010, October 12). Source GNA. World Bank to assist Ghana in youth skills training-Vice President.

Chaturvedi, S., Fues, T., et al. (Eds.). (2012). *Development cooperation and emerging powers. New partners or old patterns*. London/New York: Zed Books.

Chimero, A. (2003). Information for perception and information processing. *Minds and Machines, 13*, 577–588. The Netherlands: Kluwer Academic Publishers.

Chiriyankadath, J. Colonialism and post-colonialism development. http://www.docstoc.com/docs/110059444/2-Colonialism-and-Post-Colonial-Development

Clark, I. (2005). *Legitimacy in international society*. Oxford/London: Oxford University Press.

Cobain, I., & Hirsch, A. The tycoon, the dictator's wife and the $2.5bn Guinea mining deal. *The Guardian*. FBI investigating Beny Steinmetz's company BSGR after lucrative deal to extract iron ore from Simandou mountain range. http://www.theguardian.com/world/2013/jul/30/africa-guinea-mining-bsgr-steinmetz

Commission for Africa. (2005, March). Our common interest. Report of the commission for Africa.

Cotula, L., Vermeulen, S., Leonard, R., & Keel, J. (2009). Land grab or development opportunity? Agricultural investment and international land deals in Africa. IIED/FAO/IFAD. http://www.ifad.org/pub/land/land_grab.pdf

Dahl, R. A. (cited by Dowding) (1968). Power. In D. L. Sils (Ed.), *International encyclopedia of the social sciences* (Vol. 12). New York: Free Press.

Department of Rural Development & Ministry of Rural Development. (2010). *Strategic plan* (p. 2, 3). Government of India. 9 Feb 2010. http://www.performance.gov.in/sites/default/files/document/strategy/RD.pdf

Domhoff, G. W. (1996). Basics of studying power. *Who Rules America?* http://www2.ucsc.edu/whorulesamerica/methods/studying_power.html

Dowding, K. (1996). *Power: Concepts in social thought.* Minneapolis: Open University Press/University of Minnesota Press.

Edwards, M., & Hulme, D. (Eds.). (1996). *Beyond the magic bullet. NGO performance and accountability in the post-Cold War world.* West Hartford: Kumarian Press.

ELS, F. Mining.com. (2013). UPDATE: Court win for Israeli billionaire in fight over $50 billion African mining prize. June 10, 2013. http://www.mining.com/simandou-the-greatest-mine-ever-sold-36183/

Falk, T. The Bulletin. China invests $1.1 billion in Nigerian infrastructure. 10 July 2013. http://www.zdnet.com/article/china-invests-11-billion-in-nigerian-infrastructure/

Farias, & Bustos, E. Understanding social perception and managing diversity. Organizational behavior. University of London. http://www.angelfire.com/ak6/organizational_behav/lecture3.pdf

Faul, M in Yahoo Finance. Nigeria gets back $227 million looted by dictator. 2014-06-19. http://finance.yahoo.com/news/nigeria-gets-back-227-million-183556491.html;_ylt=A0LEVr6Zhw9V5U4Aql4lnIlQ;_ylu=X3oDMTEzamk4b3NtBHNlYwNzcgRwb3MDMwRjb2xvA2JmMQR2dGlkA1lIUzAwMV8x

Faubion, J. D. (Ed.). (1984). *Power. Michel Foucault. Essential works of Foucault 1954–1984.* In P. Rainbow, Series Editor (Vol. 3). New York: New Press

Fink, R., & Meierotto, L. (2002). *Cultural survival* CSQ Issue 26.4 (Winter2002). http://www.culturalsurvival.org/publications/cultural-survival-quarterly/mali/moratorium-talo-dam-construction-still-holding

Foucault, M. (2000). "Power" Volume 3 "*Essential works of Foucault.*". In J. D. Fabion (Ed.), P. Rainbow (Ser. Ed.). New York: The New Press.

Ghanaweb.com. (2012). Japan gives $6.8 million grant to Ghana. *Business News.* February 29, 2012. http://www.ghanaweb.com/GhanaHomePage/business/artikel.php?ID=230855. Also: ghanaweb.com. Ghana to receive support from China. *Business News*, March 22, 2006. http://www.ghanaweb.com/GhanaHomePage/business/artikel.php?ID=101401

Gibson, J. J. (1986). *The ecological approach to visual perception.* Hillsdale/New Jersey/London: Lawrence Erlbaum Associates Publishers.

Gordon, C. (Ed.). (1972–1977). Power/Knowledge by Michel Foucault. *Selected interviews & other writings.* Pantheon Books: New York

Grimes, W. (2008). Wise and fall guys, welcome to globalization. A review of the book by Glenny, M. "McMAFIA. A journey through the global criminal underworld". New York: Vintage Books. *New York Times*. April 11, 2008. See http://www.nytimes.com/2008/04/11/books/11book.html?pagewanted=all&_r=1&

Hammett, D. P. From Havana with love: A case study of South-South development cooperation operating between Cuba and South Africa in the health care sector. Centre for African Studies. University of Edinburgh. https://www.era.lib.ed.ac.uk/bitstream/id/1185/DanHCuba.pdf/;jsessionid=6B73C73C82391E7627F01F490BA80BF6

Harrington, A. Corporate social responsibility, globalization, the multinational corporation and labor: An unlikely alliance (pp. 3, 4, 5). http://www.albanylawreview.org/Articles/Vol75_1/75.1.0017_Harrington.pdf

Hirshleifer, J. (2001). *The dark side of the force. Economic foundations of conflict theory*. Cambridge, MA/New York: Cambridge University Press.

Holy Bible. (1978). New international version. The Committee on Bible Translation June 1978, revised August 1983.

Hurd, I. After Anarchy: Legitimacy and power in the United Nations security council. Princeton: University Press. http://press.princeton.edu/chapters/s8424.html

Hurd, W., & Oakland Institute. (2013). Understanding land investment deals in Africa. Country Report: Ethiopia "Ignoring abuse in Ethiopia. DFID and USAID in the Lower Omo Valley" July 2013. http://www.oaklandinstitute.org/land-deals-africa-ethiopia

Hurley, C. (2004). Perceptions of development in Ghana. In *African Diaspora* ISPs Collections. SIT Graduate Institute/SIT Study Abroad. Digital Collections @ SIT, 4-1-2004. http://digitalcollections.sit.edu/cgi/viewcontent.cgi?article=1059&context=african_diaspora_isp

Jacobs, A. & Wilford, R. Putting new approaches to NGO accountability into action. National University of Ireland in Galway. http://www.nuigalway.ie/dern/documents/19__alex_jacobs_and_robyn_wilford.pdf

Johnson, A., Martin, M., & Watts, R. (2011). Trends in International Financial Cooperation Forum for LDC. Background for preparing for the 2012 Development Cooperation Forum Department of Economic and Social Affairs. Draft 29 Apr 2011.

Kilimani, N. Study on the impact of official development (ODA) flows to Africa: The case of China. *Report for the Economic Development and NEPAD Division (EDND) of the United Nations Economic for Africa (UNECA)*.

Kindornay, S., & Samy, Y. (2012). *Establishing a legitimate development cooperation architecture in the post-Busan era*. North–South Institute. May 2012.

Kleinman, M., & Bradbury, M. (2010). Local perception of US 'hearts and minds' activities in Kenya. *Humanitarian Exchange Magazine*. Issue 47. June 2010.

http://www.odihpn.org/humanitarian-exchange-magazine/issue-47/local-perceptions-of-us-hearts-and-minds-activities-in-kenya

Kragelund, P. (2010). *The potential role of non-traditional donors in aid in Africa.* ICTSD Programme on Competitiveness and Sustainable Development. Issue Paper No.11. Geneva, February 2010.

Krishnanda, S. (2003). The Philosophy of life. *PART I*: The foundations of philosophy. Chapter 5: The theory of perception. The perceptive apparatus. Himalayas: The Divine Life Society Press. http://www.swami-krishnananda.org/phil/phil_05.html

Lancaster, C. (2007). *Foreign aid. Diplomacy, development, and domestic politics.* Chicago/London: University of Chicago Press.

Lewis, D., & Kanji, N. (2009). *Non-governmental organizations and development.* London/New York: Routledge Taylor Francis Group.

Lukes, S. (2005). *Power: A radical view. The original with two major new chapters* (2nd ed.). Basingstoke: Palgrave Macmillan in Association with the British Sociological Association.

Maclachlan, M. C., & Mcauliffe, S. C. (2010). *The aid triangle. Recognizing the human dynamics of dominance, justice and identity.* London/New York: Fernwood Publishing/Halifax/Winnipeg/Zed Books.

Malapanis, A., & Kane, R. (1995). Mandela: 'Cuba shared the trenches with us'. S. African President Praises 'Unparalleled Internationalism'. *The Militant, 59*(39).October23,1995.http://www.themilitant.com/1995/5939/5939_1.html

Mansori, K. (2011). Why Greece, Spain, and Ireland aren't to blame for Europe's woes. New Republic – *Politics, Culture Magazine*. October 11, 2011. http://www.newrepublic.com/article/economy/95989/eurozone-crisis-debt-dont-blame-greece

Martens, B., Mummert, U., Murrell, P., & Seabright, P. (2002). *The institutional economics of foreign aid.* Cambridge, MA: Cambridge University Press.

Martens, B. *Why do aid agencies exist?*. Revised draft. November 2004. Paper presented at workshops at Pompeu Fabra University (Barcelona), Bloomington: The University of Indian.

Massa, I. (2011). Impact of multilateral development finance institutions on economic growth. Overseas Development Institute. London. August 2011. http://www.odi.org/sites/odi.org.uk/files/odi-assets/publications-opinion-files/7312.pdf See also "Recipient Countries Perspectives in Evaluating Performance of Multilateral Financial Institutions. A Case Study of the Commonwealth Secretariat's Efforts." OECD. http://www.oecd.org/site/oecdgfd/37998702.pdf

Mechanic, D. Sources of power of lower participants in complex organizations. http://www.jstor.org/discover/10.2307/2390947?uid=3739704&uid=2&uid=4&uid=3739256&sid=21106472268023

Mei, H. (2010). South countries combining their strengths – the perspective of Sino-South African Cooperation in development assistance to Africa. In A brave new world of 'Emerging', 'non-DAC' donors and their differences from traditional donors. NORRAG. Network for international policies and cooperation in education and training. NN44 September 2010, pp. 53–56. http://www.norrag.org/en/publications/norrag-news/online-version/a-brave-new-world-of-emerging-non-dac-donors-and-their-differences-from-traditional-donors/detail/south-countries-combining-their-strengths-the-perspective-of-sino-south-african-cooperation-in-dev.html

Mensah, M. (1994). Policy setting and institutional framework for rural development in Africa. *Special Communication* CTA Annual Report 1994.

Moore, C. Inattentional blindness: Perception or memory and what does it matter? http://www2.psychology.uiowa.edu/labs/iapl/iAPL_people/cathleen_moore/pdfs/moore_2001_psyche.pdf

Morriss, P. (1987). *Power: A philosophical analysis.* Manchester: Manchester University Press.

Morton, B. An overview of international NGOs in development cooperation. Case Study 7 (pp. 325–352). http://www.undp.org/content/dam/china/docs/Publications/UNDP-CH11%20An%20Overview%20of%20International%20NGOs%20in%20Development%20Cooperation.pdf. p. 333.

Moyo, D. (2009). Why foreign aid is hurting Africa. *Wall Street Journal.* March 21, 2009. http://www.wsj.com/articles/SB123758895999200083#articleTabs%3Darticle

Mshomba, R. (2002, September). Northern subsidies hurt Africa. *Africa Recovery-Now called Africa Renewal, 16* (#2–3), 29. *http://www.un.org/en/africarenewal/vol16no2/162agric.htm*

Nagel, J. H. (1975). *The descriptive analysis of power.* New Haven/London: Yale University Press.

Naiman, R., & Watkins, N. (1999). A survey of the impacts of IMF structural adjustment in Africa: Growth, social spending, and debt relief. In Center for Economic and Policy Research. CEPR. April 1999 (p. 12). http://www.cepr.net/documents/publications/debt_1999_04.htm

Najam, A. (2002). Financing sustainable development: Crises of legitimacy. *Progress in Development Studies, 2*(2). http://www.oecd.org/unitedkingdom/2083553.pdf

Nampewo, A. (2013). Why damming Isimba Falls will destroy tourism on River Nile. *Daily Monitor.* September 14, 2013. Inhttp://www.monitor.co.ug/arts-culture/Travel/Why+damming+Isimba+Falls+will+destroy+tourism+on+R++Nile/-/691238/1991446/-/sc1grd/-/index.html

Neondo, H. (2001). Canada puts corrupt African leaders on notice. *News from Africa,* March 7, 2001. http://www.newsfromafrica.org/newsfromafrica/articles/art_12376.html

Ndikumana, L., & Boyce, J. K. (2011). *Africa's odious debts. How foreign loans and capital flight bled a continent*. London/New York: Zed Books.

Oakland Institute. Understanding land investment deals in Africa – Country Report: Sierra Leone. Oakland: The Oakland Institute. http://www.oaklandinstitute.org/sites/oaklandinstitute.org/files/OI_SierraLeone_Land_Investment_report_0.pdf

Ogunrotifa, B. (2012). Federal civil service reform in Nigeria: The case of democratic centralism. *A Journal of Radix International Educational and Research Consortium, 1*(10) Oct 2012. http://www.academia.edu/2046090/FEDERAL_CIVIL_SERVICE_REFORM_IN_NIGERIA_THE_CASE_OF_DEMOCRATIC_CENTRALISM

Ogwu-Arizona, C. (2009). Northernization. *Nigerians in Nigeria*. June 17, 2009. http://www.nigeriansinamerica.com/northernization/

Ouattara, A. D. (1997). "The challenges of globalization for Africa" Address at the Southern Africa economic summit, sponsored by the World Economic Forum. Harare, May 21, 1997. http://www.imf.org/external/np/speeches/1997/052197.htm

Oxfam New Zealand. Cultivating poverty: The impact of US cotton subsidies on Africa. http://www.oxfamamerica.org/static/oa3/files/cultivating-poverty.pdf. And: http://www.oxfam.org.nz/report/cultivating-poverty-the-impact-of-us-cotton-subsidies-on-africa#sthash.G53AH2vZ.dpuf

Pflanz, M. (2007). Blair will find dreams for Africa unfulfilled. Freetown. *The Telegraph* of London. May 28, 2007. http://www.telegraph.co.uk/news/worldnews/1552857/Blair-will-find-dreams-for-Africa-unfulfilled.html

Poggi, G. (2001). *Forms of power*. Cambridge, MA/Malden: Polity Press/Blackwell Publishers.

Powers, W. T. (1998). *Making sense of behavior*. New Canaan: Benchmark Publications.

Powers, W. T. (2005). *Behavior: The control of perception*. New Canaan: Benchmark Publications.

Rena, R. Rich countries and their leverage on Africa in Africa economic analysis. 04/12/2008.http://www.africaeconomicanalysis.org/articles/63/1/Rich-countries-and-their-leverage-on-Africa/Page1.html

Robinson, H. (2001). *Perception* (Series: The problem of philosophy). London/New York: Routledge.

Schacter, D., & Badagaiyan, R. (citing SQUIRE –1992, TULVING and SCHACTER 1990). Neuroimaging of priming: New perspectives on implicit and explicit memory. *Current Direction in Psychological Science*. American Psychological Society. http://www.wjh.harvard.edu/~rajendra/Schacter%26Badgaiyan%2701.pdf

Schmidt, E. (2014). Review of visions of freedom. H-Diplo *Roundtable Reviews, XV*(41). http://www.academia.edu/7721243/Review_of_Piero_Gleijeses_Visions_of_Freedom

Scott, J. (1990). *Domination and the arts of resistance. Hidden transcripts.* New Haven/London: Yale University Press.

Shah, A. (2014). Aid as a foreign policy tool to aid the donor not the recipient. *Global Issues.* September 28, 2014. http://www.globalissues.org/article/35/foreign-aid-development-assistance#Aidasaforeignpolicytooltoaidthedonornottherecipient

Shortell, T. Weber's theory of social class. http://www.brooklynsoc.org/courses/43.1/weber.html

Simensen, J. Africa: The causes of under-development and the challenges of globalization. *UTENRIKSDEPARTEMENTET.* Also in http://www.nairaland.com/2008935/africa-causes-under-development-challenges#28226589

Sodhi, J. S. (2001). Beyond GDP: The debate on globalization and development. *Indian Journal of Industrial Relations, 46*(4), 562–570 (p. 562). https://www.questia.com/read/1G1-259078485/beyond-gdp-the-debate-on-globalization-development

Spencer, C. R. (1977a). Movements in international commodity prices and the balance of trade of developing countries with particular emphasis on African Countries-1972–1974. *Bank of Sierra Leone Economic Review, 2*(4).

Spencer, C. R. (1977b). Politics, public administration and agricultural development. *Journal of Developing Areas, 12*(1), 84.

Spencer, C. R. (2012). *Politics, agricultural development, and conflict resolution. An in-depth analysis of the Moyen Bani Programme in Mali.* Lanham: University Press of America.

Stapleton, S. The five sources of a leader's power, and how (and how not) to use them. http://www.simonstapleton.com/wordpress/2007/12/17/the-five-sources-of-a-leader%E2%80%99s-power-and-how-and-how-not-to-use-them/

Stiglitz, J. E. (2003). *Globalization and its discontents.* New York/London: W.W. Norton and Company.

Stimson, T. Sources of power. CLI. http://www.consultcli.com/Sourcespower.htm

Sumner, A., & Mallett, R. (2013). *The future of foreign aid. Development cooperation and the new geography of global poverty.* New York: Palgrave Macmillan.

Tarimo, A. Politicization of ethnic identities and the common good in Kenya. Aquiline Tarimo, S.J. –Santa Clara University. http://www.scu.edu/ethics/practicing/focusareas/global_ethics/kenya.htm

Thompson, B. The constitutional history and Law of Sierra Leone (1961–1995). New Lanham/York/London: University Press of America, Inc.

Tonwe, D., Ojo, G. U., & Aghedo, I. Spoils politics and environmental struggle in the Niger Delta region of Nigeria. http://www.academia.edu/1886300/Spoils_politics_and_environmental_struggle_in_the_Niger_Delta_region_of_Nigeria

Tran, D. T. Globalization factors in income distribution and poverty in developing countries. *Indian Journal of Economics and Business*, *9*(1), 2, 3. https://www.questia.com/read/1G1-225073256/globalization-factors-in-income-distribution-and-poverty

Weber, M. (1947). *The theory of social and economic organization*. New York: Oxford University Press. (cited by LEDYAEV, V in Pp 2- "*Power and Conflict*," online http://www.socialsciences.manchester.ac.uk/medialibrary/politics/research/workingpapers/mancept/LEDYAEV.pdf

Wilson, D., & Sperber, D. Relevance theory. In L. R. Horn., & G. Ward (Eds.), *The handbook of pragmatics* (607–632 (pp. 1 & 2 of 27)). Oxford: Blackwell. http://www.dan.sperber.fr/?p=93

Xiaoguang, K., & Li, F. (2006). NGO governance in China: Achievements and dilemmas. In L. Jordan & P. Van Tuijl (Eds.), *NGO accountability. Politics, principles & innovations*. London: Earthscan.

Index

C.R. Spencer, *Western Financial Assistance to the Developing World*,
DOI 10.1057/978-1-137-58399-4